TCP/IP Sockets in C
Second Edition

The Morgan Kaufmann Practical Guides Series
Series Editor, Michael J. Donahoo

For further information on these books and for a list of forthcoming titles, please visit our Web site at *http://www.mkp.com*.

TCP/IP Sockets in C
Practical Guide for Programmers
Second Edition

Michael J. Donahoo

Kenneth L. Calvert

ELSEVIER

AMSTERDAM • BOSTON • HEIDELBERG • LONDON
NEW YORK • OXFORD • PARIS • SAN DIEGO
SAN FRANCISCO • SINGAPORE • SYDNEY • TOKYO
Morgan Kaufmann Publishers is an imprint of Elsevier

MORGAN KAUFMANN PUBLISHERS

30 Corporate Drive, Suite 400, Burlington, MA 01803, USA

Library of Congress Cataloging-in-Publication Data
Application Submitted

ISBN: 978-0-12-374540-8

For information on all Morgan Kaufmann publications, visit our Web site at *www.mkp.com* or *www.elsevierdirect.com*

Printed in The United States of America
09 10 11 12 13 14 15 16   5 4 3 2 1

Contents

Preface to the Second Edition

When we wrote the first edition of this book, it was not very common for college courses on networking to include programming components. That seems difficult to believe now, when the Internet has become so important to our world, and the pedagogical benefits of hands-on programming and real-world protocol examples are so widely accepted. Although there are now other languages that provide access to the Internet, interest in the original C-based *Berkeley Sockets* remains high. The Sockets API (application programming interface) for networking was developed at UC Berkeley in the 1980s for the BSD flavor of UNIX—one of the very first examples of what would now be called an open-source project.

The Sockets API and the Internet both grew up in a world of many competing protocol families—IPX, Appletalk, DECNet, OSI, and SNA in addition to Transmission Control Protocol/Internet Protocal (TCP/IP)—and Sockets was designed to support them all. Fewer protocol families were in common use by the time we wrote the first edition of this book, and the number today is even smaller. Nevertheless, as we predicted in the first edition, the Sockets API remains important for those who want to design and build distributed applications that use the Internet—that is, that use TCP/IP. And the interface has proven robust enough to support the new version of the Internet Protocol (IPv6), which is now supported on virtually all common computing platforms.

Two main considerations motivated this second edition. First, based on our own experience and feedback from others, we found that some topics needed to be presented in more depth and that others needed to be expanded. The second consideration is the increasing acceptance and use of IP version 6, which is now supported by essentially all current end system platforms. At this writing, it is not possible to use IPv6 to exchange messages with a large fraction of hosts on the Internet, but it *is* possible to assign an IPv6 address to many of them. Although it is still too early to tell whether IPv6 will take over the world, it is not too early to start writing applications to be prepared.

Changes from the First Edition

We have updated and considerably expanded most of the material, having added two chapters. Major changes from the first edition include:

- IP version 6 coverage. We now include three kinds of code: IPv4-specific, IPv6-specific, and generic. The code in the later chapters is designed to work with either protocol version on dual-stack machines.

- An additional chapter on socket programming in C++ (contributed by David B. Sturgill). The PracticalSocket library provides wrappers for basic socket functionality. These allow an instructor to teach socket programming to students without C programming background by giving them a library and then gradually peeling back the layers. Students can start developing immediately after understanding addresses/ports and client/server. Later they can be shown the details of socket programming by peeking inside the wrapper code. Those teaching a subject that uses networking (e.g., OS) can use the library and only selectively peel back the cover.

- Enhanced coverage of data representation issues and strategies for organizing code that sends and receives messages. In our instructional experience, we find that students have less and less understanding of how data is actually stored in memory,[1] so we have attempted to compensate with more discussion of this important issue. At the same time, internationalization will only increase in importance, and thus we have included basic coverage of wide characters and encodings.

- Omission of the reference section. The descriptions of most of the functions that make up the Sockets API have been collected into the early chapters. However, with so many online sources of reference information—including "man pages"—available, we chose to leave out the complete listing of the API in favor of more code illustrations.

- Highlighting important but subtle facts and caveats. Typographical devices call out important concepts and information that might otherwise be missed on first reading.

Although the scope of the book has expanded, we have not included everything that we might have (or even that we were asked to include); examples of topics left for more comprehensive texts (or the next edition) are raw sockets and programming with WinSock.

Intended Audience

We originally wrote this book so that we would have something to hand our students when we wanted them to learn socket programming, so we would not have to take up valuable class time

---

[1] We speculate that this is due to the widespread use of C++ and Java, which hide such details from the programmer, in undergraduate curricula.

teaching it. In the years since the first edition, we have learned a good deal about the topics that students need lots of help on, and those where they do not need as much handholding. We also found that our book was appreciated at least as much by practitioners who were looking for a gentle introduction to the subject. Therefore, this book is aimed simultaneously at two general audiences: students in introductory courses in computer networks (graduate or undergraduate) with a programming component, and practitioners who want to write their own programs that communicate over the Internet. For students, it is intended as a supplement, not as a primary text about networks. Although this second edition is significantly bigger in size and scope than the first, we hope the book will still be considered a good value in that role. For practitioners who just want to write some useful code, it should serve as a standalone *introduction*—but readers in that category should be warned that this book will not make them experts. Our philosophy of learning by doing has not changed, nor has our approach of providing a concise tutorial sufficient to get one started learning on one's own, and leaving the comprehensive details to other authors. For both audiences, our goal is to take you far enough so that you can start experimenting and learning on your own.

Assumed Background

We assume basic programming skills and experience with C and UNIX. You are expected to be conversant with C concepts such as pointers and type casting, and you should have a basic understanding of the binary representation of data. Some of our examples are factored into files that should be compiled separately; we assume that you can deal with that.

Here is a little test: If you can puzzle out what the following code fragment does, you should have no problem with the code in this book:

```
typedef struct {
  int a;
  short s[2];
} MSG;

MSG *mp, m = {4, 1, 0};
char  *fp, *tp;
mp = (MSG *) malloc(sizeof(MSG));
for (fp = (char *)m.s, tp = (char *)mp->s; tp < (char *)(mp+1);)
  *tp++ = *fp++;
```

If you do not understand this fragment, do not despair (there is nothing quite so convoluted in our code), but you might want to refer to your favorite C programming book to find out what is going on here.

You should also be familiar with the UNIX notions of process/address space, command-line arguments, program termination, and regular file input and output. The material in Chapters 4 and 6 assumes a somewhat more advanced grasp of UNIX. Some prior exposure to networking concepts such as protocols, addresses, clients, and servers will be helpful.

Platform Requirements and Portability

Our presentation is UNIX-based. When we were developing this book, several people urged us to include code for Windows as well as UNIX. It was not possible to do so for various reasons, including the target length (and price) we set for the book.

For those who only have access to Windows platforms, please note that the examples in the early chapters require minimal modifications to work with WinSock. (You have to change the include files and add a setup call at the beginning of the program and a cleanup call at the end.) Most of the other examples also require very slight additional modifications. However, some are so dependent on the UNIX programming model that it does not make sense to port them to WinSock. WinSock-ready versions of the other examples, as well as detailed descriptions of the code modifications required, are available from the book's Web site at *www.elsevierdirect.com/companions/9780123745408*. Note also that almost all of our example code works with minimal modifications under the **Cygwin** UNIX library package for Windows, which is available online.

For this second edition, we have adopted the C99 language standard. This version of the language is supported by most compilers and offers so many readability-improving advantages—including line-delimited comments, fixed-size integer types, and declarations anywhere in a block—that we could not justify not using it.

Our code makes use of the "Basic Socket Interface Extensions for IPv6" [6]. Among these extensions is a new and different interface to the name system. Because we rely completely on this new interface (getaddrinfo()), our generic code may not run on some older platforms. However, we expect that most modern systems will run our code just fine.

The example programs included here have all been tested (and should compile and run without modification) on both *NIX and MacOS. Header (.h) file locations and dependencies are, alas, not quite standard and may require some fiddling on your system. Socket option support also varies widely across systems; we have tried to focus on those that are most universally supported. Consult your API documentation for system specifics. (By API documentation we mean the "man pages" for your system. To learn about this, type "man man" or use your favorite web search tool.)

Please be aware that although we strive for a basic level of robustness, the primary goal of our code examples is pedagogy, and the code is **not production quality.** We have sacrificed some robustness for brevity and clarity, especially in the generic server code. (It turns out to be nontrivial to write a server that works under all combinations of IPv4 and IPv6 protocol configurations and also maximizes the likelihood of successful client connection under all circumstances.)

This Book Will Not Make You an Expert!

We hope this second edition will be useful as a resource, even to those who already know quite a bit about sockets. As with the first edition, we learned some things in writing it. But becoming an expert takes years of experience, as well as other, more comprehensive sources [3, 16].

The first chapter is intended to give "just enough" of the big picture to get you ready to write code. Chapter 2 shows you how to write TCP clients and servers using either IPv4 or IPv6. Chapter 3 shows how to make your clients and servers use the network's name service, and also describes how to make them IP-version-independent. Chapter 4 covers User Datagram Protocol (UDP). Chapters 5 and 6 provide background needed to write more programs, while Chapter 7 relates some of what is going on in the Sockets implementation to the API calls; these three are essentially independent and may be presented in any order. Finally, Chapter 8 presents a C++ class library that provides simplified access to socket functionality.

Throughout the book, certain statements are highlighted like this: **This book will not make you an expert!** Our goal is to bring to your attention those subtle but important facts and ideas that one might miss on first reading. The marks in the margin tell you to "**note well**" whatever is in bold.

Acknowledgments

Many people contributed to making this book a reality. In addition to all those who helped us with the first edition (Michel Barbeau, Steve Bernier, Arian Durresi, Gary Harkin, Ted Herman, Lee Hollaar, David Hutchison, Shunge Li, Paul Linton, Ivan Marsic, Willis Marti, Kihong Park, Dan Schmitt, Michael Scott, Robert Strader, Ben Wah, and Ellen Zegura), we especially thank David B. Sturgill, who contributed code and text for Chapter 8, and Bobby Krupczak for his help in reviewing the draft of this second edition. Finally, to the folks at Morgan Kaufmann/Elsevier— Rick Adams, our editor, assistant editor Maria Alonso, and project manager Melinda Ritchie— thank you for your patience, help, and caring about the quality of our book.

Feedback

We are very interested in weeding out errors and otherwise improving future editions/ printings, so if you find any errors, please send an e-mail to either of us. We will maintain an errata list on the book's Web page.

M.J.D. jeff_donahoo@baylor.edu

K.L.C. calvert@netlab.uky.edu

chapter **1**

Introduction

$\mathbf{T}$oday people use computers to make phone calls, watch TV, send instant messages to their friends, play games with other people, and buy most anything you can think of—from songs to automobiles. The ability of programs to communicate over the Internet makes all this possible. It's hard to say how many individual computers are now reachable over the Internet, but we can safely say that it is growing rapidly; it won't be long before the number is in the billions. Moreover, new applications are being developed every day. With the push for ever increasing bandwidth and access, the impact of the Internet will continue to grow for the forseeable future.

How *does* a program communicate with another program over a network? The goal of this book is to *start* you on the road to understanding the answer to that question, in the context of the C programming language. For a long time, C was the language of choice for implementing network communication softward. Indeed, the application programming interface (API) known as *Sockets* was first developed in C.

Before we delve into the details of sockets, however, it is worth taking a brief look at the big picture of networks and protocols to see where our code will fit in. Our goal here is *not* to teach you how networks and TCP/IP work—many fine texts are available for that purpose [1, 3, 10, 15, 17]—but rather to introduce some basic concepts and terminology.

1.1 Networks, Packets, and Protocols

A computer network consists of machines interconnected by communication channels. We call these machines *hosts* and *routers*. Hosts are computers that run applications such as your Web browser, your IM agent, or a file-sharing program. The application programs running on hosts are the real "users" of the network. Routers (also called *gateways*) are machines whose job is to relay, or *forward*, information from one communication channel to another. They may run programs but typically do not run application programs. For our purposes, a *communication channel* is a means of conveying sequences of bytes from one host to another; it may be a wired (e.g., Ethernet), a wireless (e.g., WiFi), or other connection.

Routers are important simply because it is not practical to connect every host directly to every other host. Instead, a few hosts connect to a router, which connects to other routers, and so on to form the network. This arrangement lets each machine get by with a relatively small number of communication channels; most hosts need only one. Programs that exchange information over the network, however, do not interact directly with routers and generally remain blissfully unaware of their existence.

By *information* we mean sequences of bytes that are constructed and interpreted by programs. In the context of computer networks, these byte sequences are generally called *packets*. A packet contains control information that the network uses to do its job and sometimes also includes user data. An example is information identifying the packet's destination. Routers use such control information to figure out how to forward each packet.

A *protocol* is an agreement about the packets exchanged by communicating programs and what they mean. A protocol tells how packets are structured—for example, where the destination information is located in the packet and how big it is—as well as how the information is to be interpreted. A protocol is usually designed to solve a specific problem using given capabilities. For example, the *HyperText Transfer Protocol (HTTP)* solves the problem of transferring hypertext objects between servers, where they are stored or generated, and Web browsers that make them visible and useful to users. Instant messaging protocols solve the problem of enabling two or more users to exchange brief text messages.

Implementing a useful network requires solving a large number of different problems. To keep things manageable and modular, different protocols are designed to solve different sets of problems. TCP/IP is one such collection of solutions, sometimes called a *protocol suite*. It happens to be the suite of protocols used in the Internet, but it can be used in stand-alone private networks as well. Henceforth when we talk about the *network*, we mean any network that uses the TCP/IP protocol suite. The main protocols in the TCP/IP suite are the Internet Protocol (IP), the Transmission Control Protocol (TCP), and the User Datagram Protocol (UDP).

It turns out to be useful to organize protocols into *layers*; TCP/IP and virtually all other protocol suites are organized this way. Figure 1.1 shows the relationships among the protocols, applications, and the Sockets API in the hosts and routers, as well as the flow of data from one application (using TCP) to another. The boxes labeled TCP and IP represent implementations of those protocols. Such implementations typically reside in the operating system of a host. Applications access the services provided by UDP and TCP through the Sockets API, represented as a dashed line. The arrow depicts the flow of data from the application, through the TCP and IP implementations, through the network, and back up through the IP and TCP implementations at the other end.

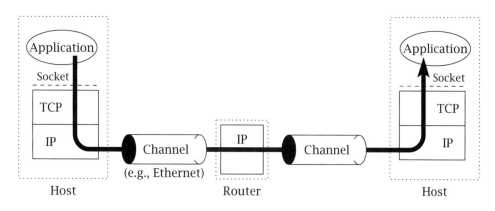

Figure 1.1: A TCP/IP network.

In TCP/IP, the bottom layer consists of the underlying communication channels—for example, Ethernet or dial-up modem connections. Those channels are used by the *network layer*, which deals with the problem of forwarding packets toward their destination (i.e., what routers do). The single-network layer protocol in the TCP/IP suite is the Internet Protocol; it solves the problem of making the sequence of channels and routers between any two hosts look like a single host-to-host channel.

The Internet Protocol provides a *datagram* service: every packet is handled and delivered by the network independently, like letters or parcels sent via the postal system. To make this work, each IP packet has to contain the *address* of its destination, just as every package that you mail is addressed to somebody. (We'll say more about addresses shortly.) Although most delivery companies guarantee delivery of a package, IP is only a best-effort protocol: it attempts to deliver each packet, but it can (and occasionally does) lose, reorder, or duplicate packets in transit through the network.

The layer above IP is called the *transport layer*. It offers a choice between two protocols: TCP and UDP. Each builds on the service provided by IP, but they do so in different ways to provide different kinds of transport, which are used by *application protocols* with different needs. TCP and UDP have one function in common: addressing. Recall that IP delivers packets to hosts; clearly, a finer granularity of addressing is needed to get a packet to a particular application program, perhaps one of many using the network on the same host. Both TCP and UDP use addresses, called *port numbers*, to identify applications within hosts. TCP and UDP are called *end-to-end transport protocols* because they carry data all the way from one program to another (whereas IP only carries data from one host to another).

TCP is designed to detect and recover from the losses, duplications, and other errors that may occur in the host-to-host channel provided by IP. TCP provides a *reliable byte-stream* channel, so that applications do not have to deal with these problems. It is a *connection-oriented* protocol: before using it to communicate, two programs must first establish a TCP connection, which involves completing an exchange of *handshake messages* between the TCP implementations on the two communicating computers. Using TCP is also similar in many ways to file input/output (I/O). In fact, a file that is written by one program and read by another is a reasonable model of communication over a TCP connection. UDP, on the other hand, does not attempt to recover from errors experienced by IP; it simply extends the IP best-effort datagram service so that it works between application programs instead of between hosts. Thus, applications that use UDP must be prepared to deal with losses, reordering, and so on.

1.2   About Addresses

When you mail a letter, you provide the address of the recipient in a form that the postal service can understand. Before you can talk to someone on the phone, you must supply a phone number to the telephone system. In a similar way, before a program can communicate with another program, it must tell the network something to identify the other program. In TCP/IP, it takes two pieces of information to identify a particular program: an *Internet address*, used by IP, and a *port number*, the additional address interpreted by the transport protocol (TCP or UDP).

Internet addresses are binary numbers. They come in two flavors, corresponding to the two versions of the Internet Protocol that have been standardized. The most common is version 4 (IPv4, [12]); the other is version 6 (IPv6, [5]), which is just beginning to be deployed. IPv4 addresses are 32 bits long; because this is only enough to identify about 4 billion distinct destinations, they are not really big enough for today's Internet. (That may seem like a lot, but because of the way they are allocated, many are wasted. More than half of the total IPv4 address space has already been allocated.) For that reason, IPv6 was introduced. IPv6 addresses are 128 bits long.

1.2.1   Writing Down IP Addresses

In representing Internet addresses for human consumption (as opposed to using them inside programs), different conventions are used for the two versions of IP. IPv4 addresses are conventionally written as a group of four decimal numbers separated by periods (e.g., 10.1.2.3); this is called the *dotted-quad* notation. The four numbers in a dotted-quad string represent the contents of the four bytes of the Internet address—thus, each is a number between 0 and 255.

The 16 bytes of an IPv6 address, on the other hand, by convention are represented as groups of hexadecimal digits, separated by colons (e.g., 2000:fdb8:0000:0000:0001:00ab:853c: 39a1). Each group of digits represents 2 bytes of the address; leading zeros may be omitted, so the fifth and sixth groups in the foregoing example might be rendered as just :1:ab:. Also, one sequence of groups that contains only zeros may be omitted altogether (while leaving the colons that would separate them from the rest of the address). So the example above could be written as 2000:fdb8::1:00ab:853c:39a1.

Technically, each Internet address refers to the connection between a host and an underlying communication channel—in other words, a *network interface*. A host may have several interfaces; it is not uncommon, for example, for a host to have connections to both wired (Ethernet) and wireless (WiFi) networks. Because each such network connection belongs to a single host, an Internet address identifies a host as well as its connection to the network. However, the converse is not true, because a single host can have multiple interfaces, and each interface can have multiple addresses. (In fact, the same interface can have both IPv4 and IPv6 addresses.)

1.2.2 Dealing with Two Versions

When the first edition of this book was written, IPv6 was not widely supported. Today most systems are capable of supporting IPv6 "out of the box." To smooth the transition from IPv4 to IPv6, most systems are *dual-stack*, simultaneously supporting both IPv4 and IPv6. In such systems, each network interface (channel connection) may have at least one IPv4 address and one IPv6 address.

The existence of two versions of IP complicates life for the socket programmer. In general, you will need to choose either IPv4 or IPv6 as the underlying protocol when you create a socket to communicate. So how can you write an application that works with both versions? Fortunately, dual-stack systems handle interoperability by supporting both protocol versions and allowing IPv6 sockets to communicate with either IPv4 or IPv6 applications. Of course, IPv4 and IPv6 addresses are quite different; however, IPv4 addresses can be mapped into IPv6 addresses using *IPv4 mapped addresses*. An IPv4 mapped address is formed by prefixing the four bytes in the IPv4 address with ::ffff. For example, the IPv4 mapped address for 132.3.23.7 is ::ffff:132.3.23.7. To aid in human readability, the last four bytes are typically written in dotted-quad notation. We discuss protocol interoperability in greater detail in Chapter 3.

Unfortunately, having an IPv6 Internet address is *not* sufficient to enable you to communicate with every other IPv6-enabled host across the Internet. To do that, you must also arrange with your Internet Service Provider (ISP) to provide IPv6 forwarding service.

1.2.3 Port Numbers

We mentioned earlier that it takes *two* pieces of address to get a message to a program. The *port number* in TCP or UDP is always interpreted relative to an Internet address. Returning to our earlier analogies, a port number corresponds to a room number at a given street address, say, that of a large building. The postal service uses the street address to get the letter to a mailbox; whoever empties the mailbox is then responsible for getting the letter to the proper room within the building. Or consider a company with an internal telephone system: to speak to an individual in the company, you first dial the company's main phone number to connect to the internal telephone system and then dial the extension of the particular telephone of the individual with whom you wish to speak. In these analogies, the Internet address is the street address or the company's main number, whereas the port corresponds to the room number or telephone extension. Port numbers are the same in both IPv4 and IPv6: 16-bit unsigned binary numbers. Thus, each one is in the range 1 to 65,535 (0 is reserved).

1.2.4   Special Addresses

In each version of IP, certain special-purpose addresses are defined. One of these that is worth knowing is the *loopback address*, which is always assigned to a special *loopback interface*, a virtual device that simply echoes transmitted packets right back to the sender. The loopback interface is very useful for testing, because packets sent to that address are immediately returned to the destination. Moreover, it is present on every host and can be used even when a computer has no other interfaces (i.e., is not connected to the network). The loopback address for IPv4 is 127.0.0.1;[1] for IPv6 it is 0:0:0:0:0:0:0:1 (or just ::1).

Another group of IPv4 addresses reserved for a special purpose includes those reserved for "private use." This group includes all IPv4 addresses that start with 10 or 192.168, as well as those whose first number is 172 and whose second number is between 16 and 31. (There is no corresponding class for IPv6.) These addresses were originally designated for use in private networks that are *not* part of the global Internet. Today they are often used in homes and small offices that are connected to the Internet through a *network address translation* (NAT) [7] device. Such a device acts like a router that translates (rewrites) the addresses and ports in packets as it forwards them. More precisely, it maps (private address, port) pairs in packets on one of its interfaces to (public address, port) pairs on the other interface. This enables a small group of hosts (e.g., those on a home network) to effectively "share" a single IP address. The importance of these addresses is that *they cannot be reached from the global Internet*. If you are trying out the code in this book on a machine that has an address in the private-use class (e.g., on your home network), and you are trying to communicate with another host that does *not* have one of these addresses, in general you will not succeed unless the host with the private address initiates communication—and even then you may fail.

A related class contains the *link-local*, or "autoconfiguration" addresses. For IPv4, such addresses begin with 169.254. For IPv6, any address whose first 16-bit chunk is FE80, FE90, FEA0, or FEB0 is a link-local address. These addresses can *only* be used for communication between hosts connected to the same network; routers will not forward packets that have such addresses as their destination.

Finally, another class consists of *multicast* addresses. Whereas regular IP (sometimes called "unicast") addresses refer to a single destination, multicast addresses potentially refer to an arbitrary number of destinations. Multicasting is an advanced subject that we cover briefly in Chapter 6. In IPv4, multicast addresses in dotted-quad format have a first number in the range 224 to 239. In IPv6, multicast addresses start with FF.

---

[1]Technically, any IPv4 address beginning with 127 should loop back.

1.3   About Names

Most likely you are accustomed to referring to hosts by *name* (e.g., host.example.com). However, the Internet protocols deal with addresses (binary numbers), not names. You should understand that the use of names instead of addresses is a convenience feature that is independent of the basic service provided by TCP/IP—you can write and use TCP/IP applications without ever using a name. When you use a name to identify a communication end point, the system does some extra work to *resolve* the name into an address. This extra step is often worth it, for a couple of reasons. First, names are obviously easier for humans to remember than dotted-quads (or, in the case of IPv6, strings of hexadecimal digits). Second, names provide a level of indirection, which insulates users from IP address changes. During the writing of the first edition of this book, the address of the Web server *www.mkp.com* changed. Because we always refer to that Web server by name, *www.mkp.com* resolves to the current Internet address instead of 208.164.121.48. The change in IP address is transparent to programs that use the name to access the Web server.

The name-resolution service can access information from a wide variety of sources. Two of the primary sources are the *Domain Name System (DNS)* and local configuration databases. The DNS [8] is a distributed database that maps *domain names* such as *www.mkp.com* to Internet addresses and other information; the DNS protocol [9] allows hosts connected to the Internet to retrieve information from that database using TCP or UDP. Local configuration databases are generally OS-specific mechanisms for local name-to-Internet address mappings.

1.4   Clients and Servers

In our postal and telephone analogies, each communication is initiated by one party, who sends a letter or makes the telephone call, while the other party responds to the initiator's contact by sending a return letter or picking up the phone and talking. Internet communication is similar. The terms *client* and *server* refer to these roles: The client program initiates communication, while the server program waits passively for and then responds to clients that contact it. Together, the client and server compose the *application*. The terms *client* and *server* are descriptive of the typical situation in which the server makes a particular capability—for example, a database service—available to any client able to communicate with it.

Whether a program is acting as a client or server determines the general form of its use of the Sockets API to establish communication with its *peer*. (The client is the peer of the server and vice versa.) In addition, the client-server distinction is important because the client needs to know the server's address and port initially, but not vice versa. With the Sockets API, the server can, if necessary, learn the client's address information when it receives the initial communication from the client. This is analogous to a telephone call—in order to be called, a person does not need to know the telephone number of the caller. As with a telephone call, once the connection is established, the distinction between server and client disappears.

How does a client find out a server's IP address and port number? Usually, the client knows the name of the server it wants—for example, from a *Universal Resource Locator (URL)* such as *http://www.mkp.com*—and uses the name-resolution service to learn the corresponding Internet address.

Finding a server's port number is a different story. In principle, servers can use any port, but the client must be able to learn what it is. In the Internet, there is a convention of assigning well-known port numbers to certain applications. The Internet Assigned Number Authority (IANA) oversees this assignment. For example, port number 80 has been assigned to the *Hyper-Text Transfer Protocol (HTTP)*. When you run an HTTP client browser, it tries to contact the Web server on that port by default. A list of all the assigned port numbers is maintained by the numbering authority of the Internet (see *http://www.iana.org/assignments/port-numbers*).

You may have heard of an alternative to client-server called peer-to-peer (P2P). In P2P, applications both consume and provide service, unlike the traditional client-server architecture in which servers provide service and clients consume. In fact, P2P nodes are sometimes called "servents," combining the words server and client. So do you need to learn a different set of technologies to program for P2P instead of client-server? No. In Sockets, client vs. server merely distinguishes who makes the initial connection and who waits for connections. P2P applications typically both initiate connections (to existing P2P nodes) and accept connections (from other P2P nodes). After reading this book, you'll be able to write P2P applications just as well as client-server.

1.5   What Is a Socket?

A *socket* is an abstraction through which an application may send and receive data, in much the same way as an open-file handle allows an application to read and write data to stable storage. A socket allows an application to plug in to the network and communicate with other applications that are plugged in to the same network. Information written to the socket by an application on one machine can be read by an application on a different machine and vice versa.

Different types of sockets correspond to different underlying protocol suites and different stacks of protocols within a suite. This book deals only with the TCP/IP protocol suite. The main types of sockets in TCP/IP today are *stream sockets* and *datagram sockets*. Stream sockets use TCP as the end-to-end protocol (with IP underneath) and thus provide a reliable byte-stream service. A TCP/IP stream socket represents one end of a TCP connection. Datagram sockets use UDP (again, with IP underneath) and thus provide a best-effort datagram service that applications can use to send individual messages up to about 65,500 bytes in length. Stream and datagram sockets are also supported by other protocol suites, but this book deals only with TCP stream sockets and UDP datagram sockets. A TCP/IP socket is uniquely identified by an Internet address, an end-to-end protocol (TCP or UDP), and a port number. As you proceed, you will encounter several ways for a socket to become bound to an address.

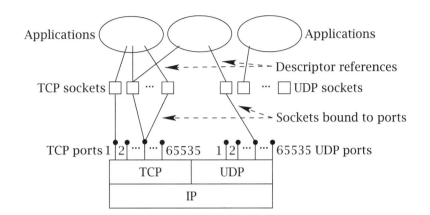

Figure 1.2: Sockets, protocols, and ports.

Figure 1.2 depicts the logical relationships among applications, socket abstractions, protocols, and port numbers within a single host. There are several things to note about these relationships. First, a program can have multiple sockets in use at the same time. Second, multiple programs can be using the same socket abstraction at the same time, although this is less common. The figure shows that each socket has an associated local TCP or UDP port, which is used to direct incoming packets to the application that is supposed to receive them. Earlier we said that a port identifies an application on a host. Actually, a port identifies a socket on a host. There is more to it than this, however, because as Figure 1.2 shows, more than one socket can be associated with one local port. This is most common with TCP sockets; fortunately, you need not understand the details to write client-server programs that use TCP sockets. The full story will be revealed in Chapter 7.

Exercises

1. Report your IP addresses using the ifconfig command in *NIX or the ipconfig command in Windows. Identify the addresses that are IPv6.

2. Report the name of the computer on which you are working by using the hostname command.

3. Can you find the IP address of any of your directly connected routers?

4. Use Internet search to try and discover what happened to IPv5.

5. Write the following IPv6 address using as few characters as possible: 2345:0000:0000:A432:0000:0000:0000:0023

6. Can you think of a real-life example of communication that does not fit the client-server model?

7. To how many different kinds of networks is your home connected? How many support two-way transport?

8. IP is a best-effort protocol, requiring that information be broken down into datagrams, which may be lost, duplicated, or reordered. TCP hides all of this, providing a reliable service that takes and delivers an unbroken stream of bytes. How might you go about providing TCP service on top of IP? Why would anybody use UDP when TCP is available?

chapter 2

Basic TCP Sockets

It's time to learn about writing your own socket applications. We'll start with TCP. By now you're probably ready to get your hands dirty with some actual code, so we begin by going through a working example of a TCP client and server. Then we present the details of the socket API used in basic TCP. To keep things simpler, we'll present code initially that works for one particular version of IP: IPv4, which at the time this is being written is still the dominant version of the Internet Protocol, by a wide margin. At the end of this chapter we present the (minor) modifications required to write IPv6 versions of our clients and servers. In Chapter 3 we will demonstrate the creation of protocol-independent applications.

Our example client and server implement the *echo* protocol. It works as follows: the client connects to the server and sends its data. The server simply echoes whatever it receives back to the client and disconnects. In our application, the data that the client sends is a string provided as a command-line argument. Our client will print the data it receives from the server so we can see what comes back. Many systems include an echo service for debugging and testing purposes.

2.1 IPv4 TCP Client

The distinction between client and server is important because each uses the sockets interface differently at certain steps in the communication. We first focus on the client. Its job is to initiate communication with a server that is passively waiting to be contacted.

The typical TCP client's communication involves four basic steps:

1. Create a TCP socket using socket().

2. Establish a connection to the server using connect().

3. Communicate using send and recv().

4. Close the connection with close().

TCPEchoClient4.c is an implementation of a TCP echo client for IPv4.

TCPEchoClient4.c

```
 1  #include <stdio.h>
 2  #include <stdlib.h>
 3  #include <string.h>
 4  #include <unistd.h>
 5  #include <sys/types.h>
 6  #include <sys/socket.h>
 7  #include <netinet/in.h>
 8  #include <arpa/inet.h>
 9  #include "Practical.h"
10
11  int main(int argc, char *argv[]) {
12
13    if (argc < 3 || argc > 4) // Test for correct number of arguments
14      DieWithUserMessage("Parameter(s)",
15          "<Server Address> <Echo Word> [<Server Port>]");
16
17    char *servIP = argv[1];     // First arg: server IP address (dotted quad)
18    char *echoString = argv[2]; // Second arg: string to echo
19
20    // Third arg (optional): server port (numeric).  7 is well-known echo port
21    in_port_t servPort = (argc == 4) ? atoi(argv[3]) : 7;
22
23    // Create a reliable, stream socket using TCP
24    int sock = socket(AF_INET, SOCK_STREAM, IPPROTO_TCP);
25    if (sock < 0)
26      DieWithSystemMessage("socket() failed");
27
28    // Construct the server address structure
29    struct sockaddr_in servAddr;            // Server address
30    memset(&servAddr, 0, sizeof(servAddr)); // Zero out structure
31    servAddr.sin_family = AF_INET;          // IPv4 address family
32    // Convert address
```

```
33    int rtnVal = inet_pton(AF_INET, servIP, &servAddr.sin_addr.s_addr);
34    if (rtnVal == 0)
35      DieWithUserMessage("inet_pton() failed", "invalid address string");
36    else if (rtnVal < 0)
37      DieWithSystemMessage("inet_pton() failed");
38    servAddr.sin_port = htons(servPort);    // Server port
39
40    // Establish the connection to the echo server
41    if (connect(sock, (struct sockaddr *) &servAddr, sizeof(servAddr)) < 0)
42      DieWithSystemMessage("connect() failed");
43
44    size_t echoStringLen = strlen(echoString); // Determine input length
45
46    // Send the string to the server
47    ssize_t numBytes = send(sock, echoString, echoStringLen, 0);
48    if (numBytes < 0)
49      DieWithSystemMessage("send() failed");
50    else if (numBytes != echoStringLen)
51      DieWithUserMessage("send()", "sent unexpected number of bytes");
52
53    // Receive the same string back from the server
54    unsigned int totalBytesRcvd = 0; // Count of total bytes received
55    fputs("Received: ", stdout);       // Setup to print the echoed string
56    while (totalBytesRcvd < echoStringLen) {
57      char buffer[BUFSIZE]; // I/O buffer
58      /* Receive up to the buffer size (minus 1 to leave space for
59       a null terminator) bytes from the sender */
60      numBytes = recv(sock, buffer, BUFSIZE - 1, 0);
61      if (numBytes < 0)
62        DieWithSystemMessage("recv() failed");
63      else if (numBytes == 0)
64        DieWithUserMessage("recv()", "connection closed prematurely");
65      totalBytesRcvd += numBytes; // Keep tally of total bytes
66      buffer[numBytes] = '\0';    // Terminate the string!
67      fputs(buffer, stdout);      // Print the echo buffer
68    }
69
70    fputc('\n', stdout); // Print a final linefeed
71
72    close(sock);
73    exit(0);
74  }
```

TCPEchoClient4.c

Our TCPEchoClient4.c does the following:

1. **Application setup and parameter parsing:** lines 1–21
   - ▪ **Include files:** lines 1–9
     These header files declare the standard functions and constants of the API. Consult your documentation (e.g., man pages) for the appropriate include files for socket functions and data structures on your system. We utilize our own include file, Practical.h, with prototypes for our own functions, which we describe below.

   - ▪ **Typical parameter parsing and sanity checking:** lines 13–21
     The IPv4 address and string to echo are passed in as the first two parameters. Optionally, the client takes the server port as the third parameter. If no port is provided, the client uses the well-known echo protocol port, 7.

2. **TCP socket creation:** lines 23–26
   We create a socket using the socket() function. The socket is for IPv4 (AF_INET) using the stream-based protocol (SOCK_STREAM) called TCP (IPPROTO_TCP). socket() returns an integer-valued descriptor or "handle" for the socket if successful. If socket fails, it returns –1, and we call our error-handling function, DieWithSystemMessage() (described later), to print an informative hint and exit.

3. **Prepare address and establish connection:** lines 28–42
   - ▪ **Prepare sockaddr_in structure to hold server address:** lines 29–30
     To connect a socket, we have to specify the address and port to connect to. The **sockaddr_in** structure is defined to be a "container" for this information. The call to memset() ensures that any parts of the structure that we do not explicitly set contain zero.

   - ▪ **Filling in the sockaddr_in:** lines 31–38
     We must set the address family (AF_INET), Internet address, and port number. The function inet_pton() converts the string representation of the server's Internet address (passed as a command-line argument in dotted-quad notation) into a 32-bit binary representation. The server's port number was converted from a command-line string to binary earlier; the call to htons() ("host to network short") ensures that the binary value is formatted as required by the API. (Reasons for this are described in Chapter 5.)

   - ▪ **Connecting:** lines 40–42
     The connect() function establishes a connection between the given socket and the one identified by the address and port in the **sockaddr_in** structure. Because the Sockets API is generic, the pointer to the **sockaddr_in** address structure (which is specific to IPv4 addresses) needs to be *cast* to the generic type (**sockaddr***), and the actual size of the address data structure must be supplied.

4. **Send echo string to server:** lines 44–51
   We find the length of the argument string and save it for later use. A pointer to the echo string is passed to the send() call; the string itself was stored somewhere (like all command-line arguments) when the application was started. We do not really care where

it is; we just need to know the address of the first byte and how many bytes to send. (Note that we do not send the end-of-string marker character (0) that is at the end of the argument string—and all strings in C). `send()` returns the number of bytes sent if successful and -1 otherwise. If `send()` fails or sends the wrong number of bytes, we must deal with the error. Note that sending the wrong number of bytes will not happen here. Nevertheless, it's a good idea to include the test because errors can occur in some contexts.

5. **Receive echo server reply:** lines 53-70

   TCP is a byte-stream protocol. One implication of this type of protocol is that `send()` boundaries are not preserved. In other words: **The bytes sent by a call to send() on one end of a connection may not all be returned by a single call to recv() on the other end.** (We discuss this issue in more detail in Chapter 7.) So we need to repeatedly receive bytes until we have received as many as we sent. In all likelihood, this loop will only be executed once because the data from the server will in fact be returned all at once; however, that is not *guaranteed* to happen, and so we have to allow for the possibility that multiple reads are required. This is a basic principle of writing applications that use sockets: **you must never assume anything about what the network and the program at the other end are going to do.**

   - **Receive a block of bytes:** lines 57-65

     `recv()` blocks until data is available, returning the number of bytes copied into the buffer or −1 in case of failure. A return value of zero indicates that the application at the other end closed the TCP connection. Note that the size parameter passed to `recv()` reserves space for adding a terminating null character.

   - **Print buffer:** lines 66-67

     We print the data sent by the server as it is received. We add the terminating null character (0) at the end of each chunk of received data so that it can be treated as a string by `fputs()`. We do not check whether the bytes received are the same as the bytes sent. The server may send something completely different (up to the length of the string we sent), and it will be written to the standard output.

   - **Print newline:** line 70

     When we have received as many bytes as we sent, we exit the loop and print a newline.

6. **Terminate connection and exit:** lines 72-73

   The `close()` function informs the remote socket that communication is ended, and then deallocates local resources of the socket.

Our client application (and indeed all the programs in this book) makes use of two error-handling functions:

```
DieWithUserMessage(const char *msg, const char *detail)
DieWithSystemMessage(const char *msg)
```

Both functions print a user-supplied message string (*msg*) to *stderr*, followed by a detail message string; they then call `exit()` with an error return code, causing the application to terminate.

The only difference is the source of the detail message. For DieWithUserMessage(), the detail message is user-supplied. For DieWithSystemMessage(), the detail message is supplied by the system based on the value of the special variable *errno* (which describes the reason for the most recent failure, if any, of a system call). We call DieWithSystemMessage() only if the error situation results from a call to a system call that sets *errno*. (To keep our programs simple, our examples do not contain much code devoted to recovering from errors—they simply punt and exit. Production code generally should not give up so easily.)

Occasionally, we need to supply information to the user without exiting; we use printf() if we need formatting capabilities, and fputs() otherwise. In particular, we try to avoid using printf() to output fixed, preformatted strings. **One thing that you should *never* do is to pass text received from the network as the first argument to printf(). It creates a serious security vulnerability. Use fputs() instead.**

Note: the DieWith...() functions are *declared* in the header "Practical.h." However, the actual *implementation* of these functions is contained in the file DieWithMessage.c, which should be compiled and linked with *all* example applications in this text.

DieWithMessage.c

```
1   #include <stdio.h>
2   #include <stdlib.h>
3
4   void DieWithUserMessage(const char *msg, const char *detail) {
5     fputs(msg, stderr);
6     fputs(": ", stderr);
7     fputs(detail, stderr);
8     fputc('\n', stderr);
9     exit(1);
10  }
11
12  void DieWithSystemMessage(const char *msg) {
13    perror(msg);
14    exit(1);
15  }
```

DieWithMessage.c

If we compile TCPEchoClient4.c and DieWithMessage.c to create program TCPEchoClient4, we can communicate with an echo server with Internet address 169.1.1.1 as follows:

```
% TCPEchoClient4 169.1.1.1 "Echo this!"
Received: Echo this!
```

For our client to work, we need a server. Many systems include an echo server for debugging and testing purposes; however, for security reasons, such servers are often initially disabled. If you don't have access to an echo server, that's okay because we're about to write one.

2.2 IPv4 TCP Server

We now turn our focus to constructing a TCP server. The server's job is to set up a communication endpoint and passively wait for a connection from the client. There are four general steps for basic TCP server communication:

1. Create a TCP socket using socket().
2. Assign a port number to the socket with bind().
3. Tell the system to allow connections to be made to that port, using listen().
4. Repeatedly do the following:
   - Call accept() to get a new socket for each client connection.
   - Communicate with the client via that new socket using send() and recv().
   - Close the client connection using close().

Creating the socket, sending, receiving, and closing are the same as in the client. The differences in the server's use of sockets have to do with binding an address to the socket and then using the socket as a way to obtain other sockets that are connected to clients. (We'll elaborate on this in the comments following the code.) The server's communication with each client is as simple as can be: it simply receives data on the client connection and sends the same data back over to the client; it repeats this until the client closes its end of the connection, at which point no more data will be forthcoming.

TCPEchoServer4.c

```
 1  #include <stdio.h>
 2  #include <stdlib.h>
 3  #include <string.h>
 4  #include <sys/types.h>
 5  #include <sys/socket.h>
 6  #include <netinet/in.h>
 7  #include <arpa/inet.h>
 8  #include "Practical.h"
 9
10  static const int MAXPENDING = 5; // Maximum outstanding connection requests
11
12  int main(int argc, char *argv[]) {
```

```
13
14   if (argc != 2) // Test for correct number of arguments
15     DieWithUserMessage("Parameter(s)", "<Server Port>");
16
17   in_port_t servPort = atoi(argv[1]); // First arg:  local port
18
19   // Create socket for incoming connections
20   int servSock; // Socket descriptor for server
21   if ((servSock = socket(AF_INET, SOCK_STREAM, IPPROTO_TCP)) < 0)
22     DieWithSystemMessage("socket() failed");
23
24   // Construct local address structure
25   struct sockaddr_in servAddr;                    // Local address
26   memset(&servAddr, 0, sizeof(servAddr));         // Zero out structure
27   servAddr.sin_family = AF_INET;                  // IPv4 address family
28   servAddr.sin_addr.s_addr = htonl(INADDR_ANY);   // Any incoming interface
29   servAddr.sin_port = htons(servPort);            // Local port
30
31   // Bind to the local address
32   if (bind(servSock, (struct sockaddr*) &servAddr, sizeof(servAddr)) < 0)
33     DieWithSystemMessage("bind() failed");
34
35   // Mark the socket so it will listen for incoming connections
36   if (listen(servSock, MAXPENDING) < 0)
37     DieWithSystemMessage("listen() failed");
38
39   for (;;) { // Run forever
40     struct sockaddr_in clntAddr; // Client address
41     // Set length of client address structure (in-out parameter)
42     socklen_t clntAddrLen = sizeof(clntAddr);
43
44     // Wait for a client to connect
45     int clntSock = accept(servSock, (struct sockaddr *) &clntAddr, &clntAddrLen);
46     if (clntSock < 0)
47       DieWithSystemMessage("accept() failed");
48
49     // clntSock is connected to a client!
50
51     char clntName[INET_ADDRSTRLEN]; // String to contain client address
52     if (inet_ntop(AF_INET, &clntAddr.sin_addr.s_addr, clntName,
53         sizeof(clntName)) != NULL)
54       printf("Handling client %s/%d\n", clntName, ntohs(clntAddr.sin_port));
55     else
56       puts("Unable to get client address");
57
```

```
58        HandleTCPClient(clntSock);
59    }
60    // NOT REACHED
61  }
```

TCPEchoServer4.c

1. **Program setup and parameter parsing:** lines 1-17
   We convert the port number from string to numeric value using atoi(); if the first argument is not a number, atoi() will return 0, which will cause an error later when we call bind().

2. **Socket creation and setup:** lines 19-37
   - **Create a TCP socket:** lines 20-22
     We create a stream socket just like we did in the client.

   - **Fill in desired endpoint address:** lines 25-29
     On the server, we need to associate our server socket with an address and port number so that client connections get to the right place. Since we are writing for IPv4, we use a **sockaddr_in** structure for this. Because we don't much care which address we are on (any one assigned to the machine the server is running on will be OK), we let the system pick it by specifying the wildcard address INADDR_ANY as our desired Internet address. (This is usually the right thing to do for servers, and it saves the server from having to find out any actual Internet address.) Before setting both address and port number in the **sockaddr_in**, we convert each to network byte order using htonl() and htons(). (See Section 5.1.2 for details.)

   - **Bind socket to specified address and port:** lines 32-33
     As noted above, the server's socket needs to be associated with a local address and port; the function that accomplishes this is bind(). Notice that **while the client has to supply the server's address to connect(), the server has to specify its** *own* **address to bind().** It is this piece of information (i.e., the server's address and port) that they have to agree on to communicate; neither one really needs to know the client's address. Note that bind() may fail for various reasons; one of the most important is that some other socket is already bound to the specified port (see Section 7.5). Also, on some systems special privileges are required to bind to certain ports (typically those with numbers less than 1024).

   - **Set the socket to listen:** lines 36-37
     The listen() call tells the TCP implementation to allow incoming connections from clients. Before the call to listen(), any incoming connection requests to the socket's address would be silently rejected—that is, the connect() would fail at the client.

3. **Iteratively handle incoming connections:** lines 39-59
   - **Accept an incoming connection:** lines 40-47

As discussed above, a TCP socket on which listen() has been called is used differently than the one we saw in the client application. Instead of sending and receiving on the socket, the server application calls accept(), which blocks until an incoming connection is made to the listening socket's port number. At that point, accept() returns a descriptor for a new socket, which is already connected to the initiating remote socket. The second argument points to a **sockaddr_in** structure, and the third argument is a pointer to the length of that structure. Upon success, the **sockaddr_in** contains the Internet address and port of the client to which the returned socket is connected; the address's length has been written into the integer pointed to by the third argument. Note that the socket referenced by the returned descriptor is already *connected*; among other things this means it is ready for sending and receiving. (For details about what happens in the underlying implementation, see Section 7.4.1 in Chapter 7.)

∎ **Report connected client:** lines 51–56
At this point *clntAddr* contains the address and port number of the connecting client; we provide a "Caller ID" function and print out the client's information. As you might expect, inet_ntop() is the inverse of inet_pton(), which we used in the client. It takes the binary representation of the client's address and converts it to a dotted-quad string. Because the implementation deals with ports and addresses in so-called network byte order (Section 5.1.2), we have to convert the port number before passing it to printf() (inet_pton() takes care of this transparently for addresses).

∎ **Handle echo client:** line 58
HandleTCPClient() takes care of the "application protocol." We discuss it below. Thus, we have factored out the "echo"-specific part of the server.

We have factored out the function that implements the "echo" part of our echo server. Although this *application protocol* only takes a few lines to implement, it's good design practice to isolate its details from the rest of the server code. This promotes code reuse.

HandleTCPClient() receives data on the given socket and sends it back on the same socket, iterating as long as recv() returns a positive value (indicating that something was received). recv() blocks until something is received or the client closes the connection. When the client closes the connection normally, recv() returns 0. You can find HandleTCPClient() in the file TCPServerUtility.c.

HandleTCPClient()

```
1  void HandleTCPClient(int clntSocket) {
2    char buffer[BUFSIZE]; // Buffer for echo string
3
4    // Receive message from client
5    ssize_t numBytesRcvd = recv(clntSocket, buffer, BUFSIZE, 0);
6    if (numBytesRcvd < 0)
7      DieWithSystemMessage("recv() failed");
```

```
8
9    // Send received string and receive again until end of stream
10   while (numBytesRcvd > 0) { // 0 indicates end of stream
11     // Echo message back to client
12     ssize_t numBytesSent = send(clntSocket, buffer, numBytesRcvd, 0);
13     if (numBytesSent < 0)
14       DieWithSystemMessage("send() failed");
15     else if (numBytesSent != numBytesRcvd)
16       DieWithUserMessage("send()", "sent unexpected number of bytes");
17
18     // See if there is more data to receive
19     numBytesRcvd = recv(clntSocket, buffer, BUFSIZE, 0);
20     if (numBytesRcvd < 0)
21       DieWithSystemMessage("recv() failed");
22   }
23
24   close(clntSocket); // Close client socket
25 }
```

HandleTCPClient()

Suppose we compile TCPEchoServer4.c, DieWithMessage.c, TCPServerUtility.c, and Address-Utility.c into the executable program TCPEchoServer4, and run that program on a host with Internet (IPv4) address 169.1.1.1, port 5000. Suppose also that we run our client on a host with Internet address 169.1.1.2 and connect it to the server. The server's output should look like this:

```
% TCPEchoServer4 5000
Handling client 169.1.1.2
```

While the client's output looks like this:

```
% TCPEchoClient4 169.1.1.1 "Echo this!" 5000
Received: Echo this!
```

The server binds its socket to port 5000 and waits for a connection request from the client. The client connects, sends the message "Echo this!" to the server, and receives the echoed response. In this command we have to supply TCPEchoClient with the port number on the command line because it is talking to our echo server, which is on port 5000 rather than the well-known port 7.

We have mentioned that a key principle for coding network applications using sockets is **Defensive Programming: your code must not make assumptions about anything received over the network**. What if you want to "play" with your TCP server to see how it responds to various incorrect client behaviors? You could write a TCP client that sends bogus messages and prints results; this, however, can be tedious and time-consuming. A quicker alternative is to use the **telnet** program available on most systems. This is a command-line tool that connects to a server, sends whatever text you type, and prints the response. Telnet takes two parameters: the server and port. For example, to telnet to our example echo server from above, try

```
% telnet 169.1.1.1 5000
```

Now type your string to echo and telnet will print the server response. The behavior of telnet differs between implementations, so you may need to research the specifics of its use on your system.

Now that we've seen a complete client and server, let's look at the individual functions that make up the Sockets API in a bit more detail.

2.3   Creating and Destroying Sockets

To communicate using TCP or UDP, a program begins by asking the operating system to create an instance of the socket abstraction. The function that accomplishes this is socket(); its parameters specify the flavor of socket needed by the program.

---

int socket(**int** *domain*, **int** *type*, **int** *protocol*)

The first parameter determines the communication *domain* of the socket. Recall that the Sockets API provides a generic interface for a large number of communication domains; however, we are only interested in IPv4 (AF_INET) and IPv6 (AF_INET6). Note that you may see some programs use PF_XXX here instead of AF_XXX. Typically, these values are equal, in which case they are interchangeable, but this is (alas) not guaranteed.[1]

The second parameter specifies the *type* of the socket. The type determines the semantics of data transmission with the socket—for example, whether transmission is reliable, whether message boundaries are preserved, and so on. The constant SOCK_STREAM specifies a socket with reliable byte-stream semantics, whereas SOCK_DGRAM specifies a best-effort datagram socket.

The third parameter specifies the particular *end-to-end protocol* to be used. For both IPv4 and IPv6, we want TCP (identified by the constant IPPROTO_TCP) for a stream socket, or UDP (identified by IPPROTO_UDP) for a datagram socket. Supplying the constant 0 as the third parameter causes the system to select the *default* end-to-end protocol for the specified protocol family and type. Because there is currently only one choice for stream sockets in the TCP/IP protocol family, we could specify 0 instead of giving the protocol number explicitly. Someday, however, there might be other end-to-end protocols in the Internet protocol family

---

[1] Truth be told, this is an ugly part of the Sockets interface, and the documentation is simply not helpful.

that implement the same semantics. In that case, specifying 0 might result in the use of a different protocol, which might or might not be desirable. The main thing is to ensure that the communicating programs are using the same end-to-end protocol.

We said earlier that socket() returns a *handle* for the communication instance. On UNIX-derived systems, it is an integer: a nonnegative value for success and −1 for failure. A nonfailure value should be treated as an opaque handle, like a file descriptor. (In reality, it *is* a file descriptor, taken from the same space as the numbers returned by open().) This handle, which we call a *socket descriptor*, is passed to other API functions to identify the socket abstraction on which the operation is to be carried out.

When an application is finished with a socket, it calls close(), giving the descriptor for the socket that is no longer needed.

---

int close(**int** *socket*)

---

close() tells the underlying protocol stack to initiate any actions required to shut down communications and deallocate any resources associated with the socket. close() returns 0 on success or −1 on failure. Once close() has been called, invoking other operations (e.g., send() and recv()) on the socket results in an error.

2.4   Specifying Addresses

Applications using sockets need to be able to identify the remote endpoint(s) with which they will communicate. We've already seen that a client must specify the address and port number of the server application with which it needs to communicate. In addition, the sockets layer sometimes needs to pass addresses to the application. For example, a feature analogous to "Caller ID" in the telephone network lets a server know the address and port number of each client that communicates with it.

In this section, we describe the data structures used as containers for this information by the Sockets API.

2.4.1   Generic Addresses

The Sockets API defines a generic data type—the **sockaddr** structure—for specifying addresses associated with sockets:

```
struct sockaddr {
    sa_family_t sa_family;    // Address family (e.g., AF_INET)
    char sa_data[14];         // Family-specific address information
};
```

The first part of this address structure defines the address family—the space to which the address belongs. For our purposes, we will always use the system-defined constants AF_INET and AF_INET6, which specify the Internet address families for IPv4 and IPv6, respectively. The second part is a blob of bits whose exact form depends on the address family. (This is a typical way of dealing with heterogeneity in operating systems and networking.) As we discussed in Section 1.2, socket addresses for the Internet protocol family have two parts: a 32-bit (IPv4) or 128-bit (IPv6) Internet address and a 16-bit port number.[2]

2.4.2   IPv4 Addresses

The particular form of the **sockaddr** structure that is used for TCP/IP socket addresses depends on the IP version. For IPv4, use the **sockaddr_in** structure.

```
struct in_addr {
    uint32_t s_addr;        // Internet address (32 bits)
};

struct sockaddr_in {
    sa_family_t sin_family;    // Internet protocol (AF_INET)
    in_port_t sin_port;        // Address port (16 bits)
    struct in_addr sin_addr;   // IPv4 address (32 bits)
    char sin_zero[8];          // Not used
};
```

As you can see, the **sockaddr_in** structure has fields for the port number and Internet address in addition to the address family. It is important to understand that **sockaddr_in** is just a more detailed view of the data in a **sockaddr** structure, tailored to sockets using IPv4. Thus, we can fill in the fields of a **sockaddr_in** and then cast (a pointer to) it to a (pointer to a) **sockaddr** and pass it to the socket functions, which look at the sa_family field to learn the actual type, then cast back to the appropriate type.

2.4.3   IPv6 Addresses

For IPv6, use the **sockaddr_in6** structure.

```
struct in_addr {
    uint32_t s_addr[16];       // Internet address (128 bits)
};

struct sockaddr_in6 {
    sa_family_t sin6_family;    // Internet protocol (AF_INET6)
    in_port_t sin6_port;        // Address port (16 bits)
    uint32_t sin6_flowinfo;     // Flow information
```

---

[2]The astute reader may have noticed that the generic **sockaddr** structure is not big enough to hold both a 16-byte IPv6 address and a 2-byte port number. We'll deal with this difficulty shortly.

```
    struct in6_addr sin6_addr; // IPv6 address (128 bits)
    uint32_t sin6_scope_id;    // Scope identifier
};
```

The **sockaddr_in6** structure has additional fields beyond those of a **sockaddr_in**. These are intended for capabilities of the IPv6 protocol that are not commonly used. They will be (mostly) ignored in this book.

As with **sockaddr_in**, we must cast (a pointer to) the **sockaddr_in6** to (a pointer to) a **sockaddr** in order to pass it to the various socket functions. Again, the implementation uses the address family field to determine the actual type of the argument.

2.4.4 Generic Address Storage

If you know anything about how data structures are allocated in C, you may have already noticed that a **sockaddr** is not big enough to hold a **sockaddr_in6**. (If you don't know anything about it, don't fear: much of what you need to know will be covered in Chapter 5.) In particular, what if we want to allocate an address structure, but we don't know the actual address type (e.g., IPv4 or IPv6)? The generic **sockaddr** won't work because it's too small for some address structures.[3] To solve this problem, the socket designers created the **sockaddr_storage** structure, which is guaranteed to be as large as any supported address type.

```
    struct sockaddr_storage {
        sa_family_t
        ...
        // Padding and fields to get correct length and alignment
        ...
    };
```

As with **sockaddr**, we still have the leading family field to determine the actual type of the address; however, with **sockaddr_storage** we have sufficient space for any address type. (For a hint about how this could be accomplished, refer to the discussion of how the C compiler lays out structures in memory, in Section 5.1.6.)

One final note on addresses. On some platforms, the address structures contain an additional field that stores the length of the address structure in bytes. For **sockaddr**, **sockaddr_in**, **sockaddr_in6**, and **sockaddr_storage**, the extra fields are called sa_len, sin_len, sin6_len, and ss_len, respectively. Since a length field is not available on all systems, avoid using it. Typically, platforms that use this form of structure define a value (e.g., SIN6_LEN) that can be tested for at compile time to see if the length field is present.

---

[3]You may wonder why this is so (we do). The reasons apparently have to do with backward-compatibility: the Sockets API was first specified a long time ago, before IPv6, when resources were scarcer and there was no reason to have a bigger structure. Changing it now to make it bigger would apparently break binary-compatibility with some applications.

2.4.5   Binary/String Address Conversion

For socket functions to understand addresses, they must be in "numeric" (i.e., binary) form; however, addresses for human use are generally "printable" strings (e.g., 192.168.1.1 or 1::1). We can convert addresses from printable string to numeric using the inet_pton() function (**pton** = **p**rintable **to** **n**umeric):

---

int inet_pton(**int** *addressFamily*, **const char** **src*, **void** **dst*)

The first parameter, *addressFamily*, specifies the address family of the address being converted. Recall that the Sockets API provides a generic interface for a large number of communication domains. However, we are only interested here in IPv4 (AF_INET) and IPv6 (AF_INET6). The *src* parameter references a null-terminated character string containing the address to convert. The *dst* parameter points to a block of memory in the caller's space to hold the result; its length must be sufficient to hold the result (at least 4 bytes for IPv4 and 16 bytes for IPv6). inet_pton() returns 1 if the conversion succeeds, with the address referenced by *dst* in network byte order; 0 if the string pointed to by *src* is not formatted as a valid address; and −1 if the specified address family is unknown.

We can go the other way, converting addresses from numeric to printable form, using inet_ntop() (**ntop** = **n**umeric **to** **p**rintable):

---

const char **inet_ntop(**int** *addressFamily*, **const void** **src*, **char** **dst*, **socklen_t** *dstBytes*)

The first parameter, *addressFamily*, specifies the type of the address being converted. The second parameter *src* points to the first byte of a block of memory containing the numeric address to convert. The size of the block is determined by the address family. The *dst* parameter points to a buffer (block of memory) allocated in the caller's space, into which the resulting string will be copied; its size is given by *dstBytes*. How do we know what size to make the block of memory? The system-defined constants INET_ADDRSTRLEN (for IPv4) and INET6_ADDRSTRLEN (for IPv6) indicate the longest possible resulting string (in bytes). inet_ntop() returns a pointer to the string containing the printable address (i.e., the third argument) if the conversion succeeds and NULL otherwise.

2.4.6   Getting a Socket's Associated Addresses

The system associates a local and foreign address with each connected socket (TCP or UDP). Later we'll discuss the details of how these values are assigned. We can find out these addresses using getsockname() for the local address and getpeername() for the foreign address. Both methods return a **sockaddr** structure containing the Internet address and port information.

---

int getpeername(**int** *socket*, **struct sockaddr** *remoteAddress, **socklen_t** *addressLength)
int getsockname(**int** *socket*, **struct sockaddr** *localAddress, **socklen_t** *addressLength)

The *socket* parameter is the descriptor of the socket whose address information we want. The *remoteAddress* and *localAddress* parameters point to address structures into which the address information will be placed by the implementation; they are always cast to **sockaddr** * by the caller. **If we don't know the IP protocol version a priori, we should pass in a (pointer to a) sockaddr_storage to receive the result.** As with other socket calls using **sockaddr**, the *addressLength* is an in-out parameter specifying the length of the buffer (input) and returned address structure (output) in bytes.

2.5   Connecting a Socket

A TCP socket must be connected to another socket before any data can be sent through it. In this sense using TCP sockets is something like using the telephone network. Before you can talk, you have to specify the number you want, and a connection must be established; if the connection cannot be established, you have to try again later. The connection establishment process is the biggest difference between clients and servers: The client initiates the connection while the server waits passively for clients to connect to it. (For additional details about the connection process and how it relates to the API functions, see Section 7.4.) To establish a connection with a server, we call connect() on the socket.

---

int connect(**int** *socket*, **const struct sockaddr** *foreignAddress, **socklen_t** *addressLength*)

The first argument, *socket*, is the descriptor created by socket(). *foreignAddress* is declared to be a pointer to a **sockaddr** because the Sockets API is generic; for our purposes, it will always be a pointer to either a **sockaddr_in** or **sockaddr_in6** containing the Internet address and port of the server. *addressLength* specifies the length of the address structure, typically given as sizeof(struct sockaddr_in) or sizeof(struct sockaddr_in6). When connect() returns, the socket is connected, and communication can proceed with calls to send() and recv().

2.6   Binding to an Address

As we have noted already, client and server "rendezvous" at the server's address and port. For that to work, the server must first be associated with that address and port. This is accomplished using bind(). Again, note that the client supplies the server's address to connect(), but the server has to specify its *own* address to bind(). Neither client nor server application needs to know the client's address in order for them to communicate. (Of course, the server may wish to know the client's address for logging or other purposes.)

---

int bind(int *socket*, **struct sockaddr** **localAddress*, **socklen_t** *addressSize*)

The first parameter is the descriptor returned by an earlier call to socket(). As with connect(), the address parameter is declared as a pointer to a **sockaddr**, but for TCP/IP applications, it will always point to a **sockaddr_in** (for IPv4) or **sockaddr_in6** (for IPv6), containing the Internet address of the local interface and the port to listen on. The *addressSize* parameter is the size of the address structure. bind() returns 0 on success and −1 on failure.

It is important to realize that it is not possible for a program to bind a socket to an *arbitrary* Internet address—if a specific Internet address is given (of either type), the call will only succeed if that address is assigned to the host on which the program is running. A server on a host with multiple Internet addresses might bind to a specific one because it *only wants to accept connections that arrive to that address*. Typically, however, the server wants to accept connections sent to *any* of the host's addresses, and so sets the address part of the **sockaddr** to the "wildcard" address INADDR_ANY for IPv4 or *in6addr_any* for IPv6. The semantics of the wildcard address are that it matches any specific address. For a server, this means that it will receive connections addressed to any of the host's addresses (of the specified type).

While bind() is mostly used by servers, a client can also use bind() to specify its local address/port. For those TCP clients that don't pick their own local address/port with bind(), the local Internet address and port are determined during the call to connect(). Thus, a client must call bind() *before* calling connect() if it is going to use it.

You can initialize a **in6_addr** structure to the wildcard address with IN6ADDR_ANY_INIT; however, this special constant may only be used as an "initializer" in a declaration. **Note well that while INADDR_ANY is defined to be in host byte order and, consequently, must be converted to network byte order with htonl() before being used as an argument to** bind(), *in6addr_any* **and IN6ADDR_ANY_INIT are already in network byte order.**

Finally, if you supply the port number 0 to bind(), the system will select an unused local port for you.

2.7 Handling Incoming Connections

After binding, the server socket has an address (or at least a port). Another step is required to instruct the underlying protocol implementation to listen for connections from clients; this is done by calling listen() on the socket.

---

int listen(**int** *socket*, **int** *queueLimit*)

The listen() function causes internal state changes to the given socket, so that incoming TCP connection requests will be processed and then queued for acceptance by the program. (Section 7.4 in Chapter 7 has more details about the life cycle of a TCP connection.) The *queue-Limit* parameter specifies an upper bound on the number of incoming connections that can be waiting at any time. The precise effect of *queueLimit* is very system dependent, so consult your local system's technical specifications.[4] listen() returns 0 on success and −1 on failure.

Once a socket is configured to listen, the program can begin accepting client connections on it. At first it might seem that a server should now wait for a connection on the socket that it has set up, send and receive through that socket, close it, and then repeat the process. However, that is not the way it works. The socket that has been bound to a port and marked "listening" is never actually used for sending and receiving. Instead, it is used as a way of getting *new* sockets, one for each client connection; the server then sends and receives on the *new* sockets. The server gets a socket for an incoming client connection by calling accept().

---

int accept(**int** *socket*, **struct sockaddr** *clientAddress, **socklen_t** *addressLength)

This function dequeues the next connection on the queue for *socket*. If the queue is empty, accept() blocks until a connection request arrives. When successful, accept() fills in the **sockaddr** structure pointed to by *clientAddress*, with the address and port of the client at the other end of the connection. Upon invocation, the *addressLength* parameter should specify the size of the structure pointed to by *clientAddress* (i.e., the space available); upon return it contains the size of the actual address returned. **A common beginner mistake is to fail to initialize the integer that *addressLength* points to so it contains the length of the structure that *clientAddress* points to**. The following shows the correct way:

```
struct sockaddr_storage address;
socklen_t addrLength = sizeof(address);
int newConnection = accept(sock, &address, &addrLength);
```

If successful, accept() returns a descriptor for a *new* socket that is connected to the client. The socket passed as the first parameter to accept() is unchanged (not connected to the client) and continues to listen for new connection requests. On failure, accept() returns −1. On most systems, accept() only fails when passed a bad socket descriptior. However, on some platforms it may return an error if the new socket has experienced a network-level error after being created and before being accepted.

---

[4]For information about using "man" pages, see the preface.

2.8 Communication

Once a socket is "connected," you can begin sending and receiving data. As we've seen, a client creates a connected socket by calling connect(), and a connected socket is returned by accept() on a server. After connection, the distinction between client and server effectively disappears, at least as far as the Sockets API is concerned. Through a connected TCP socket, you can communicate using send() and recv().

---

ssize_t send(**int** *socket*, **const void** **msg*, **size_t** *msgLength*, **int** *flags*)
ssize_t recv(**int** *socket*, **void** **rcvBuffer*, **size_t** *bufferLength*, **int** *flags*)

These functions have very similar arguments. The first parameter *socket* is the descriptor for the connected socket through which data is to be sent or received. For send(), *msg* points to the sequence of bytes to be sent, and *msgLength* is the number of bytes to send. The default behavior for send() is to block until all of the data is sent. (We revisit this behavior in Section 6.3 and Chapter 7.) For recv(), *rcvBuffer* points to the buffer—that is, an area in memory such as a character array—where received data will be placed, and *bufferLength* gives the length of the buffer, which is the maximum number of bytes that can be received at once. The default behavior for recv() is to block until at least some bytes can be transferred. (On most systems, the minimum amount of data that will cause the caller of recv() to unblock is 1 byte.)

The *flags* parameter in both send() and recv() provides a way to change some aspects of the default behavior of the socket call. Setting *flags* to 0 specifies the default behavior. send() and recv() return the number of bytes sent or received or −1 for failure. (See also Section 6.3.)

Remember: TCP is a byte-stream protocol, so send() boundaries are not preserved. **The number of bytes read in a single call to recv on the receiver is not necessarily determined by the number of bytes written by a single call to send().** If you call send() with 3000 bytes, it may take several calls to recv() to get all 3000 bytes, even if you pass a 5000-byte buffer to each recv() call. If you call send() with 100 bytes four times, you might receive all 400 bytes with a single call to recv(). A common mistake when writing TCP socket applications involves assuming that if you write all of the data with one send() you can read it all with one recv(). All these possibilities are illustrated in Chapter 7.

2.9 Using IPv6

So far, we've seen a client and server that work only with IPv4. What if you want to use IPv6? The changes are relatively minor and basically involve using the IPv6 equivalents for the address structure and constants. Let's look at the IPv6 version of our TCP echo server.

TCPEchoServer6.c

```
 1  #include <stdio.h>
 2  #include <stdlib.h>
 3  #include <string.h>
 4  #include <sys/types.h>
 5  #include <sys/socket.h>
 6  #include <netinet/in.h>
 7  #include <arpa/inet.h>
 8  #include "Practical.h"
 9
10  static const int MAXPENDING = 5; // Maximum outstanding connection requests
11
12  int main(int argc, char *argv[]) {
13
14    if (argc != 2) // Test for correct number of arguments
15      DieWithUserMessage("Parameter(s)", "<Server Port>");
16
17    in_port_t servPort = atoi(argv[1]); // First arg:  local port
18
19    // Create socket for incoming connections
20    int servSock = socket(AF_INET6, SOCK_STREAM, IPPROTO_TCP);
21    if (servSock < 0)
22      DieWithSystemMessage("socket() failed");
23
24    // Construct local address structure
25    struct sockaddr_in6 servAddr;            // Local address
26    memset(&servAddr, 0, sizeof(servAddr)); // Zero out structure
27    servAddr.sin6_family = AF_INET6;         // IPv6 address family
28    servAddr.sin6_addr = in6addr_any;        // Any incoming interface
29    servAddr.sin6_port = htons(servPort);    // Local port
30
31    // Bind to the local address
32    if (bind(servSock, (struct sockaddr *) &servAddr, sizeof(servAddr)) < 0)
33      DieWithSystemMessage("bind() failed");
34
35    // Mark the socket so it will listen for incoming connections
36    if (listen(servSock, MAXPENDING) < 0)
37      DieWithSystemMessage("listen() failed");
38
39    for (;;) { // Run forever
40      struct sockaddr_in6 clntAddr; // Client address
41      // Set length of client address structure (in-out parameter)
42      socklen_t clntAddrLen = sizeof(clntAddr);
43
```

```
44      // Wait for a client to connect
45      int clntSock = accept(servSock, (struct sockaddr *) &clntAddr, &clntAddrLen);
46      if (clntSock < 0)
47        DieWithSystemMessage("accept() failed");
48
49      // clntSock is connected to a client!
50
51      char clntName[INET6_ADDRSTRLEN]; // Array to contain client address string
52      if (inet_ntop(AF_INET6, &clntAddr.sin6_addr.s6_addr, clntName,
53          sizeof(clntName)) != NULL)
54        printf("Handling client %s/%d\n", clntName, ntohs(clntAddr.sin6_port));
55      else
56        puts("Unable to get client address");
57
58      HandleTCPClient(clntSock);
59    }
60    // NOT REACHED
61  }
```

TCPEchoServer6.c

1. **Socket creation:** lines 19-22
   We construct an IPv6 socket by specifying the communication domain as AF_INET6.

2. **Fill in local address:** lines 24-29
   For the local address, we use the IPv6 (**struct sockaddr_in6**) address structure and constants (AF_INET6 and *in6addr_any*). One subtle difference is that we do not have to convert *in6addr_any* to network byte order as we did with INADDR_ANY.

3. **Report connected client:** lines 51-56
   clntAddr, which contains the address of the connecting client, is declared as an IPv6 socket address structure. When we convert the numeric address representation to a string, the maximum string length is now INET6_ADDRSTRLEN. Finally, our call to inet_ntop() uses an IPv6 address.

You've now seen both IPv4- and IPv6-specific clients and servers. In Chapter 3 we will see how they can be made to work with either type of address.

Exercises

1. Experiment with the book's TCP echo server using telnet. What OS are you using? Does the server appear to echo as you type (character-by-character) or only after you complete a line?

2. Use telnet to connect to your favorite Web server on port 80 and fetch the default page. You can usually do this by sending the string "GET /" to the Web server. Report the server address/name and the text from the default page.

3. For TCPEchoServer.c we explicitly provide an address to the socket using bind(). We said that a socket must have an address for communication, yet we do not perform a bind() in TCPEchoClient.c. How is the echo client's socket given a local address?

4. Modify the client and server so that the server "talks" first, sending a greeting message, and the client waits until it has received the greeting before sending anything. What needs to be agreed upon between client and server?

5. Servers are supposed to run for a long time without stopping. Therefore, they have to be designed to provide good service no matter what their clients do. Examine the example TCPEchoServer.c and list anything you can think of that a client might do to cause the server to give poor service to other clients. Suggest improvements to fix the problems you find.

6. Using getsockname() and getpeername(), modify TCPEchoClient4.c to print the local and foreign address immediately after connect().

7. What happens when you call getpeername() on an unconnected TCP socket?

8. Using getsockname() and getpeername(), modify TCPEchoServer4.c to print the local and foreign address for the server socket immediately before and after bind() and for the client socket immediately after it's returned by accept().

9. Modify TCPEchoClient4.c to use **bind()** so that the system selects both the address and port.

10. Modify TCPEchoClient4.c so that the new version binds to a specific local address and system-selected port. If the local address changed or you moved the program to a host with a different local address, what do you think would happen?

11. What happens when you attempt to bind after calling **connect()**?

12. Why does the socket interface use a special socket to accept connections? In other words, what would be wrong with having a server create a socket, set it up using bind() and listen(), wait for a connection, send and receive through *that* socket, and then when it is finished, close it and repeat the process? (*Hint*: Think about what happens to connection requests that arrive right after the server closes the previous connection.)

chapter **3**

Of Names and Address Families

At this point, you know enough to build working TCP clients and servers. However, our examples so far, though useful enough, nevertheless have a couple of features that could be improved. First, *the only way to specify a destination is with an IP address*, such as 169.1.1.1 or FE80:1034::2A97:1001:1. This is a bit painful for most humans, who are—let's face it—not that good at dealing with long strings of numbers that have to be formatted just right. That's why most applications allow the use of *names* like www.mkp.com and server.example.com to specify destinations, in addition to Internet addresses. But the Sockets API, as we've seen, *only* takes numerical arguments, so applications need a way to convert names to the required numerical form.

Another problem with our examples so far is that *the choice of whether to use IPv4 or IPv6 is wired into the code*—each progam we've seen deals with only *one* version of the IP protocol. That was by design—to keep things simple. But wouldn't it be better if we could *hide* this choice from the rest of the code, letting the argument(s) determine whether a socket for IPv4 or IPv6 is created?

It turns out that the API provides solutions to both of these problems—and more! In this chapter we'll see how to (1) access the *name service* to convert between names and numeric quantities; and (2) write code that chooses between IPv4 and IPv6 at runtime.

3.1 Mapping Names to Numbers

Identifying endpoints with strings of dot- or colon-separated numbers is not very user friendly, but that's not the only reason to prefer names over addresses. Another is that a host's Internet address is tied to the part of the network to which it is connected. This is a source of inflexibility: If a host moves to another network or changes Internet service providers (ISPs), its Internet address generally has to change. Then everybody who refers to the host by that address has to be informed of the change, or they won't be able to access the host! When this book was written, the Web server for the publisher of this text, Morgan Kaufmann, had an Internet address of 129.35.69.7. However, we invariably refer to that Web server as *www.mkp.com*. Obviously, *www.mkp.com* is easier to remember than 129.35.69.7. In fact, this is most likely how you typically think of specifying a host on the Internet, by name. In addition, if Morgan Kaufmann's Web server changes its Internet address for some reason (e.g., new ISP, server moves to another machine), simply changing the mapping of *www.mkp.com* from 129.35.69.7 to the new Internet address allows the change to be transparent to all programs that use the name to identify the Web server.[1]

To solve these problems, most implementations of the Sockets API provide access to a *name service* that maps names to other information, including Internet addresses. You've already seen names that map to Internet addresses (*www.mkp.com*). Names for services (e.g., echo) can also be mapped to port numbers. The process of mapping a name to a numeric quantity (address or port number) is called *resolution*. There are a number of ways to resolve names into binary quantities; your system probably provides access to several of these. Some of them involve interaction with other systems "under the covers"; others are strictly local.

It is critical to remember that **a name service is not required for TCP/IP to work**. Names simply provide a level of indirection, for the reasons discussed above. The host-naming service can access information from a wide variety of sources. Two of the primary sources are the *Domain Name System* (DNS) and local configuration databases. The DNS [8] is a distributed database that maps *domain names* such as *www.mkp.com* to Internet addresses and other information; the DNS protocol [9] allows hosts connected to the Internet to retrieve information from that database using TCP or UDP. Local configuration databases are generally operating-system-specific mechanisms for name-to-Internet-address mappings. Fortunately for the programmer, the details of how the name service is *implemented* are hidden behind the API, so the only thing we need to know is how to ask it to *resolve* a name.

3.1.1 Accessing the Name Service

The preferred interface to the name service interface is through the function getaddrinfo():[2]

---

int getaddrinfo (**const char** **hostStr*, **const char** **serviceStr*,
            const struct addrinfo **hints*, **struct addrinfo** ***results*)

---

[1]MK's address was actually 208.164.121.48 when we wrote the first edition. Presumably, they changed their address to help us make this point.
[2]Historically, other functions were available for this purpose, and many applications still use them. However, they have several shortcomings and are considered obsolescent as of the POSIX 2001 standard.

The first two arguments to getaddrinfo() point to null-terminated character strings representing a host name or address and a service name or port number, respectively. The third argument describes the kind of information to be returned; we discuss it below. The last argument is the location of a **struct addrinfo** pointer, where a pointer to a linked list containing results will be stored. The return value of getaddrinfo() indicates whether the resolution was successful (0) or unsuccessful (nonzero error code).

Using getaddrinfo() entails using two other auxiliary functions:

---

void freeaddrinfo(**struct addrinfo** *addrList*)
const char *gai_strerror(**int** *errorCode*)

---

getaddrinfo() creates a dynamically allocated linked list of results, which must be deallocated after the caller is finished with the list. Given the pointer to the head of the result list, freeaddrinfo() frees all the storage allocated for the list. Failure to call this method can result in a pernicious memory leak. The method **should only be called when the program is finished with the returned information**; no information contained in the list of results is reliable after this function has returned. In case getaddrinfo() returns a nonzero (error) value, passing it to gai_strerror() yields a string that describes what went wrong.

Generally speaking, getaddrinfo() takes the name of a host/service pair as input and returns a linked list of structures containing everything needed to create a socket to connect to the named host/service, including: address/protocol family (v4 or v6), socket type (e.g., stream or datagram), protocol (TCP or UDP for the Internet protocol family), and numeric socket address. Each entry in the linked list is placed into an **addrinfo** structure, declared as follows:

```
struct addrinfo {
  int ai_flags;            // Flags to control info resolution
  int ai_family;           // Family:  AF_INET, AF_INET6, AF_UNSPEC
  int ai_socktype;         // Socket type:  SOCK_STREAM, SOCK_DGRAM
  int ai_protocol;         // Protocol: 0 (default) or IPPROTO_XXX
  socklen_t ai_addrlen;    // Length of socket address ai_addr
  struct sockaddr *ai_addr; // Socket address for socket
  char *ai_canonname;      // Canonical name
  struct addrinfo *ai_next; // Next addrinfo in linked list
};
```

The **ai_sockaddr** field contains a **sockaddr** of the appropriate type, with (numeric) address and port information filled in. It should be obvious which fields contain the address family, socket type, and protocol information. (The flags field is not used in the result; we will discuss its use shortly.) Actually, the results are returned in a pointer to a linked list of **addrinfo** structures; the *ai_next* field contains the pointers for this list.

Why a linked list? There are two reasons. First, for each combination of host and service, there might be several different combinations of address family (v4 or v6) and socket type/protocol (stream/TCP or datagramUDP) that represent possible endpoints. For example, the host "server.example.net" might have instances of the "spam" service listening on port 1001 on both IPv4/TCP and IPv6/UDP. The getaddrinfo() function returns both of these. The second reason is that a hostname can map to multiple IP addresses; getaddrinfo() helpfully returns all of these.

Thus, getaddrinfo() returns all the viable combinations for a given hostname, service pair. But wait—what if you don't *need* options, and you know exactly what you want in advance? You don't want to have to write code that searches through the returned list for a particular combination—say, IPv4/TCP. That's where the third parameter of getaddrinfo() comes in! It allows you to tell the system to *filter the results for you*. We'll see how it is used in our example program, GetAddrInfo.c.

GetAddrInfo.c

```
1   #include <stdio.h>
2   #include <stdlib.h>
3   #include <string.h>
4   #include <netdb.h>
5   #include "Practical.h"
6
7   int main(int argc, char *argv[]) {
8
9     if (argc != 3) // Test for correct number of arguments
10      DieWithUserMessage("Parameter(s)", "<Address/Name> <Port/Service>");
11
12    char *addrString = argv[1];   // Server address/name
13    char *portString = argv[2];   // Server port/service
14
15    // Tell the system what kind(s) of address info we want
16    struct addrinfo addrCriteria;                   // Criteria for address match
17    memset(&addrCriteria, 0, sizeof(addrCriteria)); // Zero out structure
18    addrCriteria.ai_family = AF_UNSPEC;             // Any address family
19    addrCriteria.ai_socktype = SOCK_STREAM;         // Only stream sockets
20    addrCriteria.ai_protocol = IPPROTO_TCP;         // Only TCP protocol
21
22    // Get address(es) associated with the specified name/service
23    struct addrinfo *addrList; // Holder for list of addresses returned
24    // Modify servAddr contents to reference linked list of addresses
25    int rtnVal = getaddrinfo(addrString, portString, &addrCriteria, &addrList);
26    if (rtnVal != 0)
27      DieWithUserMessage("getaddrinfo() failed", gai_strerror(rtnVal));
28
29    // Display returned addresses
```

```
30    for (struct addrinfo *addr = addrList; addr != NULL; addr = addr->ai_next) {
31        PrintSocketAddress(addr->ai_addr, stdout);
32        fputc('\n', stdout);
33    }
34
35    freeaddrinfo(addrList); // Free addrinfo allocated in getaddrinfo()
36
37    exit(0);
38 }
```

GetAddrInfo.c

1. **Application setup and parameter parsing:** lines 9–13

2. **Construct address specification:** lines 15–20
   The *addrCriteria* structure will indicate what kinds of results we are interested in.

   ■ **Declare and initialize addrinfo structure:** lines 16–17

   ■ **Set address family:** line 18
   We set the family to AF_UNSPEC, which allows the returned address to come from any family (including AF_INET and AF_INET6).

   ■ **Set socket type:** line 19
   We want a stream/TCP endpoint, so we set this to SOCK_STREAM. The system will filter out results that use different protocols.

   ■ **Set protocol:** line 20
   We want a TCP socket, so we set this to IPPROTO_TCP. Since TCP is the default protocol for stream sockets, leaving this field 0 would have the same result.

3. **Fetch address information:** lines 22–27

   ■ **Declare pointer for head of result linked list:** line 23

   ■ **Call getaddrinfo():** line 25
   We pass the desired hostname, port, and the constraints encoded in the *addrCriteria* structure.

   ■ **Check return value:** lines 26–27
   getaddrinfo() returns 0 if successful. Otherwise, the return value indicates the specific error. The auxiliary function gai_strerror() returns a character string error message explaining the given error return value. Note that these messages are different from the normal *errno*-based messages.

4. **Print addresses:** lines 29–33
   Iterate over the linked list of addresses, printing each to the console. The function PrintSocketAddress() takes an address to print and the stream on which to print. We present its code, which is in AddressUtility.c, later in this chapter.

5. **Free address linked list:** line 35

The system allocated storage for the linked list of **addrinfo** structures it returned. We must call the auxiliary function freeaddrinfo() to free that memory when we are finished with it.

The program GetAddrInfo.c takes two command-line parameters, a hostname (or address) and a service name (or port number), and prints the address information returned by getaddrinfo(). Suppose you want to find an address for the service named "whois" on the host named "localhost" (i.e., the one you are running on). Here's how you use it:

% **GetAddrInfo localhost whois**
127.0.0.1-43

To find the service "whois" on the host "pine.netlab.uky.edu", do this:

% **GetAddrInfo pine.uky.edu whois**
128.163.170.219-43

The program can deal with any combination of name and numerical arguments:

% **GetAddrInfo 169.1.1.100 time**
169.1.1.100-37
% **GetAddrInfo FE80:0000:0000:0000:0000:ABCD:0001:0002:0003 12345**
fe80::abcd:1:2:3-12345

These examples all return a single answer. But as we noted above, some names have multiple numeric addresses associated with them. For example, "google.com" is typically associated with a number of Internet addresses. This allows a service (e.g., search engine) to be placed on multiple hosts. Why do this? One reason is robustness. If any single host fails, the service continues because the client can use any of the hosts providing the service. Another advantage is scalability. If clients randomly select the numeric address (and corresponding host) to use, we can spread the load over multiple servers. The good news is that getaddrinfo() returns *all* of the addresses to which a name maps. You can experiment with this by executing the program with the names of popular Web sites. (Note that supplying 0 for the second argument results in only the address information being printed.)

3.1.2   Details, Details

As we noted above, getaddrinfo() is something of a "Swiss Army Knife" function. We'll cover some of the subtleties of its capabilities here. Beginning readers may wish to skip this section and come back to it later.

The third argument (**addrinfo** structure) tells the system what kinds of endpoints the caller is interested in. In GetAddrInfo.c, we set this parameter to indicate that any address family was acceptable, and we wanted a stream/TCP socket. We could have instead specified datagram/UDP or a particular address family (say, AF_INET6), or we could have set the *ai_socktype* and *ai_protocol* fields to zero, indicating that we wanted to receive *all* possibilities. It is even possible to pass a NULL pointer for the third argument; the system is supposed to treat this case as if an **addrinfo** structure had been passed with *ai_family* set to AF_UNSPEC and everything else set to 0.

The *ai_flags* field in the third parameter provides additional control over the behavior of getaddrinfo(). It is an integer, individual bits of which are interpreted as boolean variables by the system. The meaning of each flag is given below; flags can be combined using the bitwise OR operator "|" (see Section 5.1.8 for how to do this).

AI_PASSIVE If *hostStr* is NULL when this flag is set, any returned **addrinfo**s will have their addresses set to the appropriate "any" address constant—INADDR_ANY (IPv4) or IN6ADDR_ANY_INIT (IPv6).

AI_CANONNAME Just as one name can resolve to many numeric addresses, multiple names can resolve to the same IP address. However, one name is usually defined to be the official ("canonical") name. By setting this flag in *ai_flags*, we instruct getaddrinfo() to return a pointer to the canonical name (if it exists) in the **ai_canonname** field of the first **struct addrinfo** of the linked list.

AI_NUMERICHOST This flag causes an error to be returned if *hostStr* does not point to a string in valid numeric address format. Without this flag, if the *hostStr* parameter points to something that is not a valid string representation of a numeric address, an attempt will be made to resolve it via the name system; this can waste time and bandwidth on useless queries to the name service. If this flag is set, a given valid address string is simply converted and returned, a la inet_pton().

AI_ADDRCONFIG If set, getaddrinfo() returns addresses of a particular family only if the system has an interface configured for that family. So an IPv4 address would be returned only if the system has an interface with an IPv4 address, and similarly for IPv6.

AI_V4MAPPED If the *ai_family* field contains AF_INET6, and no matching IPv6 addresses are found, then getaddrinfo() returns IPv4-mapped IPv6 addresses. This technique can be used to provide limited interoperation between IPv4-only and IPv6 hosts.

3.2 Writing Address-Generic Code

A famous bard once wrote "To v6 or not to v6, that is the question." Fortunately, the Socket interface allows us to postpone answering that question until execution time. In our earlier TCP client and server examples, we specified a particular IP protocol version to both the socket creation and address string conversion functions using AF_INET or AF_INET6. However, getaddrinfo() allows us to write code that works with either address family, without having to duplicate steps for each version. In this section we'll use its capabilities to modify our version-specific client and server code to make them generic.

Before we do that, here's a handy little method that prints a socket address (of either flavor). Given a **sockaddr** structure containing an IPv4 or IPv6 address, it prints the address to the given output stream, using the proper format for its address family. Given any other kind of address, it prints an error string. This function takes a generic **struct sockaddr** pointer and prints the address to the specified stream. You can find our implementation of PrintSocketAddr() in AddressUtility.c with the function prototype included in Practical.h.

PrintSocketAddr()

```
1   void PrintSocketAddress(const struct sockaddr *address, FILE *stream) {
2     // Test for address and stream
3     if (address == NULL || stream == NULL)
4       return;
5
6     void *numericAddress; // Pointer to binary address
7     // Buffer to contain result (IPv6 sufficient to hold IPv4)
8     char addrBuffer[INET6_ADDRSTRLEN];
9     in_port_t port; // Port to print
10    // Set pointer to address based on address family
11    switch (address->sa_family) {
12    case AF_INET:
13      numericAddress = &((struct sockaddr_in *) address)->sin_addr;
14      port = ntohs(((struct sockaddr_in *) address)->sin_port);
15      break;
16    case AF_INET6:
17      numericAddress = &((struct sockaddr_in6 *) address)->sin6_addr;
18      port = ntohs(((struct sockaddr_in6 *) address)->sin6_port);
19      break;
20    default:
21      fputs("[unknown type]", stream);    // Unhandled type
22      return;
23    }
24    // Convert binary to printable address
25    if (inet_ntop(address->sa_family, numericAddress, addrBuffer,
26        sizeof(addrBuffer)) == NULL)
27      fputs("[invalid address]", stream); // Unable to convert
28    else {
29      fprintf(stream, "%s", addrBuffer);
30      if (port != 0)                  // Zero not valid in any socket addr
31        fprintf(stream, "-%u", port);
32    }
33  }
```

PrintSocketAddr()

3.2.1 Generic TCP Client

Using getaddrinfo(), we can write clients and servers that are not specific to one IP version or the other. Let's begin by converting our TCP client to make it version-independent; we'll drop the version number and call it TCPEchoClient.c. The general strategy is to set up arguments to getaddrinfo() that make it return both IPv4 and IPv6 addresses and use the first address that works. Since our address search functionality may be useful elsewhere, we factor out the code responsible for creating and connecting the client socket, placing it in a separate function, SetupTCPClientSocket(), in TCPClientUtility.c. The setup function takes a host and service, specified in a string, and returns a connected socket (or -1 on failure). The host or service may be specified as NULL.

TCPClientUtility.c

```
1   #include <string.h>
2   #include <unistd.h>
3   #include <sys/types.h>
4   #include <sys/socket.h>
5   #include <netdb.h>
6   #include "Practical.h"
7
8   int SetupTCPClientSocket(const char *host, const char *service) {
9     // Tell the system what kind(s) of address info we want
10    struct addrinfo addrCriteria;                   // Criteria for address match
11    memset(&addrCriteria, 0, sizeof(addrCriteria)); // Zero out structure
12    addrCriteria.ai_family = AF_UNSPEC;             // v4 or v6 is OK
13    addrCriteria.ai_socktype = SOCK_STREAM;         // Only streaming sockets
14    addrCriteria.ai_protocol = IPPROTO_TCP;         // Only TCP protocol
15
16    // Get address(es)
17    struct addrinfo *servAddr; // Holder for returned list of server addrs
18    int rtnVal = getaddrinfo(host, service, &addrCriteria, &servAddr);
19    if (rtnVal != 0)
20      DieWithUserMessage("getaddrinfo() failed", gai_strerror(rtnVal));
21
22    int sock = -1;
23    for (struct addrinfo *addr = servAddr; addr != NULL; addr = addr->ai_next) {
24      // Create a reliable, stream socket using TCP
25      sock = socket(addr->ai_family, addr->ai_socktype, addr->ai_protocol);
26      if (sock < 0)
27        continue;  // Socket creation failed; try next address
28
29      // Establish the connection to the echo server
30      if (connect(sock, addr->ai_addr, addr->ai_addrlen) == 0)
```

```
31        break;      // Socket connection succeeded; break and return socket
32
33      close(sock); // Socket connection failed; try next address
34      sock = -1;
35    }
36
37    freeaddrinfo(servAddr); // Free addrinfo allocated in getaddrinfo()
38    return sock;
39  }
```

TCPClientUtility.c

1. **Resolve the host and service:** lines 10-20
   The criteria we pass to getaddrinfo() specifies that we don't care which protocol is used
   (AF_UNSPEC), but the socket address is for TCP (SOCK_STREAM/IPPROTO_TCP).

2. **Attempt to create and connect a socket from the list of addresses:** lines 22-35
   - **Create appropriate socket type:** lines 25-27
     getaddrinfo() returns the matching domain (AF_INET or AF_INET6) and socket type/
     protocol. We pass this information on to socket() when creating the new socket. If the
     system cannot create a socket of the specified type, we move on to the next address.

   - **Connect to specified server:** lines 30-34
     We use the address obtained from getaddrinfo() to attempt to connect to the server.
     If the connection succeeds, we exit the address search loop. If the connection fails, we
     close the socket and try the next address.

3. **Free address list:** line 37
   To avoid a memory leak, we need to free the address linked list created by getaddrinfo().

4. **Return resulting socket descriptor:** line 38
   If we succeed in creating and connecting a socket, return the socket descriptor. If no
   addresses succeeded, return −1.

Now we are ready to see the generic client.

TCPEchoClient.c

```
1  #include <stdio.h>
2  #include <stdlib.h>
3  #include <string.h>
4  #include <unistd.h>
5  #include <sys/types.h>
6  #include <sys/socket.h>
7  #include <netdb.h>
8  #include "Practical.h"
```

```
9
10   int main(int argc, char *argv[]) {
11
12     if (argc < 3 || argc > 4) // Test for correct number of arguments
13       DieWithUserMessage("Parameter(s)",
14           "<Server Address/Name> <Echo Word> [<Server Port/Service>]");
15
16     char *server = argv[1];     // First arg: server address/name
17     char *echoString = argv[2]; // Second arg: string to echo
18     // Third arg (optional): server port/service
19     char *service = (argc == 4) ? argv[3] : "echo";
20
21     // Create a connected TCP socket
22     int sock = SetupTCPClientSocket(server, service);
23     if (sock < 0)
24       DieWithUserMessage("SetupTCPClientSocket() failed", "unable to connect");
25
26     size_t echoStringLen = strlen(echoString); // Determine input length
27
28     // Send the string to the server
29     ssize_t numBytes = send(sock, echoString, echoStringLen, 0);
30     if (numBytes < 0)
31       DieWithSystemMessage("send() failed");
32     else if (numBytes != echoStringLen)
33       DieWithUserMessage("send()", "sent unexpected number of bytes");
34
35     // Receive the same string back from the server
36     unsigned int totalBytesRcvd = 0; // Count of total bytes received
37     fputs("Received: ", stdout);     // Setup to print the echoed string
38     while (totalBytesRcvd < echoStringLen) {
39       char buffer[BUFSIZE]; // I/O buffer
40       // Receive up to the buffer size (minus 1 to leave space for
41       // a null terminator) bytes from the sender
42       numBytes = recv(sock, buffer, BUFSIZE - 1, 0);
43       if (numBytes < 0)
44         DieWithSystemMessage("recv() failed");
45       else if (numBytes == 0)
46         DieWithUserMessage("recv()", "connection closed prematurely");
47       totalBytesRcvd += numBytes; // Keep tally of total bytes
48       buffer[numBytes] = '\0';    // Terminate the string!
49       fputs(buffer, stdout);      // Print the buffer
50     }
51
52     fputc('\n', stdout); // Print a final linefeed
53
```

```
54    close(sock);
55    exit(0);
56  }
```

TCPEchoClient.c

After socket creation, the remainder of TCPEchoClient.c is identical to the version-specific clients. There is one caveat that must be mentioned with respect to this code. In line 25 of SetupTCPClientSocket(), we pass the *ai_family* field of the returned **addrinfo** structure as the first argument to socket(). Strictly speaking, this value identifies an *address family* (AF_XXX, whereas the first argument of socket indicates the desired *protocol family* of the socket (PF_XXX). In all implementations with which we have experience, these two families are interchangeable—in particular AF_INET and PF_INET are defined to have the same value, as are PF_INET6 and AF_INET6. **Our generic code depends on this fact.** The authors contend that these definitions will not change, but feel that full disclosure of this assumption (which allows more concise code) is important. Elimination of this assumption is straightforward enough to be left as an exercise.

3.2.2   Generic TCP Server

Our protocol-independent TCP echo server uses similar adaptations to those in the client. Recall that the typical server binds to *any* available local address. To accomplish this, we (1) specify the AI_PASSIVE flag and (2) specify NULL for the hostname. Effectively, this gets an address suitable for passing to bind(), including a wildcard for the local IP address—INADDR_ANY for IPv4 or IN6ADDR_ANY_INIT for IPv6. For systems that support *both* IPv4 and IPv6, IPv6 will generally be returned first by getaddrinfo() because it offers more options for interoperability. Note, however, that the problem of which options should be selected to maximize connectivity depends on the particulars of the environment in which the server operates—from its name service to its Internet Service Provider. **The approach we present here is essentially the simplest possible, and is likely not adequate for production servers that need to operate across a wide variety of platforms.** See the next section for additional information.

As in our protocol-independent client, we've factored the steps involved in establishing a socket into a separate function, SetupTCPServerSocket(), in TCPServerUtility.c. This setup function iterates over the addresses returned from getaddrinfo(), stopping when it can successfully bind and listen or when it's out of addresses.

SetupTCPServerSocket()

```
1  static const int MAXPENDING = 5; // Maximum outstanding connection requests
2
3  int SetupTCPServerSocket(const char *service) {
```

```
4    // Construct the server address structure
5    struct addrinfo addrCriteria;                      // Criteria for address match
6    memset(&addrCriteria, 0, sizeof(addrCriteria)); // Zero out structure
7    addrCriteria.ai_family = AF_UNSPEC;                // Any address family
8    addrCriteria.ai_flags = AI_PASSIVE;                // Accept on any address/port
9    addrCriteria.ai_socktype = SOCK_STREAM;            // Only stream sockets
10   addrCriteria.ai_protocol = IPPROTO_TCP;            // Only TCP protocol
11
12   struct addrinfo *servAddr; // List of server addresses
13   int rtnVal = getaddrinfo(NULL, service, &addrCriteria, &servAddr);
14   if (rtnVal != 0)
15     DieWithUserMessage("getaddrinfo() failed", gai_strerror(rtnVal));
16
17   int servSock = -1;
18   for (struct addrinfo *addr = servAddr; addr != NULL; addr = addr->ai_next) {
19     // Create a TCP socket
20     servSock = socket(servAddr->ai_family, servAddr->ai_socktype,
21         servAddr->ai_protocol);
22     if (servSock < 0)
23       continue;          // Socket creation failed; try next address
24
25     // Bind to the local address and set socket to list
26     if ((bind(servSock, servAddr->ai_addr, servAddr->ai_addrlen) == 0) &&
27         (listen(servSock, MAXPENDING) == 0)) {
28       // Print local address of socket
29       struct sockaddr_storage localAddr;
30       socklen_t addrSize = sizeof(localAddr);
31       if (getsockname(servSock, (struct sockaddr *) &localAddr, &addrSize) < 0)
32         DieWithSystemMessage("getsockname() failed");
33       fputs("Binding to ", stdout);
34       PrintSocketAddress((struct sockaddr *) &localAddr, stdout);
35       fputc('\n', stdout);
36       break;         // Bind and list successful
37     }
38
39     close(servSock);  // Close and try again
40     servSock = -1;
41   }
42
43   // Free address list allocated by getaddrinfo()
44   freeaddrinfo(servAddr);
45
46   return servSock;
47 }
```

SetupTCPServerSocket()

We also factor out accepting client connections into a separate function, AcceptTCPConnection(), in TCPServerUtility.c.

AcceptTCPConnection()

```
1   int AcceptTCPConnection(int servSock) {
2     struct sockaddr_storage clntAddr; // Client address
3     // Set length of client address structure (in-out parameter)
4     socklen_t clntAddrLen = sizeof(clntAddr);
5
6     // Wait for a client to connect
7     int clntSock = accept(servSock, (struct sockaddr *) &clntAddr, &clntAddrLen);
8     if (clntSock < 0)
9       DieWithSystemMessage("accept() failed");
10
11    // clntSock is connected to a client!
12
13    fputs("Handling client ", stdout);
14    PrintSocketAddress((struct sockaddr *) &clntAddr, stdout);
15    fputc('\n', stdout);
16
17    return clntSock;
18  }
```

AcceptTCPConnection()

Note that we use getsockname() to print the local socket address. When you execute TCPEchoServer.c, it will print the wildcard local network address. Finally, we use our new functions in our protocol-independent echo server.

TCPEchoServer.c

```
1   #include <stdio.h>
2   #include "Practical.h"
3   #include <unistd.h>
4
5   int main(int argc, char *argv[]) {
6
7     if (argc != 2) // Test for correct number of arguments
8       DieWithUserMessage("Parameter(s)", "<Server Port/Service>");
9
10    char *service = argv[1]; // First arg:  local port
11
12    // Create socket for incoming connections
```

```
13    int servSock = SetupTCPServerSocket(service);
14    if (servSock < 0)
15      DieWithUserMessage("SetupTCPServerSocket() failed", service);
16
17    for (;;) { // Run forever
18      // New connection creates a connected client socket
19      int clntSock = AcceptTCPConnection(servSock);
20
21      HandleTCPClient(clntSock); // Process client
22      close(clntSock);
23    }
24    // NOT REACHED
25  }
```

TCPEchoServer.c

3.2.3 IPv4–IPv6 Interoperation

Our generic client and server are oblivious to whether they are using IPv4 or IPv6 sockets. An obvious question is, "What if one is using IPv4 and the other IPv6?" The answer is that if (and only if) the program using IPv6 is a *dual-stack* system—that is, supports *both* version 4 and version 6—they should be able to interoperate. The existence of the special "v4-to-v6-mapped" address class makes this possible. This mechanism allows an IPv6 socket to be connected to an IPv4 socket. A full discussion of the implications of this and how it works is beyond the scope of this book, but the basic idea is that the IPv6 implementation in a dual-stack system recognizes that communication is desired between an IPv4 address and an IPv6 socket, and translates the IPv4 address into a "v4-to-v6-mapped" address. Thus, each socket deals with an address in its own format.

For example, if the client is a v4 socket with address 1.2.3.4, and the server is listening on a v6 socket in a dual-stack platform, when the connection request comes in, the server-side implementation will automatically do the conversion and tell the server that it is connected to a v6 socket with the v4-mapped address ::ffff:1.2.3.4. (Note that there is a bit more to it than this; in particular, the server side implementation will first try to match to a socket bound to a v4 address, and do the conversion only if it fails to find a match; see Chapter 7 for more details.)

If the server is listening on a v4 socket, the client is trying to connect from a v6 socket on a dual-stack platform, *and* the client has not bound the socket to a particular address before calling connect(), the client-side implementation will recognize that it is connecting to an IPv4 address and assign a v4-mapped IPv6 address to the socket at connect() time. The stack will "magically" convert the assigned address to an IPv4 address when the connection request is sent out. Note that, in both cases, the message that goes over the network is actually an IPv4 message.

While the v4-mapped addresses provide a good measure of interoperability, the reality is that the space of possible scenarios is very large when one considers v4-only hosts, v6-only hosts, hosts that support IPv6 but have no configured IPv6 addresses, and hosts that support IPv6 and use it on the local network, but have no wide-area IPv6 transport available (i.e., their providers do not support IPv6). Although our example code—a client that tries all possibilities returned by getaddrinfo(), and a server that sets AI_PASSIVE and binds to the first address returned by getaddrinf()—covers the most likely possibilities, **production code needs to be very carefully designed to maximize the likelihood that clients and servers will find each other under all conditions**. The details of achieving this are beyond the scope of this book; the reader should refer to RFC 4038 [11] for more details.

3.3   Getting Names from Numbers

So we can get an Internet address from a hostname, but can we perform the mapping in the other direction (hostname from an Internet address)? The answer is "usually." There is an "inverse" function called getnameinfo(), which takes a **sockaddr** address structure (really a **struct sockaddr_in** for IPv4 and **struct sockaddr_in6** for IPv6) and the address length. The function returns a corresponding node and service name in the form of a null-terminated character string—if the mapping between the number and name is stored in the name system. Callers of getnameinfo() must preallocate the space for the node and service names and pass in a pointer and length for the space. The maximum length of a node or service name is given by the constants NI_MAXHOST and NI_MAXSERV, respectively. If the caller specifies a length of 0 for node and/or service, getnameinfo() does not return the corresponding value. This function returns 0 if successful and a nonzero value if failure. The nonzero failure return code can again be passed to gai_strerror() to get the corresponding error text string.

---

int getnameinfo (**const struct sockaddr** *address*, **socklen_t** *addressLength*,
              char *node*, **socklen_t** *nodeLength*, **char** * *service*,
              socklen_t *serviceLength*, **int** *flags*)

As with getaddrinfo(), several flags control the behavior of getnameinfo(). They are described below; as before, some of them can be combined using bitwise OR ("|").

NI_NOFQDN Return only the hostname, not FQDN (Fully Qualified Domain Name), for local hosts. (The FQDN contains all parts, for example, protocols.example.com, while the hostname is only the first part, for example, "protocols".)

NI_NUMERICHOST Return the numeric form of the address instead of the name. This avoids potentially expensive name service lookups if you just want to use this service as a substitute for inet_ntop().

NI_NUMERICSERV Return the numeric form of the service instead of the name.

NI_NAMEREQD Return an error if a name cannot be found for the given address. Without this option, the numeric form of the address is returned.

NI_DGRAM Specifies datagram service; the default behavior assumes a stream service. In some cases, a service has different port numbers for TCP and UDP.

What if your program needs its own host's name? `gethostname()` takes a buffer and buffer length and copies the name of the host on which the calling program is running into the given buffer.

---

int gethostname(**char** *nameBuffer*, **size_t** *bufferLength*)

Exercises

1. `GetAddrInfo.c` requires two arguments. How could you get it to resolve a service name if you don't know any hostname?

2. Modify `GetAddrInfo.c` to take an optional third argument, containing "flags" that are passed to `getaddrinfo()` in the *ai_flags* field of the *addrinfo* argument. For example, passing "-n" as the third argument should result in the *ai_numerichost* flag being set.

3. Does `getnameinfo()` work for IPv6 addresses as well as IPv4? What does it return when given the address ::1?

4. Modify the generic `TCPEchoClient` and `TCPEchoServer` to eliminate the assumption mentioned at the end of Section 3.2.1.

chapter **4**

Using UDP Sockets

The User Datagram Protocol (UDP) provides a simpler end-to-end service than TCP provides. In fact, UDP performs only two functions: (1) It adds another layer of addressing (ports) to that of IP; and (2) it detects data corruption that may occur in transit and discards any corrupted datagrams. Because of this simplicity, UDP (datagram) sockets have some different characteristics from the TCP (stream) sockets we saw earlier.

For example, UDP sockets do not have to be connected before being used. Where TCP is analogous to telephone communication, UDP is analogous to communicating by mail: You do not have to "connect" before you send a package or letter, but you do have to specify the destination address for each one. In receiving, a UDP socket is like a mailbox into which letters or packages from many different sources can be placed.

Another difference between UDP sockets and TCP sockets is the way they deal with message boundaries: UDP sockets preserve them. This makes receiving an application message simpler, in some ways, than with TCP sockets. We will discuss this further in Section 4.3. A final difference is that the end-to-end transport service UDP provides is best effort: There is no guarantee that a message sent via a UDP socket will arrive at its destination. This means that a program using UDP sockets must be prepared to deal with loss and reordering of messages; we'll see an example of that later.

Again we introduce the UDP portion of the Sockets API through simple client and server programs. As before, they implement a trivial echo protocol. Afterward, we describe the API functionality in more detail in Sections 4.3 and 4.4.

4.1 UDP Client

Our UDP echo client, UDPEchoClient.c, looks similar to our address-family-independent TCPEchoClient.c in the way it sets up the server address and communicates with the server. However, it does not call connect(); it uses sendto() and recvfrom() instead of send() and recv(); and it only needs to do a single receive because UDP sockets preserve message boundaries, unlike TCP's byte-stream service. Of course, a UDP client only communicates with a UDP server. Many systems include a UDP echo server for debugging and testing purposes; the server simply echoes whatever messages it receives back to wherever they came from. After setting up, our echo client performs the following steps: (1) it sends the echo string to the server, (2) it receives the echo, and (3) it shuts down the program.

UDPEchoClient.c

```
 1  #include <stdio.h>
 2  #include <stdlib.h>
 3  #include <string.h>
 4  #include <unistd.h>
 5  #include <sys/socket.h>
 6  #include <netdb.h>
 7  #include "Practical.h"
 8
 9  int main(int argc, char *argv[]) {
10
11    if (argc < 3 || argc > 4) // Test for correct number of arguments
12      DieWithUserMessage("Parameter(s)",
13          "<Server Address/Name> <Echo Word> [<Server Port/Service>]");
14
15    char *server = argv[1];     // First arg: server address/name
16    char *echoString = argv[2]; // Second arg: word to echo
17
18    size_t echoStringLen = strlen(echoString);
19    if (echoStringLen > MAXSTRINGLENGTH) // Check input length
20      DieWithUserMessage(echoString, "string too long");
21
22    // Third arg (optional): server port/service
23    char *servPort = (argc == 4) ? argv[3] : "echo";
24
25    // Tell the system what kind(s) of address info we want
26    struct addrinfo addrCriteria;                   // Criteria for address match
27    memset(&addrCriteria, 0, sizeof(addrCriteria)); // Zero out structure
28    addrCriteria.ai_family = AF_UNSPEC;             // Any address family
29    // For the following fields, a zero value means "don't care"
```

```
30    addrCriteria.ai_socktype = SOCK_DGRAM;          // Only datagram sockets
31    addrCriteria.ai_protocol = IPPROTO_UDP;         // Only UDP protocol
32
33    // Get address(es)
34    struct addrinfo *servAddr; // List of server addresses
35    int rtnVal = getaddrinfo(server, servPort, &addrCriteria, &servAddr);
36    if (rtnVal != 0)
37      DieWithUserMessage("getaddrinfo() failed", gai_strerror(rtnVal));
38
39    // Create a datagram/UDP socket
40    int sock = socket(servAddr->ai_family, servAddr->ai_socktype,
41        servAddr->ai_protocol); // Socket descriptor for client
42    if (sock < 0)
43      DieWithSystemMessage("socket() failed");
44
45    // Send the string to the server
46    ssize_t numBytes = sendto(sock, echoString, echoStringLen, 0,
47        servAddr->ai_addr, servAddr->ai_addrlen);
48    if (numBytes < 0)
49      DieWithSystemMessage("sendto() failed");
50    else if (numBytes != echoStringLen)
51      DieWithUserMessage("sendto() error", "sent unexpected number of bytes");
52
53    // Receive a response
54
55    struct sockaddr_storage fromAddr; // Source address of server
56    // Set length of from address structure (in-out parameter)
57    socklen_t fromAddrLen = sizeof(fromAddr);
58    char buffer[MAXSTRINGLENGTH + 1]; // I/O buffer
59    numBytes = recvfrom(sock, buffer, MAXSTRINGLENGTH, 0,
60        (struct sockaddr *) &fromAddr, &fromAddrLen);
61    if (numBytes < 0)
62      DieWithSystemMessage("recvfrom() failed");
63    else if (numBytes != echoStringLen)
64      DieWithUserMessage("recvfrom() error", "received unexpected number of bytes");
65
66    // Verify reception from expected source
67    if (!SockAddrsEqual(servAddr->ai_addr, (struct sockaddr *) &fromAddr))
68      DieWithUserMessage("recvfrom()", "received a packet from unknown source");
69
70    freeaddrinfo(servAddr);
71
72    buffer[echoStringLen] = '\0';     // Null-terminate received data
73    printf("Received: %s\n", buffer); // Print the echoed string
74
```

```
75    close(sock);
76    exit(0);
77  }
```

UDPEchoClient.c

1. **Program setup and parameter parsing:** lines 1–23
   The server address/name and string to echo are passed in as the first two parameters. We restrict the size of our echo message; therefore, we must verify that the given string satisfies this restriction. Optionally, the client takes the server port or service name as the third parameter. If no port is provided, the client uses the well-known echo protocol service name, "echo".

2. **Get foreign address for server:** lines 25–37
   For the server, we may be given an IPv4 address, IPv6 address, or name to resolve. For the optional port, we may be given a port number or service name. We use getaddrinfo() to determine the corresponding address information (i.e., family, address, and port number). Note that we'll accept an address for any family (AF_UNSPEC) for UDP (SOCK_DGRAM and IPPROTO_UDP); specifying the latter two effectively restricts the returned address families to IPv4 and IPv6. Note also that getaddrinfo() may return multiple addresses; by simply using the first, we may fail to communicate with the server when communication is possible using an address later in the list. **A production client should be prepared to try all returned addresses.**

3. **Socket creation and setup:** lines 39–43
   This is almost identical to the TCP echo client, except that we create a datagram socket using UDP. Note that we do not need to connect() before communicating with the server.

4. **Send a single echo datagram:** lines 45–51
   With UDP we simply tell sendto() the datagram destination. If we wanted to, we could call sendto() multiple times, changing the destination on every call, thus communicating with multiple servers through the same socket. The first call to sendto() also assigns an arbitrarily chosen local port number, not in use by any other socket, to the socket identified by *sock*, because we have not previously bound the socket to a port number. We do not know (or care) what the chosen port number is, but the server will use it to send the echoed message back to us.

5. **Get and print echo reply:** lines 55–73
   - **Receive a message:** lines 55–64
     We initialize *fromAddrLen* to contain the size of the address buffer (*fromAddr*) and then pass its address as the last parameter. recvfrom() blocks until a UDP datagram addressed to this socket's port arrives. It then copies the data from the first arriving datagram into *buffer* and copies the Internet address and (UDP) port number of its source from the packet's headers into the structure *fromAddr*. Note that the data buffer

is actually one byte bigger than MAXSTRINGLENGTH, which allows us to add a null byte to terminate the string.

- **Check message source:** lines 67–70
Because there is no connection, a received message can come from any source. The output parameter *fromAddr* informs us of the datagram's source, and we check it to make sure it matches the server's Internet address. We use our own function, SockAddrsEqual(), to perform protocol-independent comparison of socket addresses. Although it is very unlikely that a packet would ever arrive from any other source, we include this check to emphasize that it is possible. There's one other complication. For applications with multiple or repeated requests, we must keep in mind that UDP messages may be reordered and arbitrarily delayed, so simply checking the source address and port may not be sufficient. (For example, the DNS protocol over UDP uses an identifier field to link requests and responses and detect duplication.) This is our last use of the address returned from getaddrinfo(), so we can free the associated storage.

- **Print received string:** lines 72–73
Before printing the received data as a string, we first ensure that it is null-terminated.

6. **Wrap-up:** lines 75–76

This example client is fine as an introduction to the UDP socket calls; it will work correctly most of the time. However, **it would not be suitable for production use, because if a message is lost going to or from the server, the call to recvfrom() blocks forever, and the program does not terminate.** Clients generally deal with this problem through the use of *timeouts*, a subject we cover later, in Section 6.3.3.

4.2   UDP Server

Our next example program implements the UDP version of the echo server, UDPEchoServer.c. The server is very simple: It loops forever, receiving a message and then sending the same message back to wherever it came from. Actually, the server only receives and sends back the first 255 characters of the message; any excess is silently discarded by the sockets implementation. (See Section 4.3 for an explanation.)

UDPEchoServer.c

```
1   #include <stdlib.h>
2   #include <string.h>
3   #include <sys/types.h>
4   #include <sys/socket.h>
5   #include <netdb.h>
6   #include "Practical.h"
```

```
7
8   int main(int argc, char *argv[]) {
9
10    if (argc != 2) // Test for correct number of arguments
11      DieWithUserMessage("Parameter(s)", "<Server Port/Service>");
12
13    char *service = argv[1]; // First arg:  local port/service
14
15    // Construct the server address structure
16    struct addrinfo addrCriteria;                  // Criteria for address
17    memset(&addrCriteria, 0, sizeof(addrCriteria)); // Zero out structure
18    addrCriteria.ai_family = AF_UNSPEC;            // Any address family
19    addrCriteria.ai_flags = AI_PASSIVE;            // Accept on any address/port
20    addrCriteria.ai_socktype = SOCK_DGRAM;         // Only datagram socket
21    addrCriteria.ai_protocol = IPPROTO_UDP;        // Only UDP socket
22
23    struct addrinfo *servAddr; // List of server addresses
24    int rtnVal = getaddrinfo(NULL, service, &addrCriteria, &servAddr);
25    if (rtnVal != 0)
26      DieWithUserMessage("getaddrinfo() failed", gai_strerror(rtnVal));
27
28    // Create socket for incoming connections
29    int sock = socket(servAddr->ai_family, servAddr->ai_socktype,
30        servAddr->ai_protocol);
31    if (sock < 0)
32      DieWithSystemMessage("socket() failed");
33
34    // Bind to the local address
35    if (bind(sock, servAddr->ai_addr, servAddr->ai_addrlen) < 0)
36      DieWithSystemMessage("bind() failed");
37
38    // Free address list allocated by getaddrinfo()
39    freeaddrinfo(servAddr);
40
41    for (;;) { // Run forever
42      struct sockaddr_storage clntAddr; // Client address
43      // Set Length of client address structure (in-out parameter)
44      socklen_t clntAddrLen = sizeof(clntAddr);
45
46      // Block until receive message from a client
47      char buffer[MAXSTRINGLENGTH]; // I/O buffer
48      // Size of received message
49      ssize_t numBytesRcvd = recvfrom(sock, buffer, MAXSTRINGLENGTH, 0,
50          (struct sockaddr *) &clntAddr, &clntAddrLen);
51      if (numBytesRcvd < 0)
```

```
52        DieWithSystemMessage("recvfrom() failed");
53
54      fputs("Handling client ", stdout);
55      PrintSocketAddress((struct sockaddr *) &clntAddr, stdout);
56      fputc('\n', stdout);
57
58      // Send received datagram back to the client
59      ssize_t numBytesSent = sendto(sock, buffer, numBytesRcvd, 0,
60          (struct sockaddr *) &clntAddr, sizeof(clntAddr));
61      if (numBytesSent < 0)
62        DieWithSystemMessage("sendto() failed)");
63      else if (numBytesSent != numBytesRcvd)
64        DieWithUserMessage("sendto()", "sent unexpected number of bytes");
65    }
66    // NOT REACHED
67  }
```

UDPEchoServer.c

1. **Program setup and parameter parsing:** lines 1-13

2. **Parse/resolve address/port args:** lines 15-26
   The port may be specified on the command line as a port number or service name. We use getaddrinfo() to determine the actual local port number. As with our UDP client, we'll accept an address for any family (AF_UNSPEC) for UDP (SOCK_DGRAM and IPPROTO_UDP). We want our UDP server to accept echo requests from any of its interfaces. Setting the AI_PASSIVE flag makes getaddrinfo() return the wildcard Internet address (INADDR_ANY for IPv4 or *in6addr_any* for IPv6). getaddrinfo() may return multiple addresses; we simply use the first.

3. **Socket creation and setup:** lines 28-39
   This is nearly identical to the TCP echo server, except that we create a datagram socket using UDP. Also, we do not need to call listen() because there is no connection setup—the socket is ready to receive messages as soon as it has an address.

4. **Iteratively handle incoming echo requests:** lines 41-65
   Several key differences between UDP and TCP servers are demonstrated in how each communicates with the client. In the TCP server, we blocked on a call to accept() awaiting a connection from a client. Since UDP servers do not establish a connection, we do not need to get a new socket for each client. Instead, we can immediately call recvfrom() with the same socket that was bound to the desired port number.

   ■ **Receive an echo request:** lines 42-52
     recvfrom() blocks until a datagram is received from a client. Since there is no connection, each datagram may come from a different sender, and we learn the source at

the same time we receive the datagram. recvfrom() puts the address of the source in *clntAddr*. The length of this address buffer is specified by *cliAddrLen*.

■ **Send echo reply:** lines 59-64
sendto() transmits the data in *buffer* back to the address specified by *clntAddr*. Each received datagram is considered a single client echo request, so we only need a single send and receive—unlike the TCP echo server, where we needed to receive until the client closed the connection.

4.3   Sending and Receiving with UDP Sockets

As soon as it is created, a UDP socket can be used to send/receive messages to/from any address and to/from many *different* addresses in succession. To allow the destination address to be specified for each message, the Sockets API provides a different sending routine that is generally used with UDP sockets: sendto(). Similarly, the recvfrom() routine returns the source address of each received message in addition to the message itself.

---

ssize_t sendto(**int** *socket*, **const void** **msg*, **size_t** *msgLength*, **int** *flags*,
                       const struct sockaddr **destAddr*, **socklen_t** *addrLen*)
ssize_t recvfrom(**int** *socket*, **void** **msg*, **size_t** *msgLength*, **int** *flags*,
                       struct sockaddr **srcAddr*, **socklen_t** **addrLen*)

The first four parameters to sendto() are the same as those for send(). The two additional parameters specify the message's destination. Again, they will invariably be a pointer to a **struct sockaddr_in** and its size, respectively, or a pointer to a **struct sockaddr_in6** and its size, respectively. Similarly, recvfrom() takes the same parameters as recv() but, in addition, has two parameters that inform the caller of the source of the received datagram. One thing to note is that *addrLen* is an *in-out* parameter in recvfrom(): On input it specifies the size of the address buffer *srcAddr*, which will typically be a **struct sockaddr_storage** in IP-version-independent code. On output, it specifies the size of the address that was actually copied into the buffer. **Two errors often made by novices are (1) passing an integer value instead of a pointer to an integer for *addrLen* and (2) forgetting to initialize the pointed-to length variable to contain the appropriate size.**

We have already pointed out a subtle but important difference between TCP and UDP, namely, that *UDP preserves message boundaries*. In particular, each call to recvfrom() returns data from at most one sendto() call. Moreover, different calls to recvfrom() will never return data from the same call to sendto() (unless you use the MSG_PEEK flag with recvfrom()—see the last paragraph of this section).

When a call to send() on a TCP socket returns, all the caller knows is that the data has been copied into a buffer for transmission; the data may or may not have actually been transmitted yet. (This is explained in more detail in Chapter 7.) However, UDP does not buffer data for possible retransmission because it does not recover from errors. This means that by the time a call to sendto() on a UDP socket returns, the message has been passed to the underlying channel for transmission and is (or soon will be) on its way out the door.

Between the time a message arrives from the network and the time its data is returned via recv() or recvfrom(), the data is stored in a first-in, first-out (FIFO) receive buffer. With a connected TCP socket, all received-but-not-yet-delivered bytes are treated as one continuous sequence (see Section 7.1). For a UDP socket, however, the bytes from different messages may have come from different senders. Therefore, the boundaries between them need to be preserved so that the data from each message can be returned with the proper address. The buffer really contains a FIFO sequence of "chunks" of data, each with an associated source address. A call to recvfrom() will never return more than one of these chunks. However, if recvfrom() is called with size parameter n, and the size of the first chunk in the receive FIFO is bigger than n, only the first n bytes of the chunk are returned. **The remaining bytes are quietly discarded, with no indication to the receiving program**.

For this reason, a receiver should always supply a buffer big enough to hold the largest message allowed by its application protocol at the time it calls recvfrom(). This technique will guarantee that no data will be lost. The maximum amount of data that can ever be returned by recvfrom() on a UDP socket is 65,507 bytes—the largest payload that can be carried in a UDP datagram.

Alternatively, the receiver can use the MSG_PEEK flag with recvfrom() to "peek" at the first chunk waiting to be received. This flag causes the received data to remain in the socket's receive FIFO so it can be received more than once. This strategy can be useful if memory is scarce, application messages vary widely in size, and each message carries information about its size in the first few bytes. The receiver first calls recvfrom() with MSG_PEEK and a small buffer, examines the first few bytes of the message to determine its size, and then calls recvfrom() again (without MSG_PEEK) with a buffer big enough to hold the entire message. In the usual case where memory is not scarce, using a buffer big enough for the largest possible message is simpler.

4.4 Connecting a UDP Socket

It is possible to call connect() on a UDP socket to fix the destination address of future datagrams sent over the socket. Once connected, you may use send() instead of sendto() to transmit datagrams because you no longer need to specify the destination address. In a similar way, you may use recv() instead of recvfrom() because a connected UDP socket can *only* receive datagrams from the associated foreign address and port, so after calling connect() you know the source address of any incoming datagrams. In fact, after connecting, you may *only* send and receive to/from the address specified to connect(). Note that connecting and then using send() and recv() with UDP does not change how UDP behaves. Message boundaries are still preserved, datagrams can be lost, and so on. You can "disconnect" by calling `connect()` with an address family of AF_UNSPEC.

Another subtle advantage to calling `connect()` on a UDP socket is that it enables you to receive error indications that result from earlier actions on the socket. The canonical example is sending a datagram to a nonexistent server or port. When this happens, the `send()` that eventually leads to the error returns with no indication of error. Some time later, an error message is delivered to your host, indicating that the sent datagram encountered a problem. Because this datagram is a *control* message and not a regular UDP datagram, the system can't always tell where to send it if your socket is unconnected, because an unconnected socket has no associated foreign address and port. However, if your socket is connected, the system is able to match the information in the error datagram with your socket's associated foreign IP address and port. (See Section 7.5 for details about this process.) Note such a control error message being delivered to your socket will result in an error return from a *subsequent* system call (for example, the `recv()` that was intended to get the reply), not the offending `send()`.

Exercises

1. Modify `UDPEchoClient.c` to use `connect()`. After the final `recv()`, show how to disconnect the UDP socket. Using `getsockname()` and `getpeername()`, print the local and foreign address before and after `connect()`, and after disconnect.

2. Modify `UDPEchoServer.c` to use `connect()`.

3. Verify experimentally the size of the largest datagram you can send and receive using a UDP socket. Is the answer different for IPv4 and IPv6?

4. While `UDPEchoServer.c` explicitly specifies its local port number using `bind()`, we do not call `bind()` in `UDPEchoClient.c`. How is the UDP echo client's socket given a port number? Note that the answer is different for UDP and TCP. We can select the client's local port using `bind()`. What difficulties might we encounter if we do this?

5. Modify `UDPEchoClient.c` and `UDPEchoServer.c` to allow the largest echo string possible where an echo request is restricted to a single datagram.

6. Modify `UDPEchoClient.c` and `UDPEchoServer.c` to allow arbitrarily large echo strings. You may ignore datagram loss and reordering (for now).

7. Using `getsockname()` and `getpeername()`, modify `UDPEchoClient.c` to print the local and foreign address for the socket immediately before and after `sendto()`.

8. You can use the same UDP socket to send datagrams to many different destinations. Modify `UDPEchoClient.c` to send and receive an echo datagram to/from two different UDP echo servers. You can use the book's server running on multiple hosts or twice on the same host with different ports.

chapter **5**

Sending and Receiving Data

Typically, you use sockets because your program needs to provide information to, or use information provided by, another program. There is no magic: any programs that exchange information must agree on how that information will be *encoded*—represented as a sequence of bits—as well as which program sends what information when, and how the information received affects the behavior of the program. This agreement regarding the form and meaning of information exchanged over a communication channel is called a *protocol*; a protocol used in implementing a particular application is an *application protocol*. In our echo example from the earlier chapters, the application protocol is trivial: neither the client's nor the server's behavior is affected by the *contents* of the messages they exchange. Because in most real applications the behavior of clients and servers depends on the information they exchange, application protocols are usually somewhat more complicated.

The TCP/IP protocols transport bytes of user data without examining or modifying them. This allows applications great flexibility in how they encode their information for transmission. Most application protocols are defined in terms of discrete *messages* made up of sequences of *fields*. Each field contains a specific piece of information encoded as a sequence of bits. The application protocol specifies exactly how these sequences of bits are to be arranged by the sender and interpreted, or *parsed*, by the receiver so that the latter can extract the meaning of each field. About the only constraint imposed by TCP/IP is that information must be sent and received in chunks whose length in bits is a multiple of eight. So from now on we consider messages to be sequences of *bytes*. Given this, it may be helpful to think of a transmitted message as a sequence or array of numbers, each between 0 and 255. That corresponds to the range of binary values that can be encoded in 8 bits: 00000000 for zero, 00000001 for one, 00000010 for two, and so on, up to 11111111 for 255.

When you build a program to exchange information via sockets with other programs, typically one of two situations applies: either you are designing/writing the programs on both sides of the socket, in which case you are free to define the application protocol yourself, or you are implementing a protocol that someone else has *already* specified, perhaps a protocol *standard*. In either case, the basic principles of encoding and decoding different types of information as bytes "on the wire" are the same. (By the way, everything in this chapter also applies if the "wire" is a file that is written by one program and then read by another.)

5.1   Encoding Integers

Let's first consider the question of how integers—that is, groups of bits that can represent whole numbers—can be sent and received via sockets. In a sense, all types of information are ultimately encoded as fixed-size integers, so the ability to send and receive them is fundamental.

5.1.1   Sizes of Integers

We have seen that TCP and UDP sockets transmit sequences of *bytes*: groups of 8 bits, which can contain whole number values in the range 0–255. Sometimes it is necessary to send integers whose value might be bigger than 255; such integers must be encoded using multiple bytes. To exchange fixed-size, multibyte integers, the sender and receiver have to agree *in advance* on several things. The first is the *size* (in bytes) of each integer to be sent.

For example, an **int** might be stored as a 32-bit quantity. In addition to **int**, the C language defines several other integer types: **short**, **char**, and **long**; the idea is that these integers can be different sizes, and the programmer can use the one that fits the application. Unlike some languages, however, the C language does *not* specify the exact size of each of these primitive types. Instead, that is left up to the implementation. Thus, the size of a **short** integer can vary from platform to platform.[1] The C language specification does say that a **char** is no bigger than a **short**, which is no bigger than an **int**, which is no bigger than a **long**, which is no bigger than a **long long**. However, the specification does *not* require that these types actually be different sizes—it is technically possible for a **char** to be the same size as a **long**! On most platforms, however, the sizes do differ, and it is a safe bet that they do on yours, too.

So how do you determine the exact size of an **int** (or **char**, or **long**, or ...) on your platform? The answer is simple: use the sizeof() operator, which returns the amount of memory (in "bytes") occupied by its argument (a type or variable) on the current platform. Here are a couple of things to note about sizeof(). First, the language specifies that sizeof(char) is

---

[1]By "platform" in this book we mean the combination of compiler, operating system, and hardware architecture. The gcc compiler with the Linux operating system, running on Intel's IA-32 architecture, is an example of a platform.

1—*always*. Thus in the C language a "byte" is the amount of space occupied by a variable of type **char**, and the units of sizeof() are actually sizeof(char). But exactly how big is a C-language "byte"? That's the second thing: the predefined constant CHAR_BIT tells how many bits it takes to represent a value of type **char**—usually 8, but possibly 10 or even 32.

Although it's always possible to write a simple program to print the values returned by sizeof() for the various primitive integer types, and thus clear up any mystery about integer sizes on your platform, C's lack of specificity about the size of its primitive integer types makes it a little tricky if you want to write portable code for sending integers of a specific size over the Internet. Consider the problem of sending a 32-bit integer over a TCP connection. Do you use an **int**, a **long**, or what? On some machines an **int** is 32 bits, while on others a **long** may be 32 bits.

The C99 language standard specification offers a solution in the form of a set of optional types: **int8_t**, **int16_t**, **int32_t**, and **int64_t** (along with their unsigned counterparts **uint8_t**, etc) all have the size (in bits) indicated by their names. On a platform where CHAR_BIT is eight,[2] these are 1, 2, 4 and 8 byte integers, respectively. Although these types may not be implemented on every platform, each *is* required to be defined if any native primitive type has the corresponding size. (So if, say, the size of an **int** on the platform is 32 bits, the "optional" type **int32_t** is *required* to be defined.) Throughout the rest of this chapter, we make use of these types to specify the precise size of the integers we want. We will also make use of the C99-defined type **long long**, which is typically larger than a long. Program TestSizes.c will print the value of CHAR_BIT, the sizes of all the primitive integer types, and the sizes of the fixed-size types defined by the C99 standard. (The program will not compile if any of the optional types are not defined on your platform.)

TestSizes.c

```
 1  #include <limits.h>
 2  #include <stdint.h>
 3  #include <stdio.h>
 4
 5  int main(int argc, char *argv[]) {
 6    printf("CHAR_BIT is %d\n\n",CHAR_BIT);        // Bits in a char (usually 8!)
 7
 8    printf("sizeof(char) is %d\n", sizeof(char));  // ALWAYS 1
 9    printf("sizeof(short) is %d\n", sizeof(short));
10    printf("sizeof(int) is %d\n", sizeof(int));
11    printf("sizeof(long) is %d\n", sizeof(long));
12    printf("sizeof(long long) is %d\n\n", sizeof(long long));
13
14    printf("sizeof(int8_t) is %d\n", sizeof(int8_t));
```

---

[2]We are not aware of any modern general-purpose computing platform where CHAR_BIT differs from eight. Throughout the rest of this book, the value of CHAR_BIT is assumed, without comment, to be 8.

```
15    printf("sizeof(int16_t) is %d\n", sizeof(int16_t));
16    printf("sizeof(int32_t) is %d\n", sizeof(int32_t));
17    printf("sizeof(int64_t) is %d\n\n", sizeof(int64_t));
18
19    printf("sizeof(uint8_t) is %d\n", sizeof(uint8_t));
20    printf("sizeof(uint16_t) is %d\n", sizeof(uint16_t));
21    printf("sizeof(uint32_t) is %d\n", sizeof(uint32_t));
22    printf("sizeof(uint64_t) is %d\n", sizeof(uint64_t));
23  }
```

TestSizes.c

To make things a little more concrete, in the remainder of this section we'll consider the problem of encoding a sequence of integers of different sizes—specifically, of 1, 2, 4, and 8 bytes, in that order. Thus, we need a total of 15 bytes, as shown in the following figure.

We'll consider several different methods of doing this, but in all cases we'll assume that the C99 fixed-size types are supported.

5.1.2   Byte Ordering

Once the sender and receiver have specified the sizes of the integers to be transmitted, they need to agree on some other aspects. For integers that require more than one byte to encode, they have to answer the question of which *order* to send the bytes in.

There are two obvious choices: start at the "right" end of the number, with the least significant bits—so-called *little-endian* order—or at the left end, with the most significant bits—*big-endian* order. (Note that the ordering of *bits within bytes* is, fortunately, handled by the implementation in a standard way.) Consider the **long long** value 123456787654321L. Its 64-bit representation (in hexadecimal) is 0x0000704885F926B1. If we transmit the bytes in big-endian order, the sequence of (decimal) byte values will look like this:

0	0	112	72	133	249	38	177

Big-endian order of transmission

If we transmit them in little-endian order, the sequence will be:

177	38	249	133	72	112	0	0

Little-endian order of transmission

The main point is that for any multibyte integer quantity, the sender and receiver need to agree on whether big-endian or little-endian order will be used.[3] If the sender were to use little-endian order to send the above integer, and the receiver were expecting big-endian, instead of the correct value, the receiver would interpret the transmitted 8-byte sequence as the value 12765164544669515776L.

Most protocols that send multibyte quantities in the Internet today use big-endian byte order; in fact, it is sometimes called *network byte order.* The byte order used by the hardware (whether it is big- or little-endian) is called the *native byte order.* C language platforms typically provide functions that allow you to convert values between native and network byte orders; you may recall that we have already encountered htons() and htonl(). Those routines, along with ntohl() and ntohs(), handle the conversion for typical integer sizes. The functions whose names end in "l" (for "long") operate on 32-bit quantities, while the ones ending in "s" (for "short") operate on 16-bit quantities. The "h" stands for "host," and the "n" for "network". Thus htons() was used in Chapter 2 to convert 16-bit port numbers from host byte order to network byte order, because *the Sockets API routines deal only with addresses and ports in network byte order.* That fact is worth repeating, because beginning programmers are often bitten by forgetting it: **addresses and ports that cross the Sockets API are always in network byte order**. We will make full use of these order-conversion functions shortly.

5.1.3 Signedness and Sign Extension

One last detail on which the sender and receiver must agree: whether the numbers transmitted will be *signed* or *unsigned.* We've said that bytes contain values in the range 0 to 255 (decimal). That's true if we don't need negative numbers, but they are necessary for many applications. Fortunately, the same 255-bit patterns can be interpreted as integers in the range -128 to 127. *Two's-complement* representation is the usual way of representing such signed numbers. For a k-bit number, the two's-complement representation of the negative integer $-n, 1 \leq n \leq 2^{k-1}$, is the binary value of $2^k - n$. The nonnegative integer $p, 0 \leq p \leq 2^{k-1} - 1$, is encoded simply by the k-bit binary value of p. Thus, given k bits, we can represent values in the range -2^{k-1} through $2^{k-1} - 1$ using two's-complement. Note that the most significant bit (msb) tells whether the value is positive (msb $= 0$) or negative (msb $= 1$). On the other hand, a k-bit *unsigned* integer can encode values in the range 0 through $2^k - 1$ directly. So for example, the 32-bit value 0xFFFFFFFF (the all-ones value) when interpreted as a signed, two's-complement number represents -1; when interpreted as an unsigned integer, it represents 4294967295. The signedness of the integers being transmitted should be determined by the range of values that need to be encoded.

Some care is required when dealing with integers of different signedness because of *sign-extension.* When a signed value is copied to any wider type, the additional bits are copied from the sign (i.e., most significant) bit. By way of example, suppose the variable *smallInt* is of type

---

[3]Other orders are possible for integers bigger than 2 bytes, but we know of no modern systems that use them.

int8_t, that is, a signed, 8-bit integer, and *widerInt* is of type **int16_t**. Suppose also that *smallInt* contains the (binary) value 01001110 (i.e., decimal 78). The assignment statement:

```
widerInt := smallInt;
```

places the binary value 0000000001001110 into *widerInt*. However, if *smallInt* has the value 11100010 (decimal −30) before the assignment statement, then afterward *widerInt* contains the binary value 1111111111100010.

Now suppose the variable *widerUInt* is of type **uint16_t**, and *smallInt* again has the value −30, and we do this assignment:

```
widerUInt := smallInt;
```

What do you think the value of *widerUInt* is afterward? The answer is again 1111111111100010, because the sign of *smallInt*'s value is extended *as it is widened* to fit in *widerUInt*, even though the latter variable is unsigned. If you print the resulting value of *widerUInt* as a decimal number, the result will be 65506. On the other hand, if we have a variable *smallUInt* of type **uint8_t**, containing the same binary value 11100010, and we copy its value to the wider unsigned variable:

```
widerUInt := smallUInt;
```

and then print the result, we get 226, because the value of an unsigned integer type is—reasonably enough—*not* sign-extended.

One final point to remember: when expressions are evaluated, values of variables are widened (if needed) to the "native" (**int**) size before any computation occurs. Thus, if you add the values of two **char** variables together, the type of the result will be **int**, not **char**:

```
char a,b;
printf("sizeof(a+b) is %d\n", sizeof(a+b));
```

On the platform used in writing this book, this code prints "sizeof(a+b) is 4". The type of the argument to sizeof()—the expression $a + b$—is **int**. This is generally not an issue, but you need to be aware that *sign-extension also occurs during this implicit widening*.

5.1.4   Encoding Integers by Hand

Having agreed on byte ordering (we'll use big-endian) and signedness (the integers are all unsigned), we're ready to construct our message. We'll first show how to do it "by hand," using shifting and masking operations. The program BruteForceCoding.c features a method EncodeIntBigEndian() that places any given primitive integer value as a sequence of the specified number of bytes at a specified location in memory, using big-endian representation. The method takes four arguments: a pointer to the starting location where the value is to be placed; the value to be encoded (represented as a 64-bit unsigned integer, which is big enough to hold any of the other types); the offset in the array at which the value should start; and the size in bytes of the value to be written. Of course, whatever we encode at the sender must be decodable at the receiver. The DecodeIntBigEndian() method handles decoding a byte sequence of a given length into a 64-bit integer, interpreting it as a big-endian sequence.

These methods treat all quantities as unsigned; see the exercises for other possibilities.

BruteForceCoding.c

```
1   #include <stdint.h>
2   #include <stdlib.h>
3   #include <stdio.h>
4   #include <limits.h>
5   #include "Practical.h"
6
7   const uint8_t val8 = 101; // One hundred and one
8   const uint16_t val16 = 10001; // Ten thousand and one
9   const uint32_t val32 = 100000001; // One hundred million and one
10  const uint64_t val64 = 1000000000001L; // One trillion and one
11  const int MESSAGELENGTH = sizeof(uint8_t) + sizeof(uint16_t) + sizeof(uint32_t)
12      + sizeof(uint64_t);
13
14  static char stringBuf[BUFSIZE];
15  char *BytesToDecString(uint8_t *byteArray, int arrayLength) {
16    char *cp = stringBuf;
17    size_t bufSpaceLeft = BUFSIZE;
18    for (int i = 0; i < arrayLength && bufSpaceLeft > 0; i++) {
19      int strl = snprintf(cp, bufSpaceLeft, "%u ", byteArray[i]);
20      bufSpaceLeft -= strl;
21      cp += strl;
22    }
23    return stringBuf;
24  }
25
26  // Warning:  Untested preconditions (e.g., 0 <= size <= 8)
27  int EncodeIntBigEndian(uint8_t dst[], uint64_t val, int offset, int size) {
28    for (int i = 0; i < size; i++) {
29      dst[offset++] = (uint8_t) (val >> ((size - 1) - i) * CHAR_BIT);
30    }
31    return offset;
32  }
33
34  // Warning:  Untested preconditions (e.g., 0 <= size <= 8)
35  uint64_t DecodeIntBigEndian(uint8_t val[], int offset, int size) {
36    uint64_t rtn = 0;
37    for (int i = 0; i < size; i++) {
38      rtn = (rtn << CHAR_BIT) | val[offset + i];
39    }
40    return rtn;
```

```
41  }
42
43  int main(int argc, char *argv[]) {
44    uint8_t message[MESSAGELENGTH]; // Big enough to hold all four values
45
46    // Encode the integers in sequence in the message buffer
47    int offset = 0;
48    offset = EncodeIntBigEndian(message, val8, offset, sizeof(uint8_t));
49    offset = EncodeIntBigEndian(message, val16, offset, sizeof(uint16_t));
50    offset = EncodeIntBigEndian(message, val32, offset, sizeof(uint32_t));
51    offset = EncodeIntBigEndian(message, val64, offset, sizeof(uint64_t));
52    printf("Encoded message:\n%s\n", BytesToDecString(message, MESSAGELENGTH));
53
54    uint64_t value =
55        DecodeIntBigEndian(message, sizeof(uint8_t), sizeof(uint16_t));
56    printf("Decoded 2-byte integer = %u\n", (unsigned int) value);
57    value = DecodeIntBigEndian(message, sizeof(uint8_t) + sizeof(uint16_t)
58        + sizeof(uint32_t), sizeof(uint64_t));
59    printf("Decoded 8-byte integer = %llu\n", value);
60
61    // Show signedness
62    offset = 4;
63    int iSize = sizeof(int32_t);
64    value = DecodeIntBigEndian(message, offset, iSize);
65    printf("Decoded value (offset %d, size %d) = %lld\n", offset, iSize, value);
66    int signedVal = DecodeIntBigEndian(message, offset, iSize);
67    printf("...same as signed value %d\n", signedVal);
68  }
```

BruteForceCoding.c

1. **Declarations and inclusions:** lines 1–12
   - **Library functions and constants:** lines 1–5
   - **Integer variables with values to be encoded:** lines 7–10
   - **Message length computation:** lines 11–12
     The language spec says the initializer expression evaluates to 15; we include it for completeness.

2. BytesToDecString(): lines 14–24
   This auxiliary routine takes an array of bytes and its length, and returns a string containing the value of each byte as a decimal integer in the range 0 to 255.

3. EncodeIntBigEndian(): lines 27–32
   We iterate over the given value *size* times. On each iteration, the right-hand side of the assignment shifts the value to be encoded to the right, so the byte we are interested in is

in the low-order 8 bits. The resulting value is then *cast* to the type **uint8_t**, which throws away all but the low-order 8 bits, and placed in the array at the appropriate location. The ending value of `offset` is returned so that the caller does not have to recompute it when encoding a sequence of integers (as we will).

4. `DecodeIntBigEndian()`: lines 35–41
We construct the value in a 64-bit integer variable. Again we iterate *size* times, each time shifting the accumulated value left and bitwise-ORing in the next byte's value.

5. **Demonstrate methods:** lines 43–68
   - **Declare buffer (array of bytes) to receive series of integers:** line 44
   - **Encode items:** lines 47–51
     The integers are encoded into the array in the sequence described earlier.
   - **Print contents of encoded array:** line 52
   - **Extract and display some values from encoded message:** lines 54–59
     Output should show the decoded values equal to the original constants.
   - **Signedness effects:** lines 62–67
     At offset 4, the byte value is 245 (decimal); because it has its high-order bit set, if it is the high-order byte of a signed value, that value will be considered negative. We show this be decoding the 4 bytes starting at offset 4 and placing the result into both a signed integer and an unsigned integer.

Note that we might consider testing several preconditions at the beginning of `EncodeIntBigEndian()` and `DecodeIntBigEndian()`, such as $0 \le size \le 8$ and `dst != NULL`. Can you name any others?

Running the program produces output showing the following (decimal) byte values:

101	39	17	5	245	225	1	0	0	0	232	212	165	16	1

byte ←→ short ←——————→ int ←————————————————→ long

As you can see, the brute-force method requires the programmer to do quite a bit of work: computing and naming the offset and size of each value, and invoking the encoding routine with the appropriate arguments. Fortunately, alternative ways to build messages are often available. We discuss these next.

5.1.5 Wrapping TCP Sockets in Streams

A way of encoding multibyte integers for transmission over a stream (TCP) socket is to use the built-in **FILE**-stream facilities—the same methods you use with *stdin*, *stdout*, and so on. To access these facilities, you need to associate one or more **FILE** streams with your socket descriptor, via the `fdopen()` call.

FILE *fdopen(**int** *socketdes,* **const char** **mode*)
int fclose(**FILE** * *stream*)
int fflush(**FILE** * *stream*)

The fdopen() function "wraps" the socket in a stream and returns the result (or NULL if an error occurs); it is as if you could call fopen() on a network address. This allows buffered I/O to be performed on the socket via operations like fgets(), fputs(), fread() and fwrite(); the "mode" argument to fdopen() takes the same values as fopen(). fflush() pushes buffered data to underlying socket. fclose() closes the stream along with the underlying socket. fflush() causes any buffered to be sent over the underlying socket.

---

size_t fwrite(**const void** * *ptr,* **size_t size, size_t nmemb, FILE** * *stream*)
size_t fread(**void** * *ptr,* **size_t size, size_t nmemb, FILE** * *stream*)

The fwrite() method writes the specified number of objects of the given size to the stream. The fread() method goes in the other direction, reading the given number of objects of the given size from the given stream and placing them sequentially in the location pointed to by *ptr*. Note that the sizes are given in units of sizeof(**char**), while the return values of these methods are the number of objects read/written, *not* the number of bytes. In particular, fread() never reads *part* of an object from the stream, and similarly fwrite() never writes a partial object. If the underlying connection terminates, these methods will return a short item count.

By giving different sizes to fwrite(), we can output our message to the stream sequentially. Assume that the variables *val8*, *val16*, and the rest are declared and initialized as in BruteForceCoding.c and that the integer variable *sock* is the descriptor of the connected TCP socket over which we want to write our message. Finally, assume that htonll() is a function that converts 64-bit integers from host to network byte order (see Exercise 2). Then we can write our message to the socket one integer at a time:

```
sock = socket(/*...*/);
/* ... connect socket ...*/
// wrap the socket in an output stream
FILE *outstream = fdopen(sock, "w");
// send message, converting each object to network byte order before sending
if (fwrite(&val8, sizeof(val8), 1, outstream) != 1) ...
val16 = htons(val16);
if (fwrite(&val16, sizeof(val16), 1, outstream) != 1) ...
val32 = htonl(val32);
if (fwrite(&val32, sizeof(val32), 1, outstream) != 1) ...
val64 = htonll(val64);
if (fwrite(&val64, sizeof(val64), 1, outstream) != 1) ...
```

```
fflush(outstream); // immediately flush stream buffer to socket
...                // do other work...
fclose(outstream); // flushes stream and closes socket
```

So much for the sending side. How does the receiver recover the transmitted values? As you might expect, the receiving side takes the analogous steps using fread(). Suppose now the variable *csock* contains the socket descriptor for a TCP connection, that the received values are to be placed in the variables *rcv8*, *rcv16*, *rcv32*, and *rcv64* of the expected types, and that ntohll() is a network-to-host byte order converter for 64-bit types.

```
/* ... csock is connected ...*/
// wrap the socket in an input stream
FILE *instream = fdopen(csock, "r");
// receive message, converting each received object to host byte order
if (fread(&rcv8, sizeof(rcv8), 1, instream) != 1) ...
if (fread(&rcv16, sizeof(rcv16), 1, instream) != 1) ...
rcv16 = ntohs(rcv16); // convert to host order
if (fread(&rcv32, sizeof(rcv32), 1, instream) != 1) ...
rcv32 = ntohl(rcv32);
if (fread(&rcv64, sizeof(rcv64), 1, instream) != 1) ...
rcv64 = ntohll(rcv64);
...
fclose(instream); // closes the socket connection!
```

Among the advantages of using buffered **FILE**-streams with sockets is the ability to "put back" a byte after reading it from the stream (via ungetc()); this can sometimes be useful when parsing messages. **We must emphasize, however, that FILE-streams can *only* be used with TCP sockets.**

5.1.6 Structure Overlays: Alignment and Padding

The most common approach to constructing messages containing binary data (i.e., multibyte integers) involves overlaying a C structure on a section of memory and assigning to the fields of the structure directly. This is possible because the C language specification *explicitly defines how structures are laid out in memory by the compiler.* It has this feature because it was designed for implementing operating systems, where efficiency is a primary concern, and it is often necessary to know precisely how data structures are represented. In combination with the facilities for byte order conversion that we saw above, this makes it rather simple to construct and parse messages made up of integers of particular sizes. (There is a significant caveat, however, that we will encounter shortly.)

Suppose for a moment that we are dealing with three integer components of an address: the number on the street, which ranges from 1 to about 12000; an apartment number that never exceeds 8000 (a nonapartment address uses an apartment number of −1); and a postal code, which is a five-digit number between 10000 and 99999. The first two components can be represented using 16-bit integers; the third is too big for that, so we'll use a 32-bit integer for it. If we want to pass those quantities around inside a program, we could declare a structure and pass around pointers to it:

```
struct addressInfo {
    uint16_t  streetAddress;
    int16_t  aptNumber;
    uint32_t   postalCode;
} addrInfo;
```

Clearly, such a structure is useful for passing data around in a program, but can we use it to pass information between programs over the Internet? The answer is yes. The C specification says that this structure will be laid out as follows in memory:

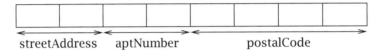

To exchange information between programs, we can simply use the layout of the structure as the message format, and take the contents directly from the structure and send them over the network (after any needed byte-order conversions). If the variable *addrInfo* declared above has been initialized to contain the values we want to send, and *sock* represents a connected socket as usual, we could send the 8-byte message using the following code:

```
// ... put values in addrInfo ...
// convert to network byte order
addrInfo.streetAddress = htons(addrInfo.streetAddress);
addrInfo.aptNumber = htons(addrInfo.aptNumber);
addrInfo.postalCode = htonl(addrInfo.postalCode);
if (send(sock, &addrInfo, sizeof(addrInfo), 0) != sizeof(addrInfo)) ...
```

On the receiving end, we can again use a buffered input stream (see previous section) and fread() to handle getting the right number of bytes into the structure. (Otherwise we have to use a loop because, as we saw earlier, there is no guarantee that all the bytes of the message will be returned in a single call to recv()). Once that's done, all we have to do is take care of byte ordering:

```
struct addressInfo addrInfo;
// ... sock is a connected socket descriptor ...
FILE *instream = fdopen(sock, "r");
if (fread(&addrInfo, sizeof(struct addressInfo), 1, instream) != 1) {
  // ... handle error
}
// convert to host byte order
addrInfo.streetAddress = ntohs(addrInfo.streetAddress);
addrInfo.aptNumber = ntohs(addrInfo.aptNumber);
addrInfo.postalCode = ntohl(addrInfo.postalCode);
// use information from message...
```

Now, it would seem that we could construct our 15-byte message using a declaration like the following:

```
struct integerMessage {
  uint8_t oneByte;
  uint16_t twoBytes;
  uint32_t fourBytes;
  uint64_t eightBytes;
}
```

Alas, this doesn't work, because the C language rules for laying out data structures include specific *alignment* requirements, including that the fields within a structure begin on certain boundaries based on their type. The main points of the requirements can be summarized as follows:

- Data structures are maximally aligned. That is, the address of any instance of a structure (including one in an array) will be divisible by the size of its largest native integer field.

- Fields whose type is a multibyte integer type are aligned to their size (in bytes). Thus, an **int32_t** integer field's beginning address is always divisible by four, and a **uint16_t** integer field's address is guaranteed to be divisible by two.

To enforce these constraints, the compiler may add *padding* between the fields of a structure. Because of this, the size of the structure declared above is not 15, but *16*. To see why, let's consider the constraints that apply. First, the whole structure must begin on an address divisible by 8. The *twoBytes* field must be at an even address, *fourBytes* must be at an address divisible by four, and *eightBytes*' address must be divisible by eight. All of these constraints will be satisfied if a single byte of padding is inserted between the *oneByte* field and the *twoBytes* field, like this:

The contents of bytes added by the compiler as padding are undefined. Thus if the declaration above is used, and the receiver is expecting the original unpadded layout, incorrect behavior is the likely result.

The best solution is to avoid the need for padding by laying out messages so that it is not needed. Unfortunately (and somewhat surprisingly), that's not always possible. In the case of our four-integer example, if we arranged the message with fields in the opposite order:

```
struct backwardMessage {
  uint64_t eightBytes;
  uint32_t fourBytes;
  uint16_t twoBytes;
  uint8_t oneByte;
}
```

no padding would be required between the fields. However, sizeof(struct backwardMessage) would nevertheless return 16, not 15. This is because one byte of padding would be required *between* instances of the structure (in an array, for example), in order to satisfy the first (maximal-alignment) constraint. (The invariant that must be maintained is that in an array of structures, the address of one element plus the sizeof() the structure yields the address of the subsequent element.) As a consequence, there is no way to specify a structure containing any multibyte integer for which sizeof() returns an odd number.

If we can't eliminate compiler-required padding, we can, as a last resort, include it in the message format specification. For our example, the message format could be defined with an *explicit* padding byte after the first field:

```
struct integerMessage2 {
  uint8_t oneByte;
  uint8_t padding;    // Required for alignment
  uint16_t twoBytes;
  uint32_t fourBytes;
  uint64_t eightBytes;
}
```

This structure is laid out in memory *exactly* like the originally declared **integerMessage**, except that the contents of the padding byte can now be controlled and accessed by the programmer. We'll see more examples of the use of structures to encode data in Section 5.2.3.

5.1.7 Strings and Text

Old-fashioned *text*—strings of printable (displayable) characters—is perhaps the most common way to represent information. We've already seen examples of sending and receiving strings of text in our echo client and server; you are probably also accustomed to having programs you write generate text output.

Text is convenient because we deal with it all the time: information is represented as strings of characters in books, newspapers, and on computer displays. Thus, once we know how to encode text for transmission, it is straightforward to send most any other kind of data: simply represent it as text, then encode the text. You know how to represent numbers and boolean values as strings of text—for example "123478962", "6.02e23", "true", "false". In this section we deal with the question of encoding such strings as byte sequences.

To that end, we first need to recognize that text is made up of sequences of symbols, or *characters*. The C language includes the primitive type **char** for representing characters, but does not include a primitive type for strings. Strings in C are traditionally represented as arrays of **char**. A **char** value in C is represented internally as an integer. For example, the character 'a', that is, the symbol for the letter 'a', corresponds to the integer 97. The character 'X' corresponds to 88, and the symbol '!' (exclamation mark) corresponds to 33.

A mapping between a set of symbols and a set of integers is called a *coded character set*. You may have heard of the coded character set known as *ASCII*—American Standard Code for Information Interchange. ASCII maps the letters of the English alphabet, digits, punctuation, and some other special (nonprintable) symbols to integers between 0 and 127. It has been used for data transmission since the 1960s, and is used extensively in application protocols such as HTTP (the protocol used for the World Wide Web), even today. The C language specifies a *basic character set* that is a subset of ASCII. The importance of ASCII (and the C basic character set) is that strings containing only characters from the basic set can be encoded using one byte per character. (Note that in our echo client and server from Chapter 2 the encoding was *irrelevant*, because the server did not interpret the received data at all.)

This is well and good if you speak and use a language (like English) that can be represented using a small number of symbols. However, consider that no more than 256 distinct symbols can be encoded using one byte per symbol, and that a large fraction of the world's people use languages that have more than 256 symbols, and therefore have to be encoded using more than 8 bits per character. Clearly, the use of C presents significant challenges for implementing code that is "internationalizable." Mandarin is just one prominent example of a language that requires thousands of symbols.

The C99 extensions standard defines a type **wchar_t** ("wide character") to store characters from charsets that may use more than one byte per symbol. In addition, various library functions are defined that support conversion between byte sequences and arrays of **wchar_t**, in both directions. (In fact, there is a wide character string version of virtually every library function that operates on character strings.) To convert back and forth between wide strings and encoded char (byte) sequences suitable for transmission over the network, we would use the wcstombs() ("wide character string to multibyte string") and mbstowcs() functions.

```
#include <stdlib.h>
size_t wcstombs(char *restrict s, const wchar_t *restrict pwcs, size_t n);
size_t mbstowcs(wchar_t *restrict pwcs, const char *restrict s, size_t n);
```

The first of these converts a sequence of wide characters from the array pointed to by *pwcs* into a sequence of multibyte characters, and stores these multibyte characters into the array pointed to by *s*, stopping if the next conversion would exceed the limit of *n* total bytes or if a null character is stored. The second does the same thing in the other direction.

As we have seen, for a coded character set that requires larger integer values, there is more than one way to encode those values for transmission over the network. Thus, it is necessary that sender and receiver agree on how those integers will be encoded as byte sequences.

As an example, consider a platform that uses 16-bit integers internally to represent characters, and whose character set includes ASCII as a subset—that is, the character 'a' maps to 97, 'X' to 88, and so on. Using the wide character facilities, we can declare a wide character string:

```
wchar_t testString[] = "Test!";
```

The internal representation of this string uses six 16-bit integers (including one for the terminating null (0) character). However, there are several ways to encode those integers as a sequence of 8-bit bytes:

- Each character can be represented using 2 bytes, in big-endian order. In that case, the result of calling wcstombs() on the wide string **"Test!"** would be the following sequence: 0, 84, 0, 101, 0, 115, 0, 116, 0, 33.

- Alternatively, we could use 2 bytes in little-endian order, which would give: 84, 0, 101, 0, 115, 0, 116, 0, 33, 0.

- We could use an encoding that maps symbols in the original ASCII character set to single bytes (the same as their ASCII encoding), and uses 2 bytes for symbols beyond ASCII. If the high-order bit of a byte is set, it indicates the next symbol is encoded with 2 bytes; otherwise it is an ASCII symbol encoded with a single byte. In this case the result after calling `wcstombs()` would be the 5-byte sequence 84, 101, 115, 116, 33.

Note that in these examples we did *not* include the terminating null (0) character. The terminating null is an artifact of the language, and not part of the string itself. It therefore should not be transmitted with the string unless the protocol explicitly specifies that method of marking the end of the string.

The bad news is that C99's wide character facilities are *not* designed to give the programmer explicit control over the encoding scheme. Indeed, they assume a single, fixed charset defined according to the "locale" of the platform. Although the facilities support a variety of charsets, they do not even provide the programmer any way to learn which charset or encoding is in use. In fact, the C99 standard states in several situations that the effect of changing the locale's charset at runtime is undefined. What this means is that if you want to implement a protocol using a particular charset, you'll have to implement the encoding yourself.

5.1.8   Bit-Diddling: Encoding Booleans

Bitmaps are a very compact way to encode boolean information, which is often used in protocols. The idea of a bitmap is that each of the bits of an integer type can encode one boolean value—typically with 0 representing false and 1 representing true. To be able to manipulate bitmaps, you need to know how to set and clear individual bits using C's "bit-diddling" operations. A *mask* is an integer value that has one or more specific bits set to 1, and all others cleared (i.e., 0). We'll deal here mainly with 32-bit maps and masks, but everything we say applies to types of other sizes as well.

Let's number the bits of an integer's binary representation from 0 to 31, where bit 0 is the least significant bit. In general, the **uint32_t** value that has a 1 in bit position i, and a zero in all other bit positions, is just 2^i. So bit 5 corresponds to the number 32, bit 12 to 4096, and so forth. Here are some example mask declarations:

```
const int BIT5 = (1<<5);
const int BIT7 = 0x80;
const int BITS2AND3 = 12;    // 8+4
int bitmap = 128;
```

To *set* a particular bit in an **int** variable, combine it with the mask for that bit using the bitwise-OR operation (|):

```
bitmap |= BIT5;
// bit 5 is now one
```

To *clear* a particular bit, bitwise-AND it with the *bitwise complement* of the mask for that bit (which has ones everywhere except the particular bit, which is zero). The bitwise-AND operation in C is &, while the bitwise-complement operator is ~.

```
bitmap &= ~BIT7;
// bit 7 is now zero
```

You can set and clear multiple bits at once by OR-ing together the corresponding masks:

```
// clear bits 2, 3 and 5
bitmap &= ~(BITS2AND3|BIT5);
```

To test whether a bit is set, compare the result of the bitwise-AND of the mask and the value with zero:

```
bool bit6Set = (bitmap & (1<<6)) != 0;
```

5.2 Constructing, Framing, and Parsing Messages

We close this chapter with an example illustrating the application of the foregoing techniques in implementing a protocol specified by someone else. The example is a simple "voting" protocol as shown in Figure 5.1. Here a client sends a *request* message to the server; the message contains a candidate ID, which is an integer between 0 and 1000. Two types of requests are supported. An *inquiry* asks the server how many votes have been cast for the given candidate. The server sends back a *response* message containing the original candidate ID and the vote total as of the time the request was received for that candidate. A *voting* request actually casts a vote for the indicated candidate. The server again responds with a message containing the candidate ID and the vote total (which now includes the vote just cast). The protocol runs over stream sockets using TCP.

Normally, the "wire format" of the protocol messages would be precisely defined as part of the protocol. As we have seen, we might encode it in a number of ways: we could represent the information using strings of text, or as binary numbers. In order to illustrate all the

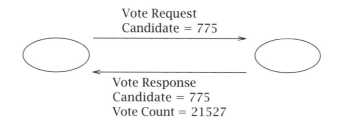

Figure 5.1: Voting protocol.

techniques described above, we will specify several different versions of the "wire format." This also helps us to make a point about protocol implementation.

When implementing any protocol, it is good practice to hide the details of the way messages are encoded from the main program logic. We'll illustrate that here by using a generic structure in the main programs to pass information to/from functions that process messages sent/received over the socket. This allows us to use the same client and server code with different implementations of the "wire format" processing. The **VoteInfo** structure, defined in VoteProtocol.h, contains everything needed to construct a message: the candidate ID number (an integer), the count of votes for that candidate (a 64-bit integer), a boolean indicating whether the message is an "inquiry" (inquiries do not affect the vote count), and another boolean indicating whether the message to be sent is a response sent from client to server (true), or a request (false). Also defined in this file are constants for the largest allowable candidate ID number and the maximum length of an encoded message on the wire. (The latter helps the programs to size their buffers.)

```
struct VoteInfo {
    uint64_t count;    // invariant: !isResponse => count==0
    int candidate;     // invariant: 0 <= candidate <= MAX_CANDIDATE
    bool isInquiry;
    bool isResponse;
};

typedef struct VoteInfo VoteInfo;

enum {
    MAX_CANDIDATE = 1000,
    MAX_WIRE_SIZE = 500
};
```

Note that we have defined a single **VoteInfo** structure for the information contained in *both* request messages and response messages. This, along with a proper control structure, allows reuse of the same message-processing code for both client and server, and both request and response.

The message-processing code is responsible for encoding the information from a **VoteInfo** structure and transmitting it over a stream socket, as well as for receiving data from a TCP socket, parsing the incoming vote protocol message (if any), and filling in a **VoteInfo** structure with the received information.

A clean design further decomposes the process into two parts. The first is concerned with *framing*, or marking the boundaries of the message, so the receiver can find it in the stream. The second is concerned with the actual encoding of the message, whether it is represented using text or binary data. Notice that these two parts can be independent of each other, and in a well-designed protocol they *should* be separated. In other words, we can specify the mechanism for framing the message as a whole separately from the encoding of its different fields. And that is what we shall do. Our job will be somewhat easier if we can use stream-processing functions, so we will have the client and server wrap the connected socket in a **FILE** stream for input and another for output.

The interface to the framing code is defined as follows in Framer.h.

```
int GetNextMsg(FILE *in, uint8_t *buf, size_t bufSize);
int PutMsg(uint8_t buf[], size_t msgSize, FILE *out);
```

The method GetNextMsg() reads data from the given stream and places it in the given buffer until it runs out of room or determines that it has received a complete message. It returns the number of bytes placed in the buffer (all framing information is stripped). The method PutMsg() adds framing information to the message contained in the given buffer, and writes both message and framing information to the given stream. Note that neither of these methods needs to know *anything* about the message content.

The interface to the encoding and parsing code is defined in VoteEncoding.h as follows:

```
bool Decode(uint8_t *inBuf, size_t mSize, VoteInfo *v);
size_t Encode(VoteInfo *v, uint8_t *outBuf, size_t bufSize);
```

The Encode() method takes a **VoteInfo** structure as input and converts it to a sequence of bytes according to a particular wire format encoding; it returns the size of the resulting byte sequence. The Decode() method takes a byte sequence of a specified size and parses it as a message according to the protocol, filling in the **VoteInfo** with the information from the message. It returns TRUE if the message was successfully parsed, and FALSE otherwise.

Given these interfaces to the framing and parsing code, we can now describe the voting client and server programs that will use these methods. The client is straightforward: the candidate ID is given as a command-line argument, along with a flag indicating that the transaction is an inquiry (by default it is a vote request). Upon sending the request, the client waits for the response and then closes the connection when it is received.

VoteClientTCP.c

```
 1  #include <stdio.h>
 2  #include <string.h>
 3  #include <stdlib.h>
 4  #include <stdint.h>
 5  #include <unistd.h>
 6  #include <errno.h>
 7  #include <sys/socket.h>
 8  #include <netinet/in.h>
 9  #include <arpa/inet.h>
10  #include <netdb.h>
11  #include "Practical.h"
12  #include "VoteProtocol.h"
13  #include "Framer.h"
14  #include "VoteEncoding.h"
15
16  int main(int argc, char *argv[]) {
17    if (argc < 4 || argc > 5)  // Test for correct # of args
```

```
18    DieWithUserMessage("Parameter(s)", "<Server> <Port/Service> <Candidate> [I]");
19
20  char *server = argv[1];    // First arg: server address/name
21  char *service = argv[2];   // Second arg: string to echo
22  // Third arg: server port/service
23  int candi = atoi(argv[3]);
24  if (candi < 0 || candi > MAX_CANDIDATE)
25    DieWithUserMessage("Candidate # not valid", argv[3]);
26
27  bool inq = argc > 4 && strcmp(argv[4], "I") == 0;
28
29  // Create a connected TCP socket
30  int sock = SetupTCPClientSocket(server, service);
31  if (sock < 0)
32    DieWithUserMessage("SetupTCPClientSocket() failed", "unable to connect");
33
34  FILE *str = fdopen(sock,"r+"); // Wrap for stream I/O
35  if (str == NULL)
36    DieWithSystemMessage("fdopen() failed");
37
38  // Set up info for a request
39  VoteInfo vi;
40  memset(&vi, 0, sizeof(vi));
41
42  vi.isInquiry = inq;
43  vi.candidate = candi;
44
45  // Encode for transmission
46  uint8_t outbuf[MAX_WIRE_SIZE];
47  size_t reqSize = Encode(&vi, outbuf, MAX_WIRE_SIZE);
48
49  // Print info
50  printf("Sending %d-byte %s for candidate %d...\n", reqSize,
51         (inq ? "inquiry" : "vote"), candi);
52
53  // Frame and send
54  if (PutMsg(outbuf, reqSize, str) < 0)
55    DieWithSystemMessage("PutMsg() failed");
56
57  // Receive and print response
58  uint8_t inbuf[MAX_WIRE_SIZE];
59  size_t respSize = GetNextMsg(str, inbuf, MAX_WIRE_SIZE); // Get the message
60  if (Decode(inbuf, respSize, &vi)) { // Parse it
61    printf("Received:\n");
62    if (vi.isResponse)
```

```
63        printf(" Response to ");
64      if (vi.isInquiry)
65        printf("inquiry ");
66      else
67        printf("vote ");
68      printf("for candidate %d\n", vi.candidate);
69      if (vi.isResponse)
70        printf("  count = %llu\n", vi.count);
71    }
72
73    // Close up
74    fclose(str);
75
76    exit(0);
77  }
```

VoteClientTCP.c

1. **Access to library functions and constants:** lines 1–14

2. **Argument processing:** lines 17–27

3. **Get connected socket:** lines 30–32

4. **Wrap the socket in a stream:** lines 34–36
   We open a stream using fdopen() (mode "r+" opens for both reading and writing).

5. **Prepare and send request message:** lines 38–55
   - **Prepare a VoteInfo structure with the candidate ID:** lines 39–43
   - **Encode into wire format:** line 47
   - **Print encoded message before framing:** lines 50–51
   - **Add framing and send over the output stream:** lines 54–55

6. **Receive, parse, and process response:** lines 58–71
   - **Call GetNextMsg():** line 59
     The method handles all the messy details of receiving enough data through the socket to make up the next message; like **recv()**, it may block indefinitely.
   - **Pass the result to be parsed:** line 60
   - **Process the response if it is correctly formed:** lines 61–70
     Invalid responses are ignored.

7. **Close the stream:** line 74

Turning now to the server, it needs a way to keep track of the vote counts of all the candidates. Because there are at most 1001 candidates, an array of 64-bit integers will serve nicely. The server prepares its socket and waits for incoming connections like the other servers we have seen. When a connection arrives, our program receives and processes messages over that connection until the client closes it. Note that, because of the very basic interface to the framing/parsing code, our client and server are quite simple-minded when it comes to handling errors in received messages; the server simply ignores any message that is malformed and immediately closes the connection.

VoteServerTCP.c

```
1   #include <stdio.h>
2   #include <string.h>
3   #include <stdbool.h>
4   #include <stdint.h>
5   #include <unistd.h>
6   #include <errno.h>
7   #include <sys/socket.h>
8   #include <arpa/inet.h>
9   #include "Practical.h"
10  #include "VoteProtocol.h"
11  #include "VoteEncoding.h"
12  #include "Framer.h"
13
14  static uint64_t counts[MAX_CANDIDATE + 1];
15
16  int main(int argc, char *argv[]) {
17    if (argc != 2) // Test for correct number of arguments
18      DieWithUserMessage("Parameter(s)", "<Server Port/Service>");
19
20    int servSock = SetupTCPServerSocket(argv[1]);
21    // servSock is now ready to use to accept connections
22
23    for (;;) { // Run forever
24
25      // Wait for a client to connect
26      int clntSock = AcceptTCPConnection(servSock);
27
28      // Create an input stream from the socket
29      FILE *channel = fdopen(clntSock, "r+");
30      if (channel == NULL)
31        DieWithSystemMessage("fdopen() failed");
32
33      // Receive messages until connection closes
34      int mSize;
35      uint8_t inBuf[MAX_WIRE_SIZE];
36      VoteInfo v;
37      while ((mSize = GetNextMsg(channel, inBuf, MAX_WIRE_SIZE)) > 0) {
38        memset(&v, 0, sizeof(v)); // Clear vote information
```

```
39        printf("Received message (%d bytes)\n", mSize);
40        if (Decode(inBuf, mSize, &v)) { // Parse to get VoteInfo
41          if (!v.isResponse) { // Ignore non-requests
42            v.isResponse = true;
43            if (v.candidate >= 0 && v.candidate <= MAX_CANDIDATE) {
44              if (!v.isInquiry)
45                counts[v.candidate] += 1;
46              v.count = counts[v.candidate];
47            } // Ignore invalid candidates
48          }
49          uint8_t outBuf[MAX_WIRE_SIZE];
50          mSize = Encode(&v, outBuf, MAX_WIRE_SIZE);
51          if (PutMsg(outBuf, mSize, channel) < 0) {
52            fputs("Error framing/outputting message\n", stderr);
53            break;
54          } else {
55            printf("Processed %s for candidate %d; current count is %llu.\n",
56                (v.isInquiry ? "inquiry" : "vote"), v.candidate, v.count);
57          }
58          fflush(channel);
59        } else {
60          fputs("Parse error, closing connection.\n", stderr);
61          break;
62        }
63      }
64      puts("Client finished");
65      fclose(channel);
66    } // Each client
67    // NOT REACHED
68  }
```

VoteServerTCP.c

1. **Access to library functions and constants:** lines 1-12
2. **Local declarations:** line 14
   Array to store vote counts.
3. **Declarations and argument processing:** lines 16-18
4. **Set up listening socket:** line 20
5. **Repeatedly accept and handle clients:** lines 23-66
   - **Wait for connection:** line 26
     AcceptTCPConnection() prints client info.
   - **Wrap the socket in a stream:** lines 29-31
   - **Receive and process messages until connection closes:** lines 34-63

Note that the server uses the same code as the client to parse, frame, and encode messages.

6. **Close client connection:** line 65

5.2.1   Framing

Application protocols typically deal with discrete messages, which are viewed as collections of fields. *Framing* refers to the general problem of enabling the receiver to locate the boundaries of a message (or part of one). Whether information is encoded as text, as multibyte binary numbers, or as some combination of the two, the application protocol must specify how the receiver of a message can determine when it has received all of the message.

Of course, if a complete message is sent as the payload of a UDP datagram, the problem is trivial: every send/receive operation on a datagram socket involves a single message, so the receiver knows exactly where that message ends. For messages sent over TCP sockets, however, the situation can be more complicated, because TCP has no notion of message boundaries. If the fields in a message all have fixed sizes and the message is made up of a fixed number of fields, then the size of the message is known in advance and the receiver can simply read the expected number of bytes into a buffer. (This technique was used in TCPEchoClient.c, where we knew the number of bytes to expect from the server.) However, when the message can vary in length—for example, if it contains some variable-length arbitrary text strings—we do not know beforehand how many bytes to read.

If a receiver tries to receive more bytes from a socket than were in the message, one of two things can happen. If no other message is in the channel, the receiver will block and will be prevented from processing the message; if the sender is also blocked waiting for a reply, the result will be *deadlock*: each side of the connection waiting for the other to send more information. On the other hand, if another message is already in the channel, the receiver may read some or all of it as part of the first message, leading to other kinds of errors. Therefore framing is an important consideration when using TCP sockets.

Note that some of the same considerations apply to finding the boundaries of the individual *fields* of the message: the receiver needs to know where one ends and another begins. Thus, pretty much everything we say here about framing messages also applies to fields. However, as was pointed out above, the cleanest code results if we deal with the problem of locating the end of the message separately from that of parsing it into fields.

Two general techniques enable a receiver to unambiguously find the end of the message:

■ *Delimiter-based*: The end of the message is indicated by a *unique marker*, a particular, agreed-upon byte (or sequence of bytes) that the sender transmits immediately following the data.

■ *Explicit length*: The variable-length field or message is preceded by a *length* field that tells how many bytes it contains. The length field is generally of a fixed size; this limits the maximum size message that can be framed.

A special case of the delimiter-based method can be used for the last message sent on a TCP connection: the sender simply closes the sending side of the connection after sending the message. After the receiver reads the last byte of the message, it receives an end-of-stream indication (i.e., recv() returns 0 or fread() returns EOF) and thus can tell that it has reached the end of the message.

The delimiter-based approach is often used with messages encoded as text: A particular character or sequence of characters is defined to mark the end of the message. The receiver simply scans the input (as characters) looking for the delimiter sequence; it returns the character string preceding the delimiter. The drawback is that *the message itself must not contain the delimiter*; otherwise the receiver will find the end of the message prematurely. With a delimiter-based framing method, someone has to be responsible for ensuring that this precondition is satisfied. Fortunately, so-called *stuffing* techniques allow delimiters that occur naturally in the message to be modified so the receiver will not recognize them as such. The sending side performs a transformation on delimiters that occur in the text; the receiver, as it scans for the delimiter, also recognizes the transformed delimiters and restores them so that the output message matches the original. The downside of such techniques is that *both* sender and receiver have to scan every byte of the message.

The length-based approach is simpler but requires a known upper bound on the size of the message. The sender first determines the length of the message, encodes it as an integer, and prefixes the result to the message. The upper bound on the message length determines the number of bytes required to encode the length: 1 byte if messages always contain fewer than 256 bytes, 2 bytes if they are always shorter than 65536 bytes, and so on.

The module DelimFramer.c implements delimiter-based framing using the "newline" character ("\n", byte value 10) as the delimiter. Our PutMsg() method does *not* do stuffing, but simply fails (catastrophically) if the byte sequence to be framed already contains the delimiter. The GetNextMsg() method scans the stream, copying each byte into the buffer until it reads the delimiter or runs out of space. It returns the number of bytes placed in the buffer. If the message is truncated, that is, the method returns a full buffer without encountering a delimiter, the returned count is negative. If some bytes of a message are accumulated and the stream ends without finding a delimiter, it is considered an error and a negative value is returned (i.e., this protocol does *not* accept end-of-stream as a delimiter). Thus, an empty but correctly framed message (length zero is returned) can be distinguished from the stream ending.

DelimFramer.c

```
1  #include <stdio.h>
2  #include <stdlib.h>
3  #include <stdint.h>
4  #include "Practical.h"
5
6  static const char DELIMITER = '\n';
7
8  /* Read up to bufSize bytes or until delimiter, copying into the given
9   * buffer as we go.
```

```
10    * Encountering EOF after some data but before delimiter results in failure.
11    * (That is: EOF is not a valid delimiter.)
12    * Returns the number of bytes placed in buf (delimiter NOT transferred).
13    * If buffer fills without encountering delimiter, negative count is returned.
14    * If stream ends before first byte, -1 is returned.
15    * Precondition: buf has room for at least bufSize bytes.
16    */
17   int GetNextMsg(FILE *in, uint8_t *buf, size_t bufSize) {
18     int count = 0;
19     int nextChar;
20     while (count < bufSize) {
21       nextChar = getc(in);
22       if (nextChar == EOF) {
23         if (count > 0)
24           DieWithUserMessage("GetNextMsg()", "Stream ended prematurely");
25         else
26           return -1;
27       }
28       if (nextChar == DELIMITER)
29         break;
30       buf[count++] = nextChar;
31     }
32     if (nextChar != DELIMITER) { // Out of space: count==bufSize
33       return -count;
34     } else { // Found delimiter
35       return count;
36     }
37   }
38
39   /* Write the given message to the output stream, followed by
40    * the delimiter.  Return number of bytes written, or -1 on failure.
41    */
42   int PutMsg(uint8_t buf[], size_t msgSize, FILE *out) {
43     // Check for delimiter in message
44     int i;
45     for (i = 0; i < msgSize; i++)
46       if (buf[i] == DELIMITER)
47         return -1;
48     if (fwrite(buf, 1, msgSize, out) != msgSize)
49       return -1;
50     fputc(DELIMITER, out);
51     fflush(out);
52     return msgSize;
53   }
```

DelimFramer.c

1. **Declare constant delimiter value:** line 6
2. **Input method:** GetNextMsg(): lines 17–37
   - **Initialize byte count:** line 18
   - **Iterate until buffer is full or EOF:** lines 20–37
     We get the next byte from the input stream, compare it to EOF, then the delimiter. On EOF we abort if an incomplete message is in the buffer, else return −1. On delimiter we break out of the loop. If the buffer becomes full (count==bufSize), we return the negation of the number of bytes read as an indication that the channel is not empty.
   - **Return the count of bytes transferred to buffer:** line 35
3. **Output method:** PutMsg(): lines 42–53
   - **Scan the input message looking for the delimiter:** lines 43–47
     If we find it, (we rather unhelpfully) kill the program.
   - **Write message to output stream:** line 48
   - **Write delimiter byte to output stream:** line 50
   - **Flush the output stream:** line 47
     This ensures that the message is sent over the underlying socket.

Although our implementation makes it fairly easy to change the single character used as a delimiter, some protocols make use of multiple-character delimiters. The HTTP protocol, which is used in the World Wide Web, uses text-encoded messages delimited by the four-character sequence \r\n\r\n. Extending the delimiter-based framing module to support multicharacter delimiters and to handle stuffing is left as an exercise.

The module LengthFramer.c implements the framing interface using length-based framing. It works for messages up to 65535 ($2^{16} - 1$) bytes in length. The PutMsg() method determines the length of the given message and writes it to the output stream as a 2-byte, big-endian integer, followed by the complete message. On the receiving side, the fread() method is used to read the length as an integer; after converting it to host byte order, that many bytes are read from the channel. Note that, with this framing method, the sender does not have to inspect the content of the message being framed; it needs only to check that the message does not exceed the length limit.

LengthFramer.c

```
1   #include <stdio.h>
2   #include <stdlib.h>
3   #include <stdint.h>
4   #include <netinet/in.h>
5   #include "Practical.h"
6
7   /* Read 2-byte length and place in big-endian order.
```

```
 8  * Then read the indicated number of bytes.
 9  * If the input buffer is too small for the data, truncate to fit and
10  * return the negation of the *indicated* length.  Thus a negative return
11  * other than -1 indicates that the message was truncated.
12  * (Ambiguity is possible only if the caller passes an empty buffer.)
13  * Input stream is always left empty.
14  */
15 int GetNextMsg(FILE *in, uint8_t *buf, size_t bufSize) {
16   uint16_t mSize = 0;
17   uint16_t extra = 0;
18
19   if (fread(&mSize, sizeof(uint16_t), 1, in) != 1)
20     return -1;
21   mSize = ntohs(mSize);
22   if (mSize > bufSize) {
23     extra = mSize - bufSize;
24     mSize = bufSize; // Truncate
25   }
26   if (fread(buf, sizeof(uint8_t), mSize, in) != mSize) {
27     fprintf(stderr, "Framing error: expected %d, read less\n", mSize);
28     return -1;
29   }
30   if (extra > 0) { // Message was truncated
31     uint8_t waste[BUFSIZE];
32     fread(waste, sizeof(uint8_t), extra, in); // Try to flush the channel
33     return -(mSize + extra); // Negation of indicated size
34   } else
35     return mSize;
36 }
37
38 /* Write the given message to the output stream, followed by
39  * the delimiter.  Precondition: buf[] is at least msgSize.
40  * Returns -1 on any error.
41  */
42 int PutMsg(uint8_t buf[], size_t msgSize, FILE *out) {
43   if (msgSize > UINT16_MAX)
44     return -1;
45   uint16_t payloadSize = htons(msgSize);
46   if ((fwrite(&payloadSize, sizeof(uint16_t), 1, out) != 1) || (fwrite(buf,
47       sizeof(uint8_t), msgSize, out) != msgSize))
48     return -1;
49   fflush(out);
50   return msgSize;
51 }
```

LengthFramer.c

1. **Input method:** `GetNextMsg()`: lines 15–36
   - **Read the prefix length:** lines 19–20
     The `fread()` method reads 2 bytes into the unsigned 16-bit integer *mSize*.
   - **Convert to host byte order:** line 21
   - **Truncate message if necessary:** lines 22–25
     If the indicated size is bigger than the buffer provided by the caller, we truncate the message so it will fit, and remember so we can indicate via the return value that we did so.
   - **Read the message:** line 26
   - **Flush channel:** lines 30–34
     If we are returning early because the buffer is full, we remove the extra bytes from the channel and return the negation of the header size.
   - **Return the size:** line 35
2. **Output method:** `PutMsg()`: lines 42–51
   - **Verify input length:** lines 43–44
     Because we use a 2-byte unsigned length field, the length cannot exceed 65535 (the value of UINT16_MAX).
   - **Convert length to network byte order:** line 45
   - **Output length and message:** lines 46–48
   - **Flush to ensure the message is sent:** line 49

5.2.2 Text-Based Message Encoding

Now we turn to the representation of voting messages as text. Because we only have to represent numbers and a couple of indicators, we can use the basic C charset US-ASCII. The message consists of text fields separated by one or more occurrences of the ASCII space character (decimal value 32). The message begins with a so-called magic string—a sequence of ASCII characters that allows a recipient to quickly recognize the message as a Voting protocol message, as opposed to random garbage that happened to arrive over the network. The Vote/Inquiry boolean is encoded with the character "v" for a vote or "i" for an inquiry. The message's status as a response is indicated by the presence of the character "R." Then comes the candidate ID, followed by the vote count, both encoded as strings of decimal digits. The module `VoteEncodingText.c` implements this text-based encoding.

VoteEncodingText.c

```
1   /* Routines for Text encoding of vote messages.
2    * Wire Format:
3    *    "Voting <v|i> [R]  <candidate ID>  <count>"
4    */
```

```
 5   #include <string.h>
 6   #include <stdint.h>
 7   #include <stdbool.h>
 8   #include <stdlib.h>
 9   #include <stdio.h>
10   #include <string.h>
11   #include "Practical.h"
12   #include "VoteProtocol.h"
13
14   static const char *MAGIC = "Voting";
15   static const char *VOTESTR = "v";
16   static const char *INQSTR = "i";
17   static const char *RESPONSESTR = "R";
18   static const char *DELIMSTR = " ";
19   enum {
20     BASE = 10
21   };
22
23   /* Encode voting message info as a text string.
24    * WARNING: Message will be silently truncated if buffer is too small!
25    * Invariants (e.g. 0 <= candidate <= 1000) not checked.
26    */
27   size_t Encode(const VoteInfo *v, uint8_t *outBuf, const size_t bufSize) {
28     uint8_t *bufPtr = outBuf;
29     long size = (size_t) bufSize;
30     int rv = snprintf((char *) bufPtr, size, "%s %c %s %d", MAGIC,
31        (v->isInquiry ? 'i' : 'v'), (v->isResponse ? "R" : ""), v->candidate);
32     bufPtr += rv;
33     size -= rv;
34     if (v->isResponse) {
35       rv = snprintf((char *) bufPtr, size, " %llu", v->count);
36       bufPtr += rv;
37     }
38     return (size_t) (bufPtr - outBuf);
39   }
40
41   /* Extract message information from given buffer.
42    * Note: modifies input buffer.
43    */
44   bool Decode(uint8_t *inBuf, const size_t mSize, VoteInfo *v) {
45
46     char *token;
47     token = strtok((char *) inBuf, DELIMSTR);
48     // Check for magic
49     if (token == NULL || strcmp(token, MAGIC) != 0)
```

```
50      return false;
51
52      // Get vote/inquiry indicator
53      token = strtok(NULL, DELIMSTR);
54      if (token == NULL)
55        return false;
56
57      if (strcmp(token, VOTESTR) == 0)
58        v->isInquiry = false;
59      else if (strcmp(token, INQSTR) == 0)
60        v->isInquiry = true;
61      else
62        return false;
63
64      // Next token is either Response flag or candidate ID
65      token = strtok(NULL, DELIMSTR);
66      if (token == NULL)
67        return false; // Message too short
68
69      if (strcmp(token, RESPONSESTR) == 0) { // Response flag present
70        v->isResponse = true;
71        token = strtok(NULL, DELIMSTR); // Get candidate ID
72        if (token == NULL)
73          return false;
74      } else { // No response flag; token is candidate ID;
75        v->isResponse = false;
76      }
77      // Get candidate #
78      v->candidate = atoi(token);
79      if (v->isResponse) { // Response message should contain a count value
80        token = strtok(NULL, DELIMSTR);
81        if (token == NULL)
82          return false;
83        v->count = strtoll(token, NULL, BASE);
84      } else {
85        v->count = 0L;
86      }
87      return true;
88  }
```

VoteEncodingText.c

The Encode() method uses snprintf() to construct a string containing all the fields of the message, separated by white space. It fails only if the caller provides an insufficient amount of space to hold the string.

The `Decode()` method uses the `strtok()` method to break the received message into tokens (fields). The `strtok()` library function takes a pointer to a character array and a string containing characters to be interpreted as delimiters. The first time it is called, it returns the largest initial substring consisting entirely of characters not in the delimiter string; the trailing delimiter of that string is replaced by a null byte. On subsequent calls with a NULL first argument, tokens are taken left to right from the original string until there are no more tokens, at which point NULL is returned.

`Decode()` first looks for the "Magic" string; if it is not the first thing in the message, it simply fails and returns FALSE. **Note well:** This illustrates a very important point about implementing protocols: **never assume anything about any input from the network**. Your program must always be prepared for any possible inputs, and handle them gracefully. In this case, the `Decode()` method simply ignores the rest of the message and returns FALSE if some expected part is not present or improperly formatted.[4] Otherwise, `Decode()` gets the fields token by token, using the library functions `atoi()` and `strtoll()` to convert tokens into integers.

5.2.3 Binary Message Encoding

Next we present a different way to encode the Voting protocol message. In contrast with the text-based format, the binary format uses fixed-size messages. Each message begins with a one-byte field that contains the "magic" value 010101 in its high-order 6 bits. As with the text format, this little bit of redundancy provides the receiver with a small degree of assurance that it is receiving a proper voting message. The two low-order bits of the first byte encode the two booleans; note the use of the bitwise-or operations shown earlier, in Section 5.1.8, to set the flags. The second byte of the message always contains zeros (it is effectively padding), and the third and fourth bytes contain the candidateID. The final 8 bytes of a response message (only) contain the vote count.

VoteEncodingBin.c

```
 1   /* Routines for binary encoding of vote messages
 2    * Wire Format:
 3    *                             1  1  1  1  1  1
 4    *  0  1  2  3  4  5  6  7  8  9  0  1  2  3  4  5
 5    * +--+--+--+--+--+--+--+--+--+--+--+--+--+--+--+--+
 6    * |     Magic       |Flags|        ZERO           |
 7    * +--+--+--+--+--+--+--+--+--+--+--+--+--+--+--+--+
 8    * |                 Candidate ID                  |
 9    * +--+--+--+--+--+--+--+--+--+--+--+--+--+--+--+--+
10    * |                                               |
```

---

[4]This also illustrates a key reason why it is best to do framing before parsing: recovery from a parse error when a message has only been partially received is much more complex because the receiver has to get "back in sync" with the sender.

```
11   * |           Vote Count (only in response)        |
12   * |                                                |
13   * |                                                |
14   * +--+--+--+--+--+--+--+--+--+--+--+--+--+--+--+--+
15   *
16   */
17
18   #include <string.h>
19   #include <stdbool.h>
20   #include <stdlib.h>
21   #include <stdint.h>
22   #include <netinet/in.h>
23   #include "Practical.h"
24   #include "VoteProtocol.h"
25
26   enum {
27     REQUEST_SIZE = 4,
28     RESPONSE_SIZE = 12,
29     COUNT_SHIFT = 32,
30     INQUIRE_FLAG = 0x0100,
31     RESPONSE_FLAG = 0x0200,
32     MAGIC = 0x5400,
33     MAGIC_MASK = 0xfc00
34   };
35
36   typedef struct voteMsgBin voteMsgBin;
37
38   struct voteMsgBin {
39     uint16_t header;
40     uint16_t candidateID;
41     uint32_t countHigh;
42     uint32_t countLow;
43   };
44
45   size_t Encode(VoteInfo *v, uint8_t *outBuf, size_t bufSize) {
46     if ((v->isResponse && bufSize < sizeof(voteMsgBin)) || bufSize < 2
47         * sizeof(uint16_t))
48       DieWithUserMessage("Output buffer too small", "");
49     voteMsgBin *vm = (voteMsgBin *) outBuf;
50     memset(outBuf, 0, sizeof(voteMsgBin)); // Be sure
51     vm->header = MAGIC;
52     if (v->isInquiry)
53       vm->header |= INQUIRE_FLAG;
54     if (v->isResponse)
55       vm->header |= RESPONSE_FLAG;
```

```
56    vm->header = htons(vm->header); // Byte order
57    vm->candidateID = htons(v->candidate); // Know it will fit, by invariants
58    if (v->isResponse) {
59      vm->countHigh = htonl(v->count >> COUNT_SHIFT);
60      vm->countLow = htonl((uint32_t) v->count);
61      return RESPONSE_SIZE;
62    } else {
63      return REQUEST_SIZE;
64    }
65  }
66
67  /* Extract message info from given buffer.
68   * Leave input unchanged.
69   */
70  bool Decode(uint8_t *inBuf, size_t mSize, VoteInfo *v) {
71
72    voteMsgBin *vm = (voteMsgBin *) inBuf;
73
74    // Attend to byte order; leave input unchanged
75    uint16_t header = ntohs(vm->header);
76    if ((mSize < REQUEST_SIZE) || ((header & MAGIC_MASK) != MAGIC))
77      return false;
78    /* message is big enough and includes correct magic number */
79    v->isResponse = ((header & RESPONSE_FLAG) != 0);
80    v->isInquiry = ((header & INQUIRE_FLAG) != 0);
81    v->candidate = ntohs(vm->candidateID);
82    if (v->isResponse && mSize >= RESPONSE_SIZE) {
83      v->count = ((uint64_t) ntohl(vm->countHigh) << COUNT_SHIFT)
84          | (uint64_t) ntohl(vm->countLow);
85    }
86    return true;
87  }
```

VoteEncodingBin.c

The Decode() method's job is especially simple in this version—it simply copies the values from the message into the **VoteInfo** structure, converting byte order along the way.

5.2.4 Putting It All Together

To get a working vote server, we simply compile together VoteServerTCP.c, one of the two framing modules, one of the two encoding modules, and the auxiliary modules DieWithMessage.c, TCPClientUtility.c, TCPServerUtility.c, and AddressUtility.c. For example:

```
% gcc -std=gnu99 -o vs VoteServerTCP.c DelimFramer.c VoteEncodingBin.c \
DieWithMessage.c TCPServerUtility.c AddressUtility.c
```

```
% gcc -std=gnu99 -o vc VoteClientTCP.c DelimFramer.c VoteEncodingBin.c \
DieWithMessage.c TCPClientUtility.c
```

All four possible combinations of framing method and encoding will work—provided the client and server use the same combination!

5.3   Wrapping Up

We have seen how primitive types can be represented as sequences of bytes for transmission "on the wire." We have also considered some of the subtleties of encoding text strings, as well as some basic methods of framing and parsing messages. We saw examples of both text-oriented and binary-encoded protocols.

It is probably worth reiterating something we said in the Preface: this chapter will by no means make you an expert! That takes a great deal of experience. But the code from this chapter can be used as a starting point for further explorations.

Exercises

1. If the underlying hardware platform is little-endian, and the "network" byte order is big-endian, is there any reason for the implementations of `htonl()` and `ntohl()` to be different?

2. Write the function **uint64_t** htonll(**uint64_t** *val*), which converts a 64-bit integer from little-endian to big-endian byte order.

3. Write the little-endian analogs of the method given in `BruteForceEncoding.c`, that is, `EncodeLittleEndian()` and `DecodeLittleEndian()`.

4. Write methods `EncodeBigEndianSigned()` and `DecodeBigEndianSigned()`, which return signed values. (The input buffers are still unsigned types. *Hint*: use explicit type-casting.)

5. The `EncodeIntBigEndian()` method in `BruteForceEncoding.c` only works if several preconditions such as $0 \leq size \leq 8$ are satisfied. Modify the method to test for these preconditions and return an error indication of some sort if any are violated. What are the advantages and disadvantages of having the program check the preconditions, versus relying on the caller to establish them?

6. Assuming all byte values are equally likely, what is the probability that a message consisting of random bits will pass the "magic test" in the binary encoding of the Voting protocol? Suppose an ASCII-encoded text message is sent to a program expecting a binary-encoded voteMsg. Which characters would enable the message to pass the "magic test" if they are the first in the message?

7. Suppose we use `DelimFraming.c` and `VoteEncodingBin.c` in building the Voting Client. Describe circumstances in which the client fails to send a message.

8. Extend the delimiter-based framing implementation to perform "byte stuffing," so that messages that contain the delimiter can be transmitted without the caller of PutMsg() having to worry about it. That is, the framing module transparently handles messages that contain the delimiter. (See any decent networking text for the algorithm.)

9. Extend the delimiter-based framing implementation to handle arbitrary multiple-byte delimiters. Be sure your implementation is efficient. (**Note**: this problem is *not* trivial! A naive approach will run very inefficiently in the worst case.)

10. Both GetNextMsg() implementations truncate the received message if the caller fails to provide a big enough buffer. Consider the behavior on the next call to GetNextMsg() after this happens, for both implementations. Is the behavior the same in both cases? If not, suggest modifications so that both implementations behave the same way in all cases.

chapter 6

Beyond Basic Socket Programming

Our client and server examples demonstrate the basic model for socket programming. The next step is to integrate these ideas into various programming models such as multitasking, signalling, and broadcasting. We demonstrate these principles in the context of standard UNIX programming; however, most modern operating systems support similar features (e.g., processes and threads).

6.1 Socket Options

The TCP/IP protocol developers spent a good deal of time thinking about the default behaviors that would satisfy most applications. (If you doubt this, read RFCs 1122 and 1123, which describe in excruciating detail the recommended behaviors—based on years of experience—for implementations of the TCP/IP protocols.) For most applications, the designers did a good job; however, it is seldom the case that "one-size-fits-all" really fits all. For example, each socket has an associated receive buffer. How big should it be? Each implementation has a default size; however, this value may not always be appropriate for your application (see also Section 7.1). This particular aspect of a socket's behavior, along with many others, is associated with a *socket option*: You can change the receive buffer size of a socket by modifying the value of the associated socket option. The functions getsockopt() and setsockopt() allow socket option values to be queried and set, respectively.

```
int getsockopt(int socket, int level, int optName, void *optVal, socklen_t *optLen)
int setsockopt(int socket, int level, int optName, const void *optVal, socklen_t optLen)
```

For both functions, *socket* must be a socket descriptor allocated by socket(). The available socket options are divided into levels that correspond to the layers of the protocol stack; the second parameter indicates the level of the option in question. Some options are protocol independent and are thus handled by the socket layer itself (SOL_SOCKET), some are specific to the transport protocol (IPPROTO_TCP), and some are handled by the internetwork protocol (IPPROTO_IP). The option itself is specified by the integer *optName*, which is always specified using a system-defined constant. The parameter *optVal* is a pointer to a buffer. For getsockopt(), the option's current value will be placed in that buffer by the implementation, whereas for setsockopt(), the socket option in the implementation will be set to the value in the buffer. In both calls, *optLen* specifies the length of the buffer, which must be correct for the particular option in question. Note that in getsockopt(), *optLen* is an in-out parameter, initially pointing to an integer containing the size of the buffer; on return the pointed-to integer contains the size of the option value. The following code segment demonstrates how to fetch and then double the configured size (in bytes) of the socket's receive buffer:

```
int rcvBufferSize;
// Retrieve and print the default buffer size
int sockOptSize = sizeof(rcvBufferSize);
if (getsockopt(sock, SOL_SOCKET, SO_RCVBUF, &rcvBufferSize, &sockOptSize) < 0)
    DieWithSystemMessage("getsockopt() failed");
printf("Initial Receive Buffer Size: %d\n", rcvBufferSize);

// Double the buffer size
rcvBufferSize *= 2;
if (setsockopt(sock, SOL_SOCKET, SO_RCVBUF, &rcvBufferSize, sizeof(rcvBufferSize)) < 0)
    DieWithSystemMessage("setsockopt() failed");
```

Note that value passed to setsockopt() is *not* guaranteed to be the new size of the socket buffer, even if the call apparently succeeds. Rather, it is best thought of as a "hint" to the system about the value desired by the user; the system, after all, has to manage resources for *all* users and may consider other factors in adjusting buffer size.

Table 6.1 shows some commonly used options at each level, including a description and the data type of the buffer pointed to by *optVal*.

6.2 Signals

Signals provide a mechanism for notifying programs that certain events have occurred—for example, the user typed the "interrupt" character, or a timer expired. Some of the events (and therefore the notification) may occur *asynchronously*, which means that the notification

SOL_SOCKET optname	Type	Values	Description
SO_BROADCAST	**int**	0,1	Broadcast allowed
SO_KEEPALIVE	**int**	0,1	Keepalive messages enabled (if implemented by protocol)
SO_LINGER	**linger**{}	time	Time to delay close return waiting for confirmation (see Section 7.4)
SO_RCVBUF	**int**	bytes	Bytes in the socket receive buffer (see code on page 100 and Section 7.1)
SO_RCVLOWAT	**int**	bytes	Minimum number of available bytes that will cause recv to return
SO_REUSEADDR	**int**	0,1	Binding allowed (under certain conditions) to an address or port already in use (see Section 7.4)
SO_SNDLOWAT	**int**	bytes	Minimum bytes to send
SO_SNDBUF	**int**	bytes	Bytes in the socket send buffer (see Section 7.1)

IPPROTO_TCP optname	type	Values	Description
TCP_MAX	**int**	seconds	Seconds between keepalive messages.
TCP_NODELAY	**int**	0, 1	Disallow delay from Nagle's algorithm for data merging

IPPROTO_IP optname	type	Values	Description
IP_TTL	**int**	0 - 255	Time-to-live for unicast IP packets.
IP_MULTICAST_TTL	**unsigned char**	0 - 255	Time-to-live for multicast IP packets (see MulticastSender.c on page 138)
IP_MULTICAST_LOOP	**int**	0,1	Enables multicast socket to receive packets it sent
IP_ADD_MEMBERSHIP	**ip_mreq**{}	group address	Enables reception of packets addressed to the specified multicast group (see MulticastReceiver.c on page 141) – Set only
IP_DROP_MEMBERSHIP	**ip_mreq**{}	group address	Disables reception of packets addressed to the specified multicast group – Set only

Table 6.1: *continued*

IPPROTO_IPV6 optname	type	Values	Description
IPV6_V6ONLY	**int**	0,1	Restrict IPv6 sockets to only IPv6 communication.
IPV6_UNICAST_HOPS	**int**	-1 - 255	Time-to-live for unicast IP packets.
IPV6_MULTICAST_HOPS	**int**	-1 - 255	Time-to-live for multicast IP packets (see MulticastSender.c on page 138)
IPV6_MULTICAST_LOOP	**u_int**	0,1	Enables multicast socket to receive packets it sent
IPV6_JOIN_GROUP	**ipv6_mreq**{}	group address	Enables reception of packets addressed to the specified multicast group (see MulticastReceiver.c on page 141) – Set only
IPV6_LEAVE_GROUP	**ipv6_mreq**{}	group address	Disables reception of packets addressed to the specified multicast group – Set only

Table 6.1: Socket Options

is delivered to the program regardless of which statement it is executing. When a signal is delivered to a running program, one of four things happens:

1. The signal is ignored. The process is never aware that the signal was delivered.

2. The program is forcibly terminated by the operating system.

3. Program execution is interrupted and a *signal-handling routine*, specified by (and part of) the program, is executed. This execution happens in a different thread of control from the main thread(s) of the program so that the program is not necessarily immediately aware of it.

4. The signal is *blocked*, that is, prevented from having any effect until the program takes action to allow its delivery. Each process has a *mask*, indicating which signals are currently blocked in that process. (Actually, each thread in a program can have its own signal mask.)

UNIX has dozens of different signals, each indicating the occurrence of a different type of event. Each signal has a system-defined *default behavior*, which is one of the first two possibilities listed above. For example, termination is the default behavior for SIGINT, which is delivered when the interrupt character (usually Control-C) is received via the controlling terminal for that process.

Signals are a complicated animal, and a full treatment is beyond the scope of this book. However, some signals are frequently encountered in the context of socket programming.

Moreover, **any program that sends on a TCP socket must explicitly deal with SIGPIPE in order to be robust.** Therefore, we present the basics of dealing with signals, focusing on these five:

Type	Triggering Event	Default
SIGALRM	Expiration of an alarm timer	termination
SIGCHLD	Child process exit	ignore
SIGINT	Interrupt char (Control-C) input	termination
SIGIO	Socket ready for I/O	ignore
SIGPIPE	Attempt to write to a closed socket	termination

An application program can change the default behavior[1] for a particular signal using sigaction():

---

int sigaction (**int** *whichSignal*, **const struct sigaction** **newAction*, **struct sigaction** **oldAction*)

---

sigaction() returns 0 on success and −1 on failure; details of its semantics, however, are a bit more involved.

Each signal is identified by an integer constant; *whichSignal* specifies the signal for which the behavior is being changed. The *newAction* parameter points to a **sigaction** structure that defines the new behavior for the given signal type; if the pointer *oldAction* is non-null, a **sigaction** structure describing the previous behavior for the given signal is copied into it, as shown here:

```
struct sigaction {
    void (*sa_handler)(int);    // Signal handler
    sigset_t sa_mask;           // Signals to be blocked during handler execution
    int sa_flags;               // Flags to modify default behavior
};
```

The field sa_handler (of type "pointer to function of one integer parameter that returns void") controls which of the first three possibilities occurs when a signal is delivered (i.e., when it is not masked). If its value is the special constant SIG_IGN, the signal will be ignored. If its value is SIG_DFL, the default behavior for that signal will be used. If its value is the address of a function (which is guaranteed to be different from the two constants), that function will be invoked with a parameter indicating the signal that was delivered. (If the same handler function

---

[1]For some signals, the default behavior cannot be changed, nor can the signal be blocked; however, this is not true for any of the five we consider.

is used for multiple signals, the parameter can be used to determine which one caused the invocation.)

Signals can be "nested" in the following sense: While one signal is being handled, another is delivered. As you can imagine, this can get rather complicated. Fortunately, the sigaction() mechanism allows some signals to be temporarily blocked (in addition to those that are already blocked by the process's signal mask) while the specified signal is handled. The field sa_mask specifies the signals to be blocked while handling *whichSignal*; it is only meaningful when sa_handler is not SIG_IGN or SIG_DFL. By default *whichSignal* is always blocked regardless of whether it is reflected in sa_mask. (On some systems, setting the flag SA_NODEFER in sa_flags allows the specified signal to be delivered while it is being handled.) The sa_flags field controls some further details of the way *whichSignal* is handled; these details are beyond the scope of this discussion.

sa_mask is implemented as a set of boolean flags, one for each type of signal. This set of flags can be manipulated with the following four functions:

---

int sigemptyset(**sigset_t** **set*)
int sigfillset(**sigset_t** **set*)
int sigaddset(**sigset_t** **set*, **int** *whichSignal*)
int sigdelset(**sigset_t** **set*, **int** *whichSignal*)

---

sigfillset() and sigemptyset() set and unset all of the flags in the given set. sigaddset() and sigdelset() set and unset individual flags, specified by the signal number, in the given set. All four functions return 0 for success and −1 for failure.

SigAction.c shows a simple sigaction() example to provide a handler for SIGINT by setting up a signal handler and then entering an infinite loop. When the program receives an interrupt signal, the handler function, a pointer to which is supplied to sigaction(), executes and exits the program.

SigAction.c

```
1   #include <stdio.h>
2   #include <signal.h>
3   #include <unistd.h>
4   #include <stdlib.h>
5   #include "Practical.h"
6
7   void InterruptSignalHandler(int signalType); // Interrupt signal handling function
8
9   int main(int argc, char *argv[]) {
10    struct sigaction handler; // Signal handler specification structure
11
```

```
12    // Set InterruptSignalHandler() as handler function
13    handler.sa_handler = InterruptSignalHandler;
14    // Create mask that blocks all signals
15    if (sigfillset(&handler.sa_mask) < 0)
16      DieWithSystemMessage("sigfillset() failed");
17    handler.sa_flags = 0;  // No flags
18
19    // Set signal handling for interrupt signal
20    if (sigaction(SIGINT, &handler, 0) < 0)
21      DieWithSystemMessage("sigaction() failed for SIGINT");
22
23    for (;;)
24      pause(); // Suspend program until signal received
25
26    exit(0);
27  }
28
29  void InterruptSignalHandler(int signalType) {
30    puts("Interrupt Received.  Exiting program.");
31    exit(1);
32  }
```

SigAction.c

1. **Signal handler function prototype:** line 7
2. **Set up signal handler:** lines 10-21
   - **Assign function to handle signal:** line 13
   - **Fill signal mask:** lines 15-16
   - **Set signal handler for SIGINT:** lines 20-21
3. **Loop forever until SIGINT:** lines 23-24
   pause() suspends the process until a signal is received.
4. **Function to handle signal:** lines 29-32
   InterruptSignalHandler() prints a message and exits the program.

So what happens when a signal that would otherwise be delivered is blocked, say, because another signal is being handled? Delivery is postponed until the handler completes. Such a signal is said to be *pending*. **It is important to realize that signals are *not* queued—a signal is either pending or it is not. If the same signal is delivered more than once while it is being handled, the handler is only executed once more after it completes the original execution.** Consider the case where three SIGINT signals arrive while the signal handler for SIGINT is already executing. The first of the three SIGINT signals is blocked; however, the subsequent two signals are lost. When the SIGINT signal handler function completes, the system executes the handler only *once* again. We must be prepared to handle this behavior in our applications. To see this in action, modify InterruptSignalHandler() in SigAction.c as follows:

```
void InterruptSignalHandler(int ignored) {
    printf("Interrupt Received.\n");
    sleep(3);
}
```

The signal handler for SIGINT sleeps for three seconds and returns, instead of exiting. Now when you execute the program, hit the interrupt key (Control-C) several times in succession. If you hit the interrupt key more than two times in a row, you still only see two "Interrupt Received" messages. The first interrupt signal invokes InterruptSignalHandler(), which sleeps for three seconds. The second interrupt is blocked because SIGINT is already being handled. The third and fourth interrupts are lost. Be warned that you will no longer be able to stop your program with a keyboard interrupt. You will need to explicitly send another signal (such as SIGTERM) to the process using the **kill** command.

One of the most important aspects of signals relates to the sockets interface. If a signal is delivered while the program is blocked in a socket call (such as a recv() or connect()), and a handler for that signal has been specified, as soon as the handler completes, the socket call will return −1 with *errno* set to EINTR. Thus, **your programs that catch and handle signals need to be prepared for these erroneous returns from system calls that can block.**

Later in this chapter we encounter the first four signals mentioned above. Here we briefly describe the semantics of SIGPIPE. Consider the following scenario: A server (or client) has a connected TCP socket, and the other end abruptly and unexpectedly closes the connection, say, because the program crashed. How does the server find out that the connection is broken? The answer is that it doesn't, until it tries to send or receive on the socket. If it tries to receive first, the call returns 0. If it tries to send first, at that point, SIGPIPE is delivered. Thus, SIGPIPE is delivered *synchronously* and not asynchronously. (Why not just return −1 from send()? See exercise 5 at the end of the chapter.)

This fact is especially significant for servers because the default behavior for SIGPIPE is to terminate the program. Thus, servers that don't change this behavior can be terminated by misbehaving clients. **Servers should always handle SIGPIPE so that they can detect the client's disappearance and reclaim any resources that were in use to service it.**

6.3 Nonblocking I/O

The default behavior of a socket call is to block until the requested action is completed. For example, the recv() function in TCPEchoClient.c (page 44) does not return until at least one message from the echo server is received. Of course, a process with a blocked function is suspended by the operating system.

A socket call may block for several reasons. Data reception functions (recv() and recvfrom()) block if data is not available. A send() on a TCP socket may block if there is not sufficient space to buffer the transmitted data (see Section 7.1). Connection-related functions for TCP sockets block until a connection has been established. For example, accept() in TCPEchoServer.c (page 48) blocks until a client establishes a connection with connect(). Long round-trip times, high error rate connections, or a slow (or deceased) server may cause a call to connect() to block for a significant amount of time. In all of these cases, the function returns only after the request has been satisfied.

What about a program that has other tasks to perform while waiting for call completion (e.g., update busy cursor or respond to user requests)? These programs may have no time to wait on a blocked system call. What about lost UDP datagrams? In UDPEchoClient.c (page 54), the client sends a datagram to the server and then waits to receive a response. **If either the datagram sent from the client or the echoed datagram from the server is lost, our echo client blocks indefinitely.** In this case, we need recvfrom() to unblock after some amount of time to allow the client to handle the datagram loss. Fortunately, several mechanisms are available for controlling unwanted blocking behaviors. We deal with three such solutions here: nonblocking sockets, asynchronous I/O, and timeouts.

6.3.1 Nonblocking Sockets

One obvious solution to the problem of undesirable blocking is to change the behavior of the socket so that *all* calls are *nonblocking*. For such a socket, if a requested operation can be completed immediately, the call's return value indicates success; otherwise it indicates failure (usually −1). In either case the call does not block indefinitely. In the case of failure, we need the ability to distinguish between failure due to blocking and other types of failures. If the failure occurred because the call would have blocked, the system sets *errno* to EWOULDBLOCK,[2] except for connect(), which returns an *errno* of EINPROGRESS.

We can change the default blocking behavior with a call to fcntl() ("file control").

---

int fcntl(**int** *socket*, **int** *command*, ...)

As the name suggests, this call can be used with any kind of file: *socket* must be a valid file (or socket) descriptor. The operation to be performed is given by *command*, which is *always* a system-defined constant. The behavior we want to modify is controlled by flags (*not* the same as socket options) associated with the descriptor, which we can get and set with the F_GETFL and F_SETFL commands. When setting the socket flags, we must specify the new flags in a variable-length argument list. The flag that controls nonblocking behavior is O_NONBLOCK. When getting the socket flags, the variable-length argument list is empty. We demonstrate the use of a nonblocking socket in the next section, where we describe asynchronous I/O in UDPEchoServer-SIGIO.c (page 109).

---

[2]Some sockets implementations return EAGAIN. On many systems, EAGAIN and EWOULDBLOCK are the same error number.

There are a few exceptions to this model of nonblocking sockets. For UDP sockets, there are no send buffers, so send() and sendto() never return EWOULDBLOCK. For all but the connect() socket call, the requested operation either completes before returning or none of the operation is performed. For example, recv() either receives data from the socket or returns an error. A nonblocking connect() is different. For UDP, connect() simply assigns a destination address for future data transmissions so that it never blocks. For TCP, connect() initiates the TCP connection setup. If the connection cannot be completed without blocking, connect() returns an error, setting *errno* to EINPROGRESS, indicating that the socket is still working on making the TCP connection. Of course, subsequent data sends and receives cannot happen until the connection is established. Determining when the connection is complete is beyond the scope of this text,[3] so we recommend not setting the socket to nonblocking until after the call to connect().

For eliminating blocking during individual send and receive operations, an alternative is available on some platforms. The *flags* parameter of send(), recv(), sendto(), and recvfrom() allows for modification of some aspects of the behavior on a particular call. Some implementations support the MSG_DONTWAIT flag, which causes nonblocking behavior in any call where it is set in *flags*.

6.3.2 Asynchronous I/O

The difficulty with nonblocking socket calls is that there is no way of knowing when one would succeed, except by periodically trying it until it does (a process known as "polling"). Why not have the operating system inform the program when a socket call will be successful? That way the program can spend its time doing other work until notified that the socket is ready for something to happen. This is called *asynchronous I/O*, and it works by having the SIGIO signal delivered to the process when some I/O-related event occurs on the socket.

Arranging for SIGIO involves three steps. First, we inform the system of the desired disposition of the signal using sigaction(). Then we ensure that signals related to the socket will be delivered to *this* process (because multiple processes can have access to the same socket, there might be ambiguity about which should get it) by making it the owner of the socket, using fcntl(). Finally, we mark the socket as being primed for asynchronous I/O by setting a flag (FASYNC), again via fcntl().

In our next example, we adapt UDPEchoServer.c (page 57) to use asynchronous I/O with nonblocking socket calls. The modified server is able to perform other tasks when there are no clients needing an echo. After creating and binding the socket, instead of calling recvfrom() and blocking until a datagram arrives, the asynchronous echo server establishes a signal handler for SIGIO and begins doing other work. When a datagram arrives, the SIGIO signal is delivered to the process, triggering execution of the handler function. The handler function calls recvfrom(),

---

[3]Well, mostly. Connection completion can be detected using the select() call, described in Section 6.5.

echoes back any received datagrams, and then returns, whereupon the main program continues whatever it was doing. Our description details only the code that differs from the original UDP echo server.

UDPEchoServer-SIGIO.c

```
 1  #include <stdio.h>
 2  #include <stdlib.h>
 3  #include <string.h>
 4  #include <unistd.h>
 5  #include <fcntl.h>
 6  #include <sys/file.h>
 7  #include <signal.h>
 8  #include <errno.h>
 9  #include <sys/types.h>
10  #include <sys/socket.h>
11  #include <netdb.h>
12  #include "Practical.h"
13
14  void UseIdleTime();             // Execution during idle time
15  void SIGIOHandler(int signalType); // Handle SIGIO
16
17  int servSock; // Socket -- GLOBAL for signal handler
18
19  int main(int argc, char *argv[]) {
20
21    if (argc != 2) // Test for correct number of arguments
22      DieWithUserMessage("Parameter(s)", "<Server Port/Service>");
23
24    char *service = argv[1]; // First arg:  local port
25
26    // Construct the server address structure
27    struct addrinfo addrCriteria;                     // Criteria for address
28    memset(&addrCriteria, 0, sizeof(addrCriteria)); // Zero out structure
29    addrCriteria.ai_family = AF_UNSPEC;             // Any address family
30    addrCriteria.ai_flags = AI_PASSIVE;             // Accept on any address/port
31    addrCriteria.ai_socktype = SOCK_DGRAM;          // Only datagram sockets
32    addrCriteria.ai_protocol = IPPROTO_UDP;         // Only UDP protocol
33
34    struct addrinfo *servAddr; // List of server addresses
35    int rtnVal = getaddrinfo(NULL, service, &addrCriteria, &servAddr);
36    if (rtnVal != 0)
37      DieWithUserMessage("getaddrinfo() failed", gai_strerror(rtnVal));
```

```
38
39    // Create socket for incoming connections
40    servSock = socket(servAddr->ai_family, servAddr->ai_socktype,
41        servAddr->ai_protocol);
42    if (servSock < 0)
43      DieWithSystemMessage("socket() failed");
44
45    // Bind to the local address
46    if (bind(servSock, servAddr->ai_addr, servAddr->ai_addrlen) < 0)
47      DieWithSystemMessage("bind() failed");
48
49    // Free address list allocated by getaddrinfo()
50    freeaddrinfo(servAddr);
51
52    struct sigaction handler;
53    handler.sa_handler = SIGIOHandler; // Set signal handler for SIGIO
54    // Create mask that mask all signals
55    if (sigfillset(&handler.sa_mask) < 0)
56      DieWithSystemMessage("sigfillset() failed");
57    handler.sa_flags = 0;              // No flags
58
59    if (sigaction(SIGIO, &handler, 0) < 0)
60      DieWithSystemMessage("sigaction() failed for SIGIO");
61
62    // We must own the socket to receive the SIGIO message
63    if (fcntl(servSock, F_SETOWN, getpid()) < 0)
64      DieWithSystemMessage("Unable to set process owner to us");
65
66    // Arrange for nonblocking I/O and SIGIO delivery
67    if (fcntl(servSock, F_SETFL, O_NONBLOCK | FASYNC) < 0)
68      DieWithSystemMessage(
69        "Unable to put client sock into non-blocking/async mode");
70
71    // Go off and do real work; echoing happens in the background
72
73    for (;;)
74      UseIdleTime();
75    // NOT REACHED
76  }
77
78  void UseIdleTime() {
79    puts(".");
80    sleep(3); // 3 seconds of activity
81  }
82
```

```
83   void SIGIOHandler(int signalType) {
84     ssize_t numBytesRcvd;
85     do { // As long as there is input...
86       struct sockaddr_storage clntAddr;  // Address of datagram source
87       size_t clntLen = sizeof(clntAddr); // Address length in-out parameter
88       char buffer[MAXSTRINGLENGTH];       // Datagram buffer
89
90       numBytesRcvd = recvfrom(servSock, buffer, MAXSTRINGLENGTH, 0,
91           (struct sockaddr *) &clntAddr, &clntLen);
92       if (numBytesRcvd < 0) {
93         // Only acceptable error: recvfrom() would have blocked
94         if (errno != EWOULDBLOCK)
95           DieWithSystemMessage("recvfrom() failed");
96       } else {
97         fprintf(stdout, "Handling client ");
98         PrintSocketAddress((struct sockaddr *) &clntAddr, stdout);
99         fputc('\n', stdout);
100
101        ssize_t numBytesSent = sendto(servSock, buffer, numBytesRcvd, 0,
102            (struct sockaddr *) &clntAddr, sizeof(clntAddr));
103        if (numBytesSent < 0)
104          DieWithSystemMessage("sendto() failed");
105        else if (numBytesSent != numBytesRcvd)
106          DieWithUserMessage("sendto()", "sent unexpected number of bytes");
107      }
108    } while (numBytesRcvd >= 0);
109    // Nothing left to receive
110  }
```

UDPEchoServer-SIGIO.c

1. **Program setup and parameter parsing:** lines 1–24

2. **Prototypes for signal and idle time handler:** lines 14–15
   UseIdleTime() simulates the other tasks of the UDP echo server. SIGIOHandler() handles
   SIGIO signals. **Note well:** UseIdleTime() **must be prepared for any "slow" system calls—
   such as reading from a terminal device—to return −1 as a result of the SIGIO signal** ⚠
   being delivered and handled (in which case it should simply verify that *errno* is EINTR
   and resume whatever it was doing).

3. **Server socket descriptor:** line 17
   We give the socket descriptor a global scope so that it can be accessed by the SIGIO
   handler function.

4. **Set up signal handling:** lines 52–69

handler is the **sigaction** structure that describes our desired signal-handling behavior. We fill it in, giving the address of the handling routine and the set of signals we want blocked.

- **Fill in the pointer to the desired handler:** line 53
- **Specify signals to be blocked during handling:** lines 55–56
- **Specify how to handle the SIGIO signal:** lines 59–60
- **Arrange for SIGIO to go to this process:** lines 63–64
  The F_SETOWN command identifies the process to receive SIGIO for this socket.
- **Set flags for nonblocking and asynchronous I/O:** lines 67–69
  Finally, we mark the socket (with the FASYNC flag[4]) to indicate that asynchronous I/O is in use, so SIGIO will be delivered on packet arrival. (Everything up to this point was just saying *how* to deal with SIGIO.) Because we do not want SIGIOHandler() to block in recvfrom(), we also set the O_NONBLOCK flag.

5. **Run forever using idle time when available:** lines 73–74

6. **Perform nonechoing server tasks:** lines 78–81

7. **Handle asynchronous I/O:** lines 83–110
   This code is very similar to the loop in our earlier UDPEchoServer.c (page 57). One difference is that here we loop until there are no more pending echo requests to satisfy and then return; this technique enables the main program thread to continue what it was doing.
   - **Receive echo request:** lines 90–99
     The first call to recvfrom() receives the datagram whose arrival prompted the SIGIO signal. Additional datagrams may arrive during execution of the handler, so the do/while loop continues to call recvfrom() until no more datagrams remain to be received. Because *sock* is a nonblocking socket, recvfrom() then returns −1 with *errno* set to EWOULDBLOCK, terminating the loop and the handler function.
   - **Send echo reply:** lines 101–106
     Just as in the original UDP echo server, sendto() repeats the message back to the client.

6.3.3 Timeouts

In the previous subsection, we relied on the system to notify our program of the occurrence of an I/O-related event. Sometimes, however, we may actually need to know that some I/O event has *not* happened for a certain time period. For example, we have already mentioned that UDP messages can be lost; in case of such a loss, our UDP echo client (or any other client that uses UDP, for that matter) will never receive a response to its request. Of course, the client

---

[4]The name may be different (e.g., O_ASYNC) on some platforms.

cannot tell directly whether a loss has occurred, so it sets a limit on how long it will wait for a response. For example, the UDP echo client might assume that if the server has not responded to its request within two seconds, the server will never respond. The client's reaction to this two-second *timeout* might be to give up or to try again by resending the request.

The standard method of implementing timeouts is to set an alarm before calling a blocking function.

---

unsigned int alarm(**unsigned int** *secs*)

---

alarm() starts a timer, which expires after the specified number of seconds (*secs*); alarm() returns the number of seconds remaining for any previously scheduled alarm (or 0 if no alarm was scheduled). When the timer expires, a SIGALRM signal is sent to the process, and the handler function for SIGALRM, if any, is executed.

The code we showed earlier in UDPEchoClient.c (page 54) has a problem if either the echo request or the response is lost: The client blocks indefinitely on recvfrom(), waiting for a datagram that will never arrive. Our next example program, UDPEchoClient-Timeout.c, modifies the original UDP echo client to retransmit the request message if a response from the echo server is not received within a time limit of two seconds. To implement this, the new client installs a handler for SIGALRM, and just before calling recvfrom(), it sets an alarm for two seconds. At the end of that interval of time, the SIGALRM signal is delivered, and the handler is invoked. When the handler returns, the blocked recvfrom() returns -1 with *errno* equal to EINTR. The client then resends the echo request to the server. This timeout and retransmission of the echo request happens up to five times before the client gives up and reports failure. Our program description only details the code that differs from the original UDP echo client.

UDPEchoClient–Timeout.c

```
 1  #include <stdio.h>
 2  #include <stdlib.h>
 3  #include <string.h>
 4  #include <unistd.h>
 5  #include <errno.h>
 6  #include <signal.h>
 7  #include <sys/socket.h>
 8  #include <netinet/in.h>
 9  #include <netdb.h>
10  #include "Practical.h"
11
12  static const unsigned int TIMEOUT_SECS = 2; // Seconds between retransmits
13  static const unsigned int MAXTRIES = 5;     // Tries before giving up
```

```
14
15  unsigned int tries = 0; // Count of times sent - GLOBAL for signal-handler access
16
17  void CatchAlarm(int ignored); // Handler for SIGALRM
18
19  int main(int argc, char *argv[]) {
20
21    if ((argc < 3) || (argc > 4)) // Test for correct number of arguments
22      DieWithUserMessage("Parameter(s)",
23          "<Server Address/Name> <Echo Word> [<Server Port/Service>]\n");
24
25    char *server = argv[1];     // First arg: server address/name
26    char *echoString = argv[2]; // Second arg: word to echo
27
28    size_t echoStringLen = strlen(echoString);
29    if (echoStringLen > MAXSTRINGLENGTH)
30      DieWithUserMessage(echoString, "too long");
31
32    char *service = (argc == 4) ? argv[3] : "echo";
33
34    // Tell the system what kind(s) of address info we want
35    struct addrinfo addrCriteria;                       // Criteria for address
36    memset(&addrCriteria, 0, sizeof(addrCriteria)); // Zero out structure
37    addrCriteria.ai_family = AF_UNSPEC;                 // Any address family
38    addrCriteria.ai_socktype = SOCK_DGRAM;              // Only datagram sockets
39    addrCriteria.ai_protocol = IPPROTO_UDP;             // Only UDP protocol
40
41    // Get address(es)
42    struct addrinfo *servAddr; // Holder for returned list of server addrs
43    int rtnVal = getaddrinfo(server, service, &addrCriteria, &servAddr);
44    if (rtnVal != 0)
45      DieWithUserMessage("getaddrinfo() failed", gai_strerror(rtnVal));
46
47    // Create a reliable, stream socket using TCP
48    int sock = socket(servAddr->ai_family, servAddr->ai_socktype,
49        servAddr->ai_protocol); // Socket descriptor for client
50    if (sock < 0)
51      DieWithSystemMessage("socket() failed");
52
53    // Set signal handler for alarm signal
54    struct sigaction handler; // Signal handler
55    handler.sa_handler = CatchAlarm;
56    if (sigfillset(&handler.sa_mask) < 0) // Block everything in handler
57      DieWithSystemMessage("sigfillset() failed");
58    handler.sa_flags = 0;
```

```
59
60    if (sigaction(SIGALRM, &handler, 0) < 0)
61      DieWithSystemMessage("sigaction() failed for SIGALRM");
62
63    // Send the string to the server
64    ssize_t numBytes = sendto(sock, echoString, echoStringLen, 0,
65        servAddr->ai_addr, servAddr->ai_addrlen);
66    if (numBytes < 0)
67      DieWithSystemMessage("sendto() failed");
68    else if (numBytes != echoStringLen)
69      DieWithUserMessage("sendto() error", "sent unexpected number of bytes");
70
71    // Receive a response
72
73    struct sockaddr_storage fromAddr; // Source address of server
74    // Set length of from address structure (in-out parameter)
75    socklen_t fromAddrLen = sizeof(fromAddr);
76    alarm(TIMEOUT_SECS); // Set the timeout
77    char buffer[MAXSTRINGLENGTH + 1]; // I/O buffer
78    while ((numBytes = recvfrom(sock, buffer, MAXSTRINGLENGTH, 0,
79        (struct sockaddr *) &fromAddr, &fromAddrLen)) < 0) {
80      if (errno == EINTR) {      // Alarm went off
81        if (tries < MAXTRIES) { // Incremented by signal handler
82          numBytes = sendto(sock, echoString, echoStringLen, 0,
83              (struct sockaddr *) servAddr->ai_addr, servAddr->ai_addrlen);
84          if (numBytes < 0)
85            DieWithSystemMessage("sendto() failed");
86          else if (numBytes != echoStringLen)
87            DieWithUserMessage("sendto() error", "sent unexpected number of bytes");
88        } else
89          DieWithUserMessage("No Response", "unable to communicate with server");
90      } else
91        DieWithSystemMessage("recvfrom() failed");
92    }
93
94    // recvfrom() got something -- cancel the timeout
95    alarm(0);
96
97    buffer[echoStringLen] = '\0';     // Null-terminate the received data
98    printf("Received: %s\n", buffer); // Print the received data
99
100   close(sock);
101   exit(0);
102 }
103
```

```
104  // Handler for SIGALRM
105  void CatchAlarm(int ignored) {
106    tries += 1;
107  }
```

UDPEchoClient-Timeout.c

1. **Program setup and parameter parsing:** lines 1-32

2. **Timeout setup:** lines 12-17
   tries is a global variable so that it can be accessed in the signal handler.

3. **Establish signal handler for SIGALRM:** lines 53-61
   This is similar to what we did for SIGIO in UDPEchoServer-SIGIO.c.

4. **Start the alarm timer:** line 76
   When/if the alarm timer expires, the handler CatchAlarm() will be invoked.

5. **Retransmission loop:** lines 78-92
   We have to loop here because the SIGALRM will cause the recvfrom() to return −1. When that happens, we decide whether or not it was a timeout and, if so, retransmit.

   ■ **Attempt reception:** lines 78-79

   ■ **Discover the reason for** recvfrom() **failure:** lines 80-91
   If *errno* equals EINTR, recvfrom() returned because it was interrupted by the SIGALRM while waiting for datagram arrival and not because we got a packet. In this case we assume either the echo request or reply is lost. If we have not exceeded the maximum number of retransmission attempts, we retransmit the request to the server; otherwise, we report a failure. After retransmission, we reset the alarm timer to wake us again if the timeout expires.

6. **Handle echo response reception:** lines 95-98
   ■ **Cancel the alarm timer:** line 95

   ■ **Ensure that message is null-terminated:** line 97
   printf() will output bytes until it encounters a null byte, so we need to make sure one is present (otherwise, our program may crash).

   ■ **Print the received message:** line 98

6.4 Multitasking

Our TCP echo server handles one client at a time. If additional clients connect while one is already being serviced, their connections will be established and they will be able to send their requests, but the server will not echo back their data until it has finished with the first client. This type of socket application is called an *iterative server*. **Iterative servers work best for**

applications where each client requires a small, bounded amount of work by the server. ⚠ However, if the time required to handle a client can be long, the overall connection time experienced by any waiting clients may become unacceptably long. To demonstrate the problem, add a sleep() after the connect() statement in TCPEchoClient.c (page 44) and experiment with several clients simultaneously accessing the TCP echo server. (Here, sleep() simulates an operation that takes significant time such as slow file or network I/O.)

Modern operating systems provide a solution to this dilemma. Using constructs like processes or threads, we can farm out responsibility for each client to an independently executing copy of the server. In this section, we will explore several models of such *concurrent servers*, including per-client processes, per-client threads, and constrained multitasking.

6.4.1 Per-Client Processes

Processes are independently executing programs on the same host. In a per-client process server, for each client connection request we simply create a new process to handle the communication. Processes share the resources of the server host, each servicing its client concurrently.

In UNIX, fork() attempts the creation of a new process, returning −1 on failure. On success, a new process is created that is identical to the calling process, except for its process ID and the return value it receives from fork(). The two processes thereafter execute independently. The process invoking fork() is called the *parent* process, and the newly created process is called the *child*. Since the processes are identical, how do the processes know whether they are parent or child? If the return from fork() is 0, the process knows that it is the child. To the parent, fork() returns the process ID of the new child process.

When a child process terminates, it does not automatically disappear. In UNIX parlance, the child becomes a *zombie*. Zombies consume system resources until they are "harvested" by their parent with a call to waitpid(), as demonstrated in our next example program, TCPEchoServer-Fork.c.

We demonstrate this per-client process, multitasking approach by adapting its use for the TCP echo server. The majority of the program is identical to the original TCPEchoServer.c (page 48). The main difference is that the multitasking server creates a new copy of itself each time it accepts a new connection; each copy handles one client and then terminates. No changes are required to TCPEchoClient.c (page 44) to work with this new server.

We have decomposed this new echo server to improve readability and to allow reuse in our later examples. Our program commentary is limited to differences between the new server and TCPEchoServer.c (page 48).

Figure 6.1 depicts the phases involved in connection setup between the server and a client. The server runs forever, listening for connections on a specified port, and repeatedly (1) accepts an incoming connection from a client and then (2) creates a new process to handle that connection. Note that only the original server process calls fork().

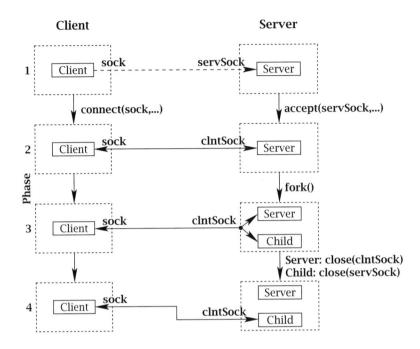

Figure 6.1: Forking TCP echo server.

TCPEchoServer-Fork.c

```
1   #include <stdio.h>
2   #include <unistd.h>
3   #include <stdlib.h>
4   #include <sys/wait.h>
5   #include "Practical.h"
6
7   int main(int argc, char *argv[]) {
8
9     if (argc != 2) // Test for correct number of arguments
10      DieWithUserMessage("Parameter(s)", "<Server Port/Service>");
11
12    char *service = argv[1]; // First arg:  local port/service
13    int servSock = SetupTCPServerSocket(service);
14    if (servSock < 0)
15      DieWithUserMessage("SetupTCPServerSocket() failed", "unable to establish");
16
17    unsigned int childProcCount = 0; // Number of child processes
18    for (;;) { // Run forever
```

```
19      // New connection creates a client socket
20      int clntSock = AcceptTCPConnection(servSock);
21      // Fork child process and report any errors
22      pid_t processID = fork();
23      if (processID < 0)
24        DieWithSystemMessage("fork() failed");
25      else if (processID == 0) { // If this is the child process
26        close(servSock);        // Child closes parent socket
27        HandleTCPClient(clntSock);
28        exit(0);                // Child process terminates
29      }
30
31      printf("with child process: %d\n", processID);
32      close(clntSock);  // Parent closes child socket descriptor
33      childProcCount++; // Increment number of child processes
34
35      while (childProcCount) { // Clean up all zombies
36        processID = waitpid((pid_t) - 1, NULL, WNOHANG); // Non-blocking wait
37        if (processID < 0) // waitpid() error?
38          DieWithSystemMessage("waitpid() failed");
39        else if (processID == 0) // No zombie to wait on
40          break;
41        else
42          childProcCount--; // Cleaned up after a child
43      }
44    }
45    // NOT REACHED
46  }
```

TCPEchoServer-Fork.c

1. **Additional include file for** waitpid(): line 4

2. **Create server socket:** lines 13–15
   SetupTCPServerSocket() allocates, binds, and marks the server socket as ready to accept incoming connections.

3. **Set up to handle multiple processes:** line 17
   childProcCount is a variable to count the number of processes.

4. **Process dispatch loop:** lines 18–44
   The parent process runs forever, forking a process for each connection request.
   - **Get the next connection:** line 20
     AcceptTCPConnection() blocks until a valid connection is established and returns the socket descriptor for that connection. Connection establishment is depicted in the transition from Phase 1 to 2 in Figure 6.1.

- **Create a child process to handle the new connection:** line 22
  fork() attempts to duplicate the calling process. If the attempt fails, fork() returns −1. If it succeeds, the child process receives a return value of 0, and the parent receives a return value of the process ID of the child process. When fork() creates a new child process, it copies the socket descriptors from the parent to the child; therefore, after fork(), both the parent and child processes have socket descriptors for the listening socket (*servSock*) and the newly created and connected client socket (*clntSock*), as shown in Phase 3 of Figure 6.1.

- **Child process execution:** lines 26-28
  The child process is only responsible for dealing with the new client so it can close the listening socket descriptor. However, since the parent process still has a descriptor for the listening socket, this close does not deallocate the socket. This is depicted in the transition from Phase 3 to 4 in Figure 6.1. It is important to note that calling close() only terminates the specified socket if no other processes have a reference to the socket. The child process then executes HandleTCPClient() to handle the connection. After handling the client, the child process calls close() to deallocate the client socket. The child process is terminated with the call to exit().

- **Parent execution continues:** lines 31-33
  Since the child is handling the new client, the parent can close the socket descriptor of the new connection socket; again, this does not deallocate the socket because the child process also contains a reference.[5] (See the transition from Phase 3 to 4 in Figure 6.1.) The parent keeps a count of the number of outstanding child processes in *childProcCount*.

- **Handle zombies:** lines 35-43
  After each connection request, the parent server process harvests the zombies created by child process termination. The server repeatedly harvests zombies by calling waitpid() until no more of them exist. The first parameter to waitpid() (−1) is a wildcard that instructs it to take any zombie, regardless of its process ID. The second parameter is a placeholder where waitpid() returns the state of the zombie. Since we do not care about the state, we specify NULL, and no state is returned. Next comes a flag parameter for customizing the behavior of waitpid(). WNOHANG causes it to return immediately if no zombies are found. waitpid() returns one of three value types: failure (returns −1), found zombie (returns *pid* of zombie), and no zombie (returns 0). If waitpid() found a zombie, we need to decrement *childProcCount* and, if more unharvested children exist (*childProcCount != 0*), look for another zombie. If waitpid() returns without finding a zombie, the parent process breaks out of the zombie harvesting loop.

---

[5]Our description of the child and parent execution assumes that the parent executes close() on the client socket before the child. However, it is possible for the client to race ahead and execute the close() call on *clntSock* before the server. In this case, the server's close() performs the actual socket deallocation, but this does not change the behavior of the server from the client's perspective.

There are several other ways to deal with zombies. On some UNIX variants, the default child termination behavior can be changed so that zombie processes are not created (e.g., SA_NOCLDWAIT flag to sigaction()). We do not use this approach because it is not portable. Another approach is to establish a handler function for the SIGCHLD signal. When a child terminates, a SIGCHLD signal is delivered to the original process invoking a specified handler function. The handler function uses waitpid() to harvest any zombies. Unfortunately, signals may interrupt at any time, including during blocked system calls (see Section 6.2). The proper method for restarting interrupted system calls differs between UNIX variants. In some systems, restarting is the default behavior. On others, the *sa_flags* field of the **sigaction** structure could be set to SA_RESTART to ensure interrupted system calls restart. On other systems, the interrupted system calls return −1 with *errno* set to EINTR. In this case, the program must restart the interrupted function. We do not use any of these approaches because they are not portable, and they complicate the program with issues that we are not addressing. We leave it as an exercise for readers to adapt our TCP echo server to use SIGCHLD on their systems.

For this and the rest of the server examples in this chapter, we have factored out the code for setting up the server socket. This code can be found in TCPServerUtility.c

SetupTCPServerSocket()

```
1   static const int MAXPENDING = 5; // Maximum outstanding connection requests
2
3   int SetupTCPServerSocket(const char *service) {
4     // Construct the server address structure
5     struct addrinfo addrCriteria;                   // Criteria for address match
6     memset(&addrCriteria, 0, sizeof(addrCriteria)); // Zero out structure
7     addrCriteria.ai_family = AF_UNSPEC;             // Any address family
8     addrCriteria.ai_flags = AI_PASSIVE;             // Accept on any address/port
9     addrCriteria.ai_socktype = SOCK_STREAM;         // Only stream sockets
10    addrCriteria.ai_protocol = IPPROTO_TCP;         // Only TCP protocol
11
12    struct addrinfo *servAddr; // List of server addresses
13    int rtnVal = getaddrinfo(NULL, service, &addrCriteria, &servAddr);
14    if (rtnVal != 0)
15      DieWithUserMessage("getaddrinfo() failed", gai_strerror(rtnVal));
16
17    int servSock = -1;
18    for (struct addrinfo *addr = servAddr; addr != NULL; addr = addr->ai_next) {
19      // Create a TCP socket
20      servSock = socket(servAddr->ai_family, servAddr->ai_socktype,
21          servAddr->ai_protocol);
22      if (servSock < 0)
23        continue;       // Socket creation failed; try next address
24
25      // Bind to the local address and set socket to list
```

```
26      if ((bind(servSock, servAddr->ai_addr, servAddr->ai_addrlen) == 0) &&
27          (listen(servSock, MAXPENDING) == 0)) {
28        // Print local address of socket
29        struct sockaddr_storage localAddr;
30        socklen_t addrSize = sizeof(localAddr);
31        if (getsockname(servSock, (struct sockaddr *) &localAddr, &addrSize) < 0)
32          DieWithSystemMessage("getsockname() failed");
33        fputs("Binding to ", stdout);
34        PrintSocketAddress((struct sockaddr *) &localAddr, stdout);
35        fputc('\n', stdout);
36        break;        // Bind and list successful
37      }
38
39      close(servSock);  // Close and try again
40      servSock = -1;
41    }
42
43    // Free address list allocated by getaddrinfo()
44    freeaddrinfo(servAddr);
45
46    return servSock;
47  }
```

SetupTCPServerSocket()

The code for getting a new client connection calls accept() and prints out information on the client's address.

AcceptTCPConnection()

```
1  int AcceptTCPConnection(int servSock) {
2    struct sockaddr_storage clntAddr; // Client address
3    // Set length of client address structure (in-out parameter)
4    socklen_t clntAddrLen = sizeof(clntAddr);
5
6    // Wait for a client to connect
7    int clntSock = accept(servSock, (struct sockaddr *) &clntAddr, &clntAddrLen);
8    if (clntSock < 0)
9      DieWithSystemMessage("accept() failed");
10
11   // clntSock is connected to a client!
12
13   fputs("Handling client ", stdout);
14   PrintSocketAddress((struct sockaddr *) &clntAddr, stdout);
15   fputc('\n', stdout);
```

```
16
17    return clntSock;
18  }
```

After connection establishment, references to the child socket are done exclusively through the socket descriptor (*clntSock* in this example). In our forking TCP echo server, the IP address and port of the client are only known temporarily in AcceptTCPConnection(). What if we want to know the IP address and port outside of AcceptTCPConnection()? If we didn't want to return that information from AcceptTCPConnection(), we could use the getpeername() and getsockname() functions described in Section 2.4.6.

6.4.2 Per-Client Thread

Forking a new process to handle each client works, but it is expensive. Every time a process is created, the operating system must duplicate the entire state of the parent process including memory, stack, file/socket descriptors, and so on. *Threads* decrease this cost by allowing multitasking within the same process: A newly created thread simply shares the same address space (code and data) with the parent, negating the need to duplicate the parent state.

The next example program, TCPEchoServer-Thread.c, demonstrates a thread-per-client multitasking approach for the TCP echo server using POSIX threads[6] ("PThreads"). The majority of the program is identical to TCPEchoServer-Fork.c (page 118). Again, no changes are required to TCPEchoClient.c (page 44) to work with this new server. The program comments are limited to code that differs from the forking echo server.

TCPEchoServer–Thread.c

```
1   #include <stdio.h>
2   #include <stdlib.h>
3   #include <string.h>
4   #include <pthread.h>
5   #include "Practical.h"
6
7   void *ThreadMain(void *arg); // Main program of a thread
8
9   // Structure of arguments to pass to client thread
10  struct ThreadArgs {
11    int clntSock; // Socket descriptor for client
```

---

[6]Other thread packages work in generally the same manner. We selected POSIX threads because a port of POSIX threads exists for most operating systems.

```
12  };
13
14  int main(int argc, char *argv[]) {
15
16    if (argc != 2) // Test for correct number of arguments
17      DieWithUserMessage("Parameter(s)", "<Server Port/Service>");
18
19    char *service = argv[1]; // First arg:  local port/service
20    int servSock = SetupTCPServerSocket(service);
21    if (servSock < 0)
22      DieWithUserMessage("SetupTCPServerSocket() failed", "unable to establish");
23    for (;;) { // Run forever
24      int clntSock = AcceptTCPConnection(servSock);
25
26      // Create separate memory for client argument
27      struct ThreadArgs *threadArgs = (struct ThreadArgs *) malloc(
28          sizeof(struct ThreadArgs));
29      if (threadArgs == NULL)
30        DieWithSystemMessage("malloc() failed");
31      threadArgs->clntSock = clntSock;
32
33      // Create client thread
34      pthread_t threadID;
35          int returnValue = pthread_create(&threadID, NULL, ThreadMain, threadArgs);
36      if (returnValue != 0)
37        DieWithUserMessage("pthread_create() failed", strerror(returnValue));
38      printf("with thread %lu\n", (unsigned long int) threadID);
39    }
40    // NOT REACHED
41  }
42
43  void *ThreadMain(void *threadArgs) {
44    // Guarantees that thread resources are deallocated upon return
45    pthread_detach(pthread_self());
46
47    // Extract socket file descriptor from argument
48    int clntSock = ((struct ThreadArgs *) threadArgs)->clntSock;
49    free(threadArgs); // Deallocate memory for argument
50
51    HandleTCPClient(clntSock);
52
53    return (NULL);
54  }
```

TCPEchoServer-Thread.c

1. **Additional include file for POSIX threads:** line 4
2. **Set up for threads:** lines 7-12
   ThreadMain() is the function for the POSIX thread to execute. pthread_create() allows the caller to pass *one* pointer as an argument to the function to be executed in the new thread. The **ThreadArgs** structure contains the "real" list of parameters. The process creating a new thread allocates and populates the structure before calling pthread_create(). In this program the thread function only needs a single argument (*clntSock*), so we could have simply passed a pointer to an integer; however, the *ThreadArgs* structure provides a more general framework for thread argument passing.
3. **Population of thread argument structure:** lines 26-31
   We only pass the client socket descriptor to the new thread.
4. **Invocation of the new thread:** lines 33-38
5. **Thread execution:** lines 43-54
   ThreadMain is the function called by pthread_create() when it creates a new thread. The required prototype for the function to be executed by a thread is ***void** *fcn(**void** *)*, a function that takes a single argument of type **void** * and returns a **void** *.

   ■ **Thread detach:** line 45
     By default, when a thread's main function returns, state is maintained about the function return code until the parent harvests the results. This is very similar to the behavior for processes. pthread_detach() allows the thread state to be immediately deallocated upon completion without parent intervention. pthread_self() provides the thread ID of the current thread as a parameter to pthread_detach(), much in the way that getpid() provides a process its process ID.

   ■ **Extracting the parameters from the ThreadArgs structure:** lines 48-49
     The **ThreadArgs** structure for this program only contains the socket descriptor of the socket connected to the client socket by accept(). Because the **ThreadArgs** structure is allocated on a per-connection basis, the new thread can deallocate **threadArgs** once the parameter(s) have been extracted.

   ■ HandleTCPClient(): line 51
     The thread function calls the same HandleTCPClient() function that we have been using all along.

   ■ **Thread return:** line 53
     After creation, the parent does not need to communicate with the thread, so the thread can return a NULL pointer.

Because the parent and thread share the same address space (and thus file/socket descriptors), the parent thread and the per-connection thread do not close the connection and listening sockets, respectively, before proceeding, as the parent and child processes did in the forking example. Figure 6.2 illustrates the actions of the threaded TCP echo server. There are a few disadvantages to using threads instead of processes:

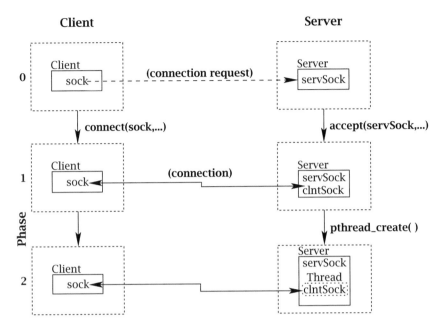

Figure 6.2: Threaded TCP echo server.

- If a child *process* goes awry, it is easy to monitor and kill it from the command line using its process identifier. Threads may not provide this capability on some platforms, so additional server functionality must be provided to monitor and kill individual threads.

- If the operating system is oblivious to the notion of threads, it may give every process the same size time slice. In that case a threaded Web server handling hundreds of clients may get the same amount of CPU time as a game of solitaire.

6.4.3   Constrained Multitasking

Process and thread creation both incur overhead. In addition, the scheduling and context switching among many processes or threads creates extra work for a system. As the number of processes or threads increases, the operating system spends more and more time dealing with this overhead. Eventually, the point is reached where adding another process or thread actually decreases overall performance. That is, a client might actually experience shorter service time if its connection request were queued until some preceding client finished, instead of creating a new process or thread to service it.

We can avoid this problem by limiting the number of processes created by the server, an approach we call *constrained-multitasking servers*. (We present a solution for processes, but it is directly applicable to threads as well.) In this solution, the server begins as the other servers by creating, binding, and listening to a socket. Then the server creates a set number (say, *N*) of processes, each of which loops forever, accepting connections from the (same) listening socket. This works because when multiple processes call accept() on the same listening socket at the same time, they all block until a connection is established. Then the system picks one process, and the socket descriptor for that new connection is returned *only in that process*; the others remain blocked until the next connection is established, another lucky winner is chosen, and so on.

Our next example program, TCPEchoServer-ForkN.c, implements this server model as a modification of the original TCPEchoServer.c (page 48), so we only comment on the differences.

TCPEchoServer-ForkN.c

```
1   #include <stdlib.h>
2   #include <unistd.h>
3   #include <stdio.h>
4   #include "Practical.h"
5
6   void ProcessMain(int servSock); // Process main
7
8   int main(int argc, char *argv[]) {
9
10    if (argc != 3) // Test for correct number of arguments
11      DieWithUserMessage("Parameter(s)", "<Server Port/Service> <Process Count>");
12
13    char *service = argv[1];                    // First arg:  local port
14    unsigned int processLimit = atoi(argv[2]); // Second arg:  number of children
15
16    // Server socket
17    int servSock = SetupTCPServerSocket(service);
18
19    // Fork limit-1 child processes
20    for (int processCt = 0; processCt < processLimit - 1; processCt++) {
21      // Fork child process and report any errors
22      pid_t processID = fork();
23      if (processID < 0)
24        DieWithSystemMessage("fork() failed");
25      else if (processID == 0) // If this is the child process
26        ProcessMain(servSock);
27    }
28
29    // Execute last process in parent
30    ProcessMain(servSock);
31    // NOT REACHED
32  }
```

```
33
34  void ProcessMain(int servSock) {
35    for (;;) { // Run forever
36      int clntSock = AcceptTCPConnection(servSock);
37      printf("with child process: %d\n", getpid());
38      HandleTCPClient(clntSock);
39    }
40  }
```

TCPEchoServer-ForkN.c

1. **Prototype for "main" of forked process:** line 6
   Each of the *N* processes executes the ProcessMain() function.

2. **Spawning *processLimit* −1 processes:** lines 19-27
   Execute loop *processLimit* −1 times, each time forking a process that calls ProcessMain() with *servSock* as the parameter.

3. **Parent becomes last thread:** line 30

4. ProcessMain(): lines 34–40
   ProcessMain() runs forever handling client requests. Effectively, it is the same as the *for(;;)* loop in TCPEchoServer.c (page 48).

Because only *N* processes are created, we limit scheduling overhead, and because each process lives forever handling client requests, we limit process creation overhead. Of course, if we spawn too few processes, we can still have clients waiting unnecessarily for service.

6.5 Multiplexing

Our programs so far have dealt with I/O over a single channel; each version of our echo server deals with only one client connection at a time. However, it is often the case that an application needs the ability to do I/O on multiple channels simultaneously. For example, we might want to provide echo service on several ports at once. The problem with this becomes clear as soon as you consider what happens after the server creates and binds a socket to each port. It is ready to accept() connections, but which socket to choose? A call to accept() (or recv()) on one socket may block, causing established connections to another socket to wait unnecessarily. This problem can be solved using nonblocking sockets, but in that case the server ends up continuously polling the sockets, which is wasteful. We would like to let the server block until *some* socket is ready for I/O.

Fortunately, UNIX provides a way to do this. With the select() function, a program can specify a list of descriptors to check for pending I/O; select() suspends the program until one of the descriptors in the list becomes ready to perform I/O and returns an indication of which descriptors are ready. Then the program can proceed with I/O on that descriptor with the assurance that the operation will not block.

---

int select(**int** *maxDescPlus1*, **fd_set** **readDescs*, **fd_set** **writeDescs*, **fd_set** **exceptionDescs*,
    struct timeval **timeout*)

---

select() monitors three separate lists of descriptors. (Note that these descriptors may refer to regular files—such as a terminal input—as well as sockets; we'll see an example of this in our example code later.)

readDescs: Descriptors in this list are checked for immediate input data availability; that is, a call to recv() (or recvfrom() for a datagram socket) would not block.

writeDescs: Descriptors in this list are checked for the ability to immediately write data; that is, a call to send() (or sendto() for a datagram socket) would not block.

exceptionDescs: Descriptors in this list are checked for pending exceptions or errors. An example of a pending exception for a TCP socket would be if the remote end of a TCP socket had closed while data were still in the channel; in such a case, the next read or write operation would fail and return ECONNRESET.

Passing NULL for any of the descriptor vectors makes select() ignore that type of I/O. For example, passing NULL for *exceptionDescs* causes select() to completely ignore exceptions on any sockets. To save space, each of these lists of descriptors is typically represented as a *bit vector*. To include a descriptor in the list, we set the bit in the bit vector corresponding to the number of its descriptor to 1. (For example, *stdin* is descriptor 0, so we would set the first bit in the vector if we want to monitor it.) Programs should not (and need not) rely on knowledge of this implementation strategy, however, because the system provides macros for manipulating instances of the type **fd_set**:

---

void FD_ZERO(**fd_set** **descriptorVector*)
void FD_CLR(**int** *descriptor*, **fd_set** **descriptorVector*)
void FD_SET(**int** *descriptor*, **fd_set** **descriptorVector*)
int FD_ISSET(**int** *descriptor*, **fd_set** **descriptorVector*)

FD_ZERO empties the list of descriptors. FD_CLR() and FD_SET() remove and add descriptors to the list, respectively. Membership of a descriptor in a list is tested by FD_ISSET(), which returns nonzero if the given descriptor is in the list, and 0 otherwise.

The maximum number of descriptors that can be contained in a list is given by the system-defined constant FD_SETSIZE. While this number can be quite large, most applications use very few descriptors. To make the implementation more efficient, the select() function allows us to pass a *hint*, which indicates the largest descriptor number that needs to be considered in any of the lists. In other words, *maxDescPlus1* is the smallest descriptor number that does *not* need to be considered, which is simply the maximum descriptor value plus one. For example, if descriptors 0, 3, and 5 are set in the descriptor list, we would set *maxDescPlus1* to the maximum descriptor value (5) plus one. Notice that *maxDescPlus1* applies for *all three* descriptor lists. If the exception descriptor list's largest descriptor is 7, while the read and write descriptor lists' largest are 5 and 2, respectively, then we set *maxDescPlus1* to 8.

What would you pay for the ability to listen simultaneously to so many descriptors for up to *three* types of I/O? Don't answer yet because select() does even more! The last parameter (*timeout*) allows control over how long select() will wait for something to happen. The *timeout* is specified with a **timeval** data structure:

```
struct timeval {
    time_t tv_sec;      // Seconds
    time_t tv_usec;     // Microseconds
};
```

If the time specified in the timeval structure elapses before any of the specified descriptors becomes ready for I/O, select() returns the value 0. If *timeout* is NULL, select() has no timeout bound and waits until some descriptor becomes ready. **Setting both *tv_sec* and *tv_usec* to 0 causes select() to return immediately, enabling polling of I/O descriptors.**

If no errors occur, select() returns the total number of descriptors prepared for I/O. To indicate the descriptors ready for I/O, select() changes the descriptor lists so that only the positions corresponding to ready descriptors are set. For example, if descriptors 0, 3, and 5 are set in the initial read descriptor list, the write and exception descriptor lists are NULL, and descriptors 0 and 5 have data available for reading, select() returns 2, and only positions 0 and 5 are set in the returned read descriptor list. An error in select() is indicated by a return value of −1.

Let's reconsider the problem of running the echo service on multiple ports. If we create a socket for each port, we could list these sockets in a *readDescriptor* list. A call to select(), given such a list, would suspend the program until an echo request arrives for at least one of the descriptors. We could then handle the connection setup and echo for that particular socket. Our next example program, TCPEchoServer-Select.c, implements this model. The user can specify an arbitrary number of ports to monitor. Notice that a connection request is considered I/O and prepares a socket descriptor for reading by select(). To illustrate that select() works on nonsocket descriptors as well, this server also watches for input from the standard input stream, which it interprets as a signal to terminate itself.

TCPEchoServer–Select.c

```
1   #include <sys/time.h>
2   #include <stdlib.h>
3   #include <stdio.h>
```

```
 4   #include <unistd.h>
 5   #include <fcntl.h>
 6   #include <stdbool.h>
 7   #include "Practical.h"
 8
 9   int main(int argc, char *argv[]) {
10
11     if (argc < 3) // Test for correct number of arguments
12       DieWithUserMessage("Parameter(s)", "<Timeout (secs.)> <Port/Service1> ...");
13
14     long timeout = atol(argv[1]); // First arg: Timeout
15     int noPorts = argc - 2;        // Number of ports is argument count minus 2
16
17     // Allocate list of sockets for incoming connections
18     int servSock[noPorts];
19     // Initialize maxDescriptor for use by select()
20     int maxDescriptor = -1;
21
22     // Create list of ports and sockets to handle ports
23     for (int port = 0; port < noPorts; port++) {
24       // Create port socket
25       servSock[port] = SetupTCPServerSocket(argv[port + 2]);
26
27       // Determine if new descriptor is the largest
28       if (servSock[port] > maxDescriptor)
29         maxDescriptor = servSock[port];
30     }
31
32     puts("Starting server:  Hit return to shutdown");
33     bool running = true; // true if server should continue running
34     fd_set sockSet;        // Set of socket descriptors for select()
35     while (running) {
36       /* Zero socket descriptor vector and set for server sockets
37        This must be reset every time select() is called */
38       FD_ZERO(&sockSet);
39       // Add keyboard to descriptor vector
40       FD_SET(STDIN_FILENO, &sockSet);
41       for (int port = 0; port < noPorts; port++)
42         FD_SET(servSock[port], &sockSet);
43
44       // Timeout specification; must be reset every time select() is called
45       struct timeval selTimeout;   // Timeout for select()
46       selTimeout.tv_sec = timeout; // Set timeout (secs.)
47       selTimeout.tv_usec = 0;      // 0 microseconds
48
```

```
49      // Suspend program until descriptor is ready or timeout
50      if (select(maxDescriptor + 1, &sockSet, NULL, NULL, &selTimeout) == 0)
51        printf("No echo requests for %ld secs...Server still alive\n", timeout);
52      else {
53        if (FD_ISSET(0, &sockSet)) { // Check keyboard
54          puts("Shutting down server");
55          getchar();
56          running = false;
57        }
58
59        // Process connection requests
60        for (int port = 0; port < noPorts; port++)
61          if (FD_ISSET(servSock[port], &sockSet)) {
62            printf("Request on port %d:  ", port);
63            HandleTCPClient(AcceptTCPConnection(servSock[port]));
64          }
65      }
66    }
67
68    // Close sockets
69    for (int port = 0; port < noPorts; port++)
70      close(servSock[port]);
71
72    exit(0);
73  }
```

TCPEchoServer-Select.c

1. **Set up a socket for each port:** lines 23–30
   We store the socket descriptors in an array, one per argument to the program.

2. **Create list of file descriptors for** select(): line 25

3. **Set timer for** select(): lines 44–47

4. select() **execution:** lines 49–65
   - **Handle timeout:** line 51
   - **Check keyboard descriptor:** lines 53–57
     If the user presses return, descriptor STDIN_FILENO will be ready for reading; in that case the server terminates itself.
   - **Check the socket descriptors:** lines 60–64
     Test each descriptor, accepting and handling the valid connections.

5. **Wrap-up:** lines 68–72
   Close all ports and exit.

`select()` is a powerful function. It can also be used to implement a timeout version of any of the blocking I/O functions (e.g., `recv()`, `accept()`) without using alarms.

6.6 Multiple Recipients

So far, all of our programs have dealt with communication involving two entities, usually a server and a client. Such one-to-one communication is sometimes called *unicast* because only one ("uni") copy of the data is sent ("cast"). Sometimes we would like to send the *same* information to more than one recipient. You probably know that computers in an office or home are often connected to a local area network, and sometimes we would like to send information that can be received by every host on the network. For example, a computer that has a printer attached may advertise it for use by other hosts on the network by sending a message this way; the operating systems of other machines receive these advertisements and make the shared resources available to their users. Instead of unicasting the message to every host on the network—which requires us not only to *know* the address of every host on the network, but also to call `sendto()` on the message once for each host—we would like to be able to call `sendto()` just once and have the *network* handle the duplication for us.

Or consider a typical case in which the sender has a single connection to the Internet, such as a cable or DSL modem. Sending the same data to multiple recipients scattered throughout the Internet with unicast requires that the same information be sent over that link many times (Figure 6.3a). If the sender's first-hop connection has limited outgoing capacity (say, one

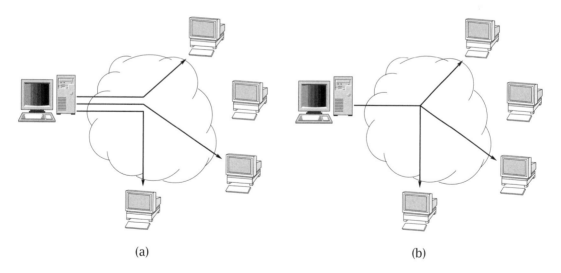

(a)   (b)

Figure 6.3: (a) Unicasting the same data to multiple recipients; (b) doing the same thing with multicast.

1 Mbps or so), it may not even be *possible* to send some kinds of information—say, a real-time video stream at 1 Mbps—to more than one recipient without exceeding the first-hop link capacity, resulting in many lost packets and poor quality. Clearly, it would be more efficient if the information could be duplicated *after* it crosses the first link, as in Figure 6.3b. This saves bandwidth *and* simplifies life for the sending program.

You may be surprised to learn that the sockets interface over TCP/IP provides access to services like this—albeit with some restrictions. There are two types of network duplication service: *broadcast* and *multicast*. With broadcast, the program calls sendto() once, and the message is automatically delivered to *all* hosts on the local network. With multicast, the message is sent once and delivered to a specific (possibly empty) *group* of hosts throughout the Internet—namely, those that have indicated to the network that they should receive messages sent to that group.

We mentioned that there are some restrictions on these services. **The first is that** *only UDP sockets can use broadcast and multicast services*. **The second is that** *broadcast only covers a local scope*, **typically a local area network. The third restriction is that** *multicast across the entire Internet is presently not supported by most Internet service providers*. In spite of these restrictions, these services can often be useful. For example, it is often useful to use multicast within a site such as a campus network, or broadcast to local hosts.

6.6.1 Broadcast

UDP datagrams can be sent to all nodes on an attached local network by sending them to a special address. In IPv4 it is called the "limited broadcast address," and it is the all-ones address (in dotted-quad notation, 255.255.255.255). In IPv6 it is called the "all-nodes address (link scope)" and has the value FF02::1. Routers do not forward packets addressed to either one of these addresses, so neither one will take a datagram beyond the local network to which the sender is connected. Each does, however, deliver the sent packet to *every* node on the network; typically, this is achieved using the hardware broadcast capability of the local network. (Not all links support broadcast; in particular, point-to-point links do not. If none of a host's interfaces support broadcast, any attempt to use it will result in an error.) Note also that a broadcast UDP datagram will actually be "heard" at a host only if some program on that host is listening for datagrams on the *port* to which the datagram is addressed.

What about a network-wide broadcast address to send a message to all hosts? There is no such address. To see why, consider the impact on the network of a broadcast to every host on the Internet. Sending a single datagram would result in an extremely large number of packet duplications by the routers, and bandwidth would be consumed on each and every network. The consequences of misuse (malicious or accidental) are too great, so the designers of IP left out such an Internet-wide broadcast facility on purpose. Even with these restrictions, broadcast on the local link can be very useful. Often it is used in state exchange for network games where the players are all on the same local area network (e.g., Ethernet).

There is one other difference between a broadcast sender and a regular sender: before sending to the broadcast address, the special socket option SO_BROADCAST must be set.

In effect, this asks the system for "permission" to broadcast. We demonstrate the use of UDP broadcast in BroadcastSender.c. Our sender broadcasts a given string every three seconds to the limited broadcast address of the address family indicated by the first argument.

BroadcastSender.c

```c
1    #include <stdio.h>
2    #include <stdlib.h>
3    #include <string.h>
4    #include <unistd.h>
5    #include <sys/socket.h>
6    #include <arpa/inet.h>
7    #include "Practical.h"
8
9    static const char *IN6ADDR_ALLNODES = "FF02::1"; // v6 addr not built in
10
11   int main(int argc, char *argv[]) {
12
13     if (argc != 4) // Test for correct number of arguments
14       DieWithUserMessage("Parameter(s)", "[4|6] <Port> <String to send>");
15
16     in_port_t port = htons((in_port_t) atoi(argv[2]));
17
18     struct sockaddr_storage destStorage;
19     memset(&destStorage, 0, sizeof(destStorage));
20
21     size_t addrSize = 0;
22     if (argv[1][0] == '4') {
23       struct sockaddr_in *destAddr4 = (struct sockaddr_in *) &destStorage;
24       destAddr4->sin_family = AF_INET;
25       destAddr4->sin_port = port;
26       destAddr4->sin_addr.s_addr = INADDR_BROADCAST;
27       addrSize = sizeof(struct sockaddr_in);
28     } else if (argv[1][0] == '6') {
29       struct sockaddr_in6 *destAddr6 = (struct sockaddr_in6 *) &destStorage;
30       destAddr6->sin6_family = AF_INET6;
31       destAddr6->sin6_port = port;
32       inet_pton(AF_INET6, IN6ADDR_ALLNODES, &destAddr6->sin6_addr);
33       addrSize = sizeof(struct sockaddr_in6);
34     } else {
35       DieWithUserMessage("Unknown address family", argv[1]);
36     }
37
38     struct sockaddr *destAddress = (struct sockaddr *) &destStorage;
```

```
39
40    size_t msgLen = strlen(argv[3]);
41    if (msgLen > MAXSTRINGLENGTH)    // Input string fits?
42      DieWithUserMessage("String too long", argv[3]);
43
44    // Create socket for sending/receiving datagrams
45    int sock = socket(destAddress->sa_family, SOCK_DGRAM, IPPROTO_UDP);
46    if (sock < 0)
47      DieWithSystemMessage("socket() failed");
48
49    // Set socket to allow broadcast
50    int broadcastPerm = 1;
51    if (setsockopt(sock, SOL_SOCKET, SO_BROADCAST, &broadcastPerm,
52        sizeof(broadcastPerm)) < 0)
53      DieWithSystemMessage("setsockopt() failed");
54
55    for (;;) {// Run forever
56      // Broadcast msgString in datagram to clients every 3 seconds
57      ssize_t numBytes = sendto(sock, argv[3], msgLen, 0, destAddress, addrSize);
58      if (numBytes < 0)
59        DieWithSystemMessage("sendto() failed");
60      else if (numBytes != msgLen)
61        DieWithUserMessage("sendto()", "sent unexpected number of bytes");
62
63      sleep(3);   // Avoid flooding the network
64    }
65    // NOT REACHED
66  }
```

BroadcastSender.c

1. **Declare constant address:** line 9
   Somewhat surprisingly, the all-nodes group address is not defined as a named system constant, so we give it a name here.

2. **Parameter processing:** lines 13-16

3. **Destination address storage:** lines 18-19
   We use a **sockaddr_storage** structure to hold the destination broadcast address, since it may be either IPv4 or IPv6.

4. **Setting up destination address:** lines 21-38
   We set the destination address according to the given type and remember the size for later use. Finally, we save the address in a pointer to a generic **sockaddr**.

5. **Socket creation:** lines 44-47

6. **Setting permission to broadcast:** lines 49-53
   By default, sockets cannot broadcast. Setting the SO_BROADCAST option for the socket enables socket broadcast.

7. **Repeatedly broadcast:** lines 55-64
   Send the argument string every three seconds to all hosts on the network.

Note that a receiver program does not need to do anything special to receive broadcast datagrams (except bind to the appropriate port). Writing a program to receive the broadcasts sent out by BroadcastSender.c is left as an exercise.

6.6.2 Multicast

For the sender using multicast is very similar to using unicast. The difference is in the form of the address. A multicast address identifies a set of receivers who have "asked" the network to deliver messages sent to that address. (This is the receiver's responsibility; see below.) A range of the address space is set aside for multicast in both IPv4 and IPv6. IPv4 multicast addresses are in the range 224.0.0.0 to 239.255.255.255. IPv6 multicast addresses are those whose first byte contains 0xFF, that is, all ones. The IPv6 multicast address space has a fairly complicated structure that is mostly beyond the scope of this book. (The reader is referred to [4] for details.) For our examples we'll use addresses beginning with FF1E; they are valid for transient use in global applications. (The third hex digit "1" indicates a multicast address that is not permanently assigned for any particular purpose, while the fourth digit "E" indicates global scope.) An example would be FF1E::1234.

Our example multicast sender, shown in file MulticastSender.c, takes a multicast address and port as an argument, and sends a given string to that address and port every three seconds.

MulticastSender.c

```
1   #include <stdlib.h>
2   #include <string.h>
3   #include <unistd.h>
4   #include <netdb.h>
5   #include "Practical.h"
6
7   int main(int argc, char *argv[]) {
8
9     if (argc < 4 || argc > 5) // Test for number of parameters
10      DieWithUserMessage("Parameter(s)",
11                         "<Multicast Address> <Port> <Send String> [<TTL>]");
12
13    char *multicastIPString = argv[1];   // First arg:  multicast IP address
14    char *service = argv[2];             // Second arg:  multicast port/service
15    char *sendString = argv[3];          // Third arg:  string to multicast
```

```
16
17   size_t sendStringLen = strlen(sendString);
18   if (sendStringLen > MAXSTRINGLENGTH)        // Check input length
19     DieWithUserMessage("String too long", sendString);
20
21   // Fourth arg (optional):  TTL for transmitting multicast packets
22   int multicastTTL = (argc == 5) ? atoi(argv[4]) : 1;
23
24   // Tell the system what kind(s) of address info we want
25   struct addrinfo addrCriteria;                    // Criteria for address match
26   memset(&addrCriteria, 0, sizeof(addrCriteria)); // Zero out structure
27   addrCriteria.ai_family = AF_UNSPEC;            // v4 or v6 is OK
28   addrCriteria.ai_socktype = SOCK_DGRAM;         // Only datagram sockets
29   addrCriteria.ai_protocol = IPPROTO_UDP;        // Only UDP please
30   addrCriteria.ai_flags |= AI_NUMERICHOST;       // Don't try to resolve address
31
32   struct addrinfo *multicastAddr;    // Holder for returned address
33   int rtnVal= getaddrinfo(multicastIPString, service,
34                           &addrCriteria, &multicastAddr);
35   if (rtnVal != 0)
36     DieWithUserMessage("getaddrinfo() failed", gai_strerror(rtnVal));
37
38   // Create socket for sending datagrams
39   int sock = socket(multicastAddr->ai_family, multicastAddr->ai_socktype,
40                     multicastAddr->ai_protocol);
41   if (sock < 0)
42     DieWithSystemMessage("socket() failed");
43
44   // Set TTL of multicast packet. Unfortunately this requires
45   // address-family-specific code
46   if (multicastAddr->ai_family == AF_INET6) { // v6-specific
47     // The v6 multicast TTL socket option requires that the value be
48     // passed in as an integer
49     if (setsockopt(sock, IPPROTO_IPV6, IPV6_MULTICAST_HOPS,
50                    &multicastTTL, sizeof(multicastTTL)) < 0)
51       DieWithSystemMessage("setsockopt(IPV6_MULTICAST_HOPS) failed");
52   } else if (multicastAddr->ai_family == AF_INET) { // v4 specific
53     // The v4 multicast TTL socket option requires that the value be
54     // passed in an unsigned char
55     u_char mcTTL = (u_char) multicastTTL;
56     if (setsockopt(sock, IPPROTO_IP, IP_MULTICAST_TTL, &mcTTL,
57                    sizeof(mcTTL)) < 0)
58       DieWithSystemMessage("setsockopt(IP_MULTICAST_TTL) failed");
59   } else {
60     DieWithUserMessage("Unable to set TTL", "invalid address family");
```

```
61   }
62
63   for (;;) { // Run forever
64     // Multicast the string to all who have joined the group
65     ssize_t numBytes = sendto(sock, sendString, sendStringLen, 0,
66                               multicastAddr->ai_addr, multicastAddr->ai_addrlen);
67     if (numBytes < 0)
68       DieWithSystemMessage("sendto() failed");
69     else if (numBytes != sendStringLen)
70       DieWithUserMessage("sendto()", "sent unexpected number of bytes");
71     sleep(3);
72   }
73   // NOT REACHED
74 }
```

MulticastSender.c

Note that unlike the broadcast sender, the multicast sender does not need to set the permission to multicast. On the other hand, the multicast sender may set the *TTL* ("time-to-live") value for the transmitted datagrams. Every packet contains a counter, which is initialized to some default value when the packet is first sent and decremented by each router that handles the packet. When this counter reaches 0, the packet is discarded. The TTL mechanism (which can be changed by setting a socket option) allows us to control the initial value of this counter and thus limit the number of hops a multicast packet can traverse. For example, by setting TTL = 1, the multicast packet will not go beyond the local network.

As mentioned earlier, the multicast network service duplicates and delivers the message only to a specific set of receivers. This set of receivers, called a *multicast group*, is identified by a particular multicast (or group) address. These receivers need some mechanism to notify the network of their interest in receiving data sent to a particular multicast address. Once notified, the network can begin forwarding the multicast messages to the receiver. This notification of the network, called "joining a group," is accomplished via a multicast request (signaling) message sent (transparently) by the underlying protocol implementation. To cause this to happen, the receiving program needs to invoke an address-family-specific multicast socket option. For IPv4 it is ip_ADD_MEMBERSHIP; for IPv6 it is (surprisingly enough) IPV6_ADD_MEMBERSHIP. This socket option takes a structure containing the address of the multicast "group" to be joined. Alas, this structure is also different for the two versions:

```
struct ip_mreq {
  struct in_addr imr_multiaddr; // Group address
  struct in_addr imr_interface; // local interface to join on
};
```

The IPv6 version differs only in the type of addresses it contains:

```
struct ipv6_mreq {
```

```
    struct in6_addr ipv6mr_multiaddr; // IPv6 multicast address of group
    unsigned int ipv6mr_interface;    // local interface to join no
    };
```

Our multicast receiver contains a fair amount of version-specific code to handle the joining process.

MulticastReceiver.c

```
1  #include <stdlib.h>
2  #include <string.h>
3  #include <unistd.h>
4  #include <netdb.h>
5  #include "Practical.h"
6
7  int main(int argc, char *argv[]) {
8
9    if (argc != 3)
10     DieWithUserMessage("Parameter(s)", "<Multicast Address> <Port>");
11
12   char *multicastAddrString = argv[1]; // First arg: multicast addr (v4 or v6!)
13   char *service = argv[2];             // Second arg: port/service
14
15   struct addrinfo addrCriteria;                    // Criteria for address match
16   memset(&addrCriteria, 0, sizeof(addrCriteria)); // Zero out structure
17   addrCriteria.ai_family = AF_UNSPEC;              // v4 or v6 is OK
18   addrCriteria.ai_socktype = SOCK_DGRAM;           // Only datagram sockets
19   addrCriteria.ai_protocol = IPPROTO_UDP;          // Only UDP protocol
20   addrCriteria.ai_flags |= AI_NUMERICHOST;         // Don't try to resolve address
21
22   // Get address information
23   struct addrinfo *multicastAddr;                  // List of server addresses
24   int rtnVal = getaddrinfo(multicastAddrString, service,
25                            &addrCriteria, &multicastAddr);
26   if (rtnVal != 0)
27     DieWithUserMessage("getaddrinfo() failed", gai_strerror(rtnVal));
28
29   // Create socket to receive on
30   int sock = socket(multicastAddr->ai_family, multicastAddr->ai_socktype,
31                     multicastAddr->ai_protocol);
32   if (sock < 0)
33     DieWithSystemMessage("socket() failed");
34
35   if (bind(sock, multicastAddr->ai_addr, multicastAddr->ai_addrlen) < 0)
36     DieWithSystemMessage("bind() failed");
37
```

```
38    // Unfortunately we need some address-family-specific pieces
39    if (multicastAddr->ai_family == AF_INET6) {
40      // Now join the multicast "group" (address)
41      struct ipv6_mreq joinRequest;
42      memcpy(&joinRequest.ipv6mr_multiaddr, &((struct sockaddr_in6 *)
43            multicastAddr->ai_addr)->sin6_addr,  sizeof(struct in6_addr));
44      joinRequest.ipv6mr_interface = 0;    // Let system choose the i/f
45      puts("Joining IPv6 multicast group...");
46      if (setsockopt(sock, IPPROTO_IPV6, IPV6_JOIN_GROUP,
47        &joinRequest, sizeof(joinRequest)) < 0)
48        DieWithSystemMessage("setsockopt(IPV6_JOIN_GROUP) failed");
49    } else if (multicastAddr->ai_family == AF_INET) {
50      // Now join the multicast "group"
51      struct ip_mreq joinRequest;
52      joinRequest.imr_multiaddr =
53        ((struct sockaddr_in *) multicastAddr->ai_addr)->sin_addr;
54      joinRequest.imr_interface.s_addr = 0;  // Let the system choose the i/f
55      printf("Joining IPv4 multicast group...\n");
56      if (setsockopt(sock, IPPROTO_IP, IP_ADD_MEMBERSHIP,
57                  &joinRequest, sizeof(joinRequest)) < 0)
58        DieWithSystemMessage("setsockopt(IPV4_ADD_MEMBERSHIP) failed");
59    } else {
60      DieWithSystemMessage("Unknown address family");
61    }
62    // Free address structure(s) allocated by getaddrinfo()
63    freeaddrinfo(multicastAddr);
64
65    char recvString[MAXSTRINGLENGTH + 1]; // Buffer to receive into
66    // Receive a single datagram from the server
67    int recvStringLen = recvfrom(sock, recvString, MAXSTRINGLENGTH, 0, NULL, 0);
68    if (recvStringLen < 0)
69      DieWithSystemMessage("recvfrom() failed");
70
71    recvString[recvStringLen] = '\0';    // Terminate the received string
72    // Note: sender did not send the terminal 0
73    printf("Received: %s\n", recvString);
74
75    close(sock);
76    exit(0);
77  }
```

MulticastReceiver.c

The multicast receiver joins the group, waits to receive a message, prints it, and then exits.

6.6.3   Broadcast vs. Multicast

The decision of using broadcast or multicast in an application depends on several issues, including the fraction of network hosts interested in receiving the data, and the knowledge of the communicating parties. Broadcast works well if a large percentage of the network hosts wish to receive the message; however, if few hosts need to receive the packet, broadcast "imposes on" all hosts in the network for the benefit of a few. Multicast is preferred because it limits the duplication of data to those that have expressed interest. The disadvantages of multicast are (1) it is presently not supported globally, and (2) the sender and receiver must agree on an IP multicast address in advance. Knowledge of an address is not required for broadcast. In some contexts (local), this makes broadcast a better mechanism for discovery than multicast. All hosts can receive broadcast by default, so it is simple to ask all hosts a question like "Where's the printer?" On the other hand, for wide-area applications, multicast is the only choice.

Exercises

1. State precisely the conditions under which an iterative server is preferable to a multiprocessing server.

2. Would you ever need to implement a timeout in a client or server that uses TCP?

3. Why do we make the server socket nonblocking in UDPEchoServer-SIGIO.c? In particular, what bad thing might happen if we did not?

4. How can you determine the minimum and maximum allowable sizes for a socket's send and receive buffers? Determine the minimums for your system.

5. This exercise considers the reasoning behind the SIGPIPE mechanism a little further. Recall that SIGPIPE is delivered when a program tries to send on a TCP socket whose connection has gone away in the meantime. An alternative approach would be to simply have the send() fail with ECONNRESET. Why might the signal-based approach be better than conveying this information by return value?

6. What do you think will happen if you use the program in MulticastReceiver.c while the program BroadcastSender.c is running on a host connected to the same LAN?

chapter **7**

Under the Hood

Some of the subtleties of network programming are difficult to grasp without some understanding of the data structures associated with each socket in the implementation and certain details of how the underlying protocols work. This is especially true of stream (TCP) sockets. This chapter describes some of what goes on "under the hood" when you create and use a socket. The initial discussion and Section 7.5 apply to both datagram (UDP) and stream (TCP) sockets; the rest applies only to TCP sockets. Please note that this description covers only the normal sequence of events and glosses over many details. Nevertheless, we believe that even this basic level of understanding is helpful. Readers who want the full story are referred to the TCP specification [13] or to one of the more comprehensive treatises on the subject [2, 17].

Figure 7.1 is a simplified view of some of the information associated with a socket—that is, the object created by a call to socket(). The integer returned by socket() is best thought of as a "handle" that identifies the collection of data structures for one communication endpoint that we refer to in this chapter as the "socket structure." As the figure indicates, more than one descriptor can refer to the same socket structure. In fact, descriptors in *different processes* can refer to the same underlying socket structure.

By "socket structure" here we mean all data structures in the socket layer and TCP implementation that contain state information relevant to this socket abstraction. Thus, the socket structure contains send and receive queues and other information, including the following:

- The local and remote Internet addresses and port numbers associated with the socket. The local Internet address (labeled "Local IP" in the figure) is one of those assigned to the

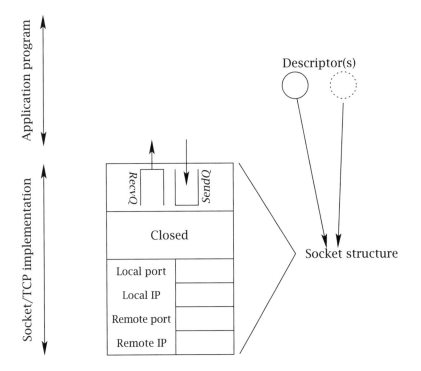

Figure 7.1: Data structures associated with a socket.

local host; the local port is set at bind() time. The remote address and port identify the remote socket, if any, to which the local socket is connected. We will say more about how and when these values are determined shortly. (Section 7.5 contains a concise summary.)

- A FIFO queue ("*RecvQ*") of received data waiting to be delivered and a FIFO queue ("*SendQ*") for data waiting to be transmitted.

- For a TCP socket, additional protocol state information relevant to the opening and closing TCP handshakes. In Figure 7.1, the state is "Closed"; all sockets start out in the Closed state.

Some general-purpose operating systems provide tools that enable users to obtain a "snapshot" of these underlying data structures. On such tool is netstat, which is typically available on both UNIX (Linux) and Windows platforms. Given appropriate options, netstat displays exactly the information indicated in Figure 7.1: number of bytes in *SendQ* and *RecvQ*, local and remote IP addresses and port numbers, and the connection state. Command-line options may vary, but the output should look something like this:

```
Active Internet connections (servers and established)
Proto Recv-Q Send-Q Local Address          Foreign Address      State
tcp       0      0 0.0.0.0:36045          0.0.0.0:*            LISTEN
tcp       0      0 0.0.0.0:111            0.0.0.0:*            LISTEN
tcp       0      0 0.0.0.0:53363          0.0.0.0:*            LISTEN
tcp       0      0 127.0.0.1:25           0.0.0.0:*            LISTEN
tcp       0      0 128.133.190.219:34077  4.71.104.187:80     TIME_WAIT
tcp       0      0 128.133.190.219:43346  79.62.132.8:22      ESTABLISHED
tcp       0      0 128.133.190.219:875    128.133.190.43:2049 ESTABLISHED
tcp6      0      0 :::22                  :::*                LISTEN
```

The first four lines and the last line depict server sockets listening for connections. (The last line is a listening socket bound to an IPv6 address.) The fifth line corresponds to a connection to a Web server (port 80) that is partially shut down (see Section 7.4.2). The next-to-last two lines are existing TCP connections. You may want to play with netstat, if it is available on your system, to examine the status of connections in the scenarios depicted in Figures 7.8–7.11. Be aware, however, that because the transitions between states depicted in the figures happen so quickly, it may be difficult to catch them in the "snapshot" provided by netstat.

Knowing that these data structures exist and how they are affected by the underlying protocols is useful because they control various aspects of the behavior of the socket. For example, because TCP provides a *reliable* byte-stream service, a copy of any data sent over a TCP socket must be kept *by the TCP implementation* until it has been successfully received at the other end of the connection. Completion of a call to send() on a TCP socket does *not*, in general, imply that the data has actually been transmitted—only that it has been copied into the local buffer. Under normal conditions, it will be transmitted soon, but the exact moment is under the control of TCP, not the application. Moreover, the nature of the byte-stream service means that message boundaries are *not* necessarily preserved in the input stream. As we saw in Section 5.2.1, this means that most application protocols need a *framing* mechanism, so the receiver can tell when it has received an entire message.

On the other hand, with a datagram (UDP) socket, packets are *not* buffered for retransmission, and by the time a call to send/sendto() returns, the data has been given to the network subsystem for transmission. If the network subsystem cannot handle the message for some reason, the packet is silently dropped (but this is rare).

The next three sections deal with some of the subtleties of sending and receiving with TCP's byte-stream service. Then, Section 7.4 considers the connection establishment and termination of the TCP protocol. Finally, Section 7.5 discusses the process of matching incoming packets to sockets and the rules about binding to port numbers.

7.1 Buffering and TCP

As a programmer, the most important thing to remember when using a TCP socket is this:

You cannot assume any correspondence between the sizes of writes to one end of the connection and sizes of reads from the other end.

In particular, data passed in a single invocation of send() at the sender can be spread across multiple invocations of recv() at the other end; a single call to recv() may return data passed in multiple calls to send().

To see this, consider a program that does the following:

```
rv = connect(s,...);
...
rv = send(s, buffer0, 1000, 0);
...
rv = send(s, buffer1, 2000, 0);
...
rv = send(s, buffer2, 5000, 0);
...
close(s);
```

where the ellipses represent code that sets up the data in the buffers but contains no other calls to send(). This TCP connection transfers 8000 bytes to the receiver. The way these 8000 bytes are grouped for delivery at the receiving end of the connection depends on the timing between the calls to send() and recv() at the two ends of the connection—as well as the size of the buffers provided to the recv() calls.

We can think of the sequence of all bytes sent (in one direction) on a TCP connection up to a particular instant in time as being divided into three FIFO queues:

1. *SendQ*: Bytes buffered in the underlying implementation at the sender that have been written to the output stream but not yet successfully transmitted to the receiving host.

2. *RecvQ*: Bytes buffered in the underlying implementation at the receiver waiting to be delivered to the receiving program—that is, read from the input stream.

3. *Delivered*: Bytes already read from the input stream by the receiver.

A call to send() at the sender appends bytes to *SendQ*. The TCP protocol is responsible for moving bytes—in order—from *SendQ* to *RecvQ*. It is important to realize that this transfer cannot be controlled or directly observed by the user program, and that it occurs in chunks whose sizes are more or less independent of the size of the buffers passed in sends. Bytes are moved from *RecvQ* to *Delivered* by calls to recv(); the size of the transferred chunks depends on the amount of data in *RecvQ* and the size of the buffer given to recv().

Figure 7.2 shows one possible state of the three queues *after* the three sends in the example above, but *before* any calls to recv() at the other end. The different shading patterns denote bytes passed in the three different invocations of send() shown above.

The output of netstat on the sending host at the instant depicted in this figure would contain a line like:

```
Active Internet connections
Proto Recv-Q Send-Q Local Address        Foreign Address      State
tcp        0   6500 10.21.44.33:43346    192.0.2.8:22         ESTABLISHED
```

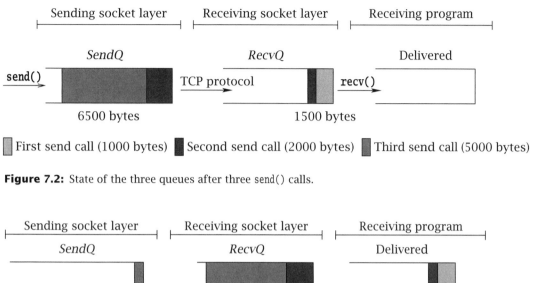

Figure 7.2: State of the three queues after three send() calls.

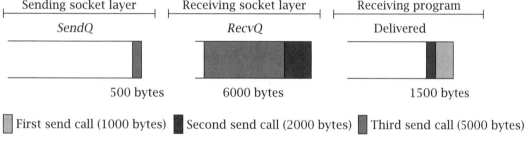

Figure 7.3: After first recv().

On the receiving host, netstat shows:

```
Active Internet connections
Proto Recv-Q Send-Q Local Address          Foreign Address      State
tcp     1500      0 192.0.2.8:22           10.21.44.33:43346    ESTABLISHED
```

Now suppose the receiver calls recv() with a byte array of size 2000. The recv() call will move all of the 1500 bytes present in the waiting-for-delivery (*RecvQ*) queue into the byte array and return the value 1500. Note that this data includes bytes passed in both the first and second calls to send(). At some time later, after TCP has completed transfer of more data, the three partitions might be in the state shown in Figure 7.3.

If the receiver now calls recv() with a buffer of size 4000, that many bytes will be moved from the waiting-for-delivery (*RecvQ*) queue to the already-delivered (*Delivered*) queue; this includes the remaining 1500 bytes from the second send(), plus the first 2500 bytes from the third send(). The resulting state of the queues is shown in Figure 7.4.

The number of bytes returned by the next call to recv() depends on the size of the buffer and the timing of the transfer of data over the network from the send-side socket/TCP implementation to the receive-side implementation. The movement of data from the *SendQ* to

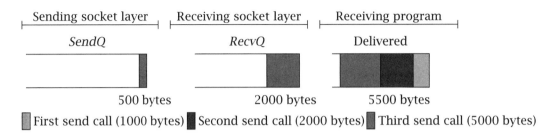

Figure 7.4: After another recv().

the *RecvQ* buffer has important implications for the design of application protocols. We have already encountered the challenge of parsing messages as they are received via a socket when in-band delimiters are used for framing (see Section 5.2). In the following sections, we consider two more subtle ramifications.

7.2 Deadlock Danger

Application protocols have to be designed with some care to avoid *deadlock*—that is, a state in which each peer is blocked waiting for the other to do something. For example, it is pretty obvious that if both client and server try to receive immediately after a connection is established, deadlock will result. Deadlock can also occur in less immediate ways.

The buffers *SendQ* and *RecvQ* in the implementation have limits on their capacity. Although the actual amount of memory they use may grow and shrink dynamically, a hard limit is necessary to prevent all of the system's memory from being gobbled up by a single TCP connection under control of a misbehaving program. Because these buffers are finite, they can fill up. It is this fact, coupled with TCP's *flow control* mechanism, that leads to the possibility of another form of deadlock.

Once *RecvQ* is full, the TCP flow control mechanism kicks in and prevents the transfer of any bytes from the sending host's *SendQ* until space becomes available in *RecvQ* as a result of the receiver calling recv(). (The purpose of the flow control mechanism is to ensure that the sender does not transmit data faster than the receiving system can handle.) A sending program can continue to call send() until *SendQ* is full. However, once *SendQ* is full, a send() will block until space becomes available, that is, until some bytes are transferred to the receiving socket's *RecvQ*. If *RecvQ* is also full, everything stops until the receiving program calls recv and some bytes are transferred to *Delivered*.

Let's assume the sizes of *SendQ* and *RecvQ* are *SQS* and *RQS*, respectively. A call to send() passing in a buffer of size n such that $n > SQS$ will not return until at least $n - SQS$ bytes have been transferred to *RecvQ* at the receiving host. If n exceeds $(SQS + RQS)$, send() cannot return until after the receiving program has read at least $n - (SQS + RQS)$ bytes from the input stream. If the receiving program does not call recv(), a large send() may not complete successfully.

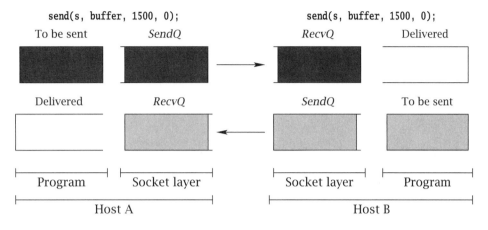

Figure 7.5: Deadlock due to simultaneous sends to output streams at opposite ends of the connection.

In particular, if both ends of the connection call send() simultaneously, each passing a buffer bigger than $SQS + RQS$ bytes, deadlock *will* result: neither write will ever complete, and both programs will remain blocked forever.

As a concrete example, consider a connection between a program on Host A and a program on Host B. Assume SQS and RQS are 500 at both A and B. Figure 7.5 shows what happens when both programs try to send 1500 bytes at the same time. The first 500 bytes of data in the program at Host A have been transferred to the other end; another 500 bytes have been copied into $SendQ$ at Host A. The remaining 500 bytes cannot be sent—and therefore send() will not return—until space frees up in $RecvQ$ at Host B. Unfortunately, the same situation holds in the program at Host B. Therefore, neither program's call to send() call will ever return!

> The moral of the story: Design the protocol carefully to avoid sending large quantities of data simultaneously in both directions.

7.3 Performance Implications

The TCP implementation's need to copy user data into $SendQ$ before sending it also has implications for performance. In particular, the sizes of the $SendQ$ and $RecvQ$ buffers affect the throughput achievable over a TCP connection. "Throughput" is the *rate* at which bytes of user data from the sender are made available to the receiving program; in programs that transfer a large amount of data, we want to maximize the number of bytes delivered per second. In the absence of network capacity or other limitations, *bigger buffers generally result in higher throughput.*

The reason for this has to do with the cost of transferring data into and out of the buffers in the underlying implementation. If you want to transfer n bytes of data (where n is large), it is generally much more efficient to call send() once with a buffer of size n than it is to call it n times with a single byte.[1] However, if you call send() with a size parameter that is much larger than SQS (the size of $SendQ$), the system has to transfer the data from the user address space in SQS-sized chunks. That is, the socket implementation fills up the $SendQ$ buffer, waits for data to be transferred out of it by the TCP protocol, refills $SendQ$, waits some more, and so on. Each time the socket implementation has to wait for data to be removed from $SendQ$, some time is wasted in the form of overhead (a context switch occurs). This overhead is comparable to that incurred by a completely new call to send(). Thus the *effective* size of a call to send() is limited by the actual SQS. The same thing applies at the receiving end: however large the buffer we pass to recv(), data will be copied out in chunks no larger than RQS, with overhead incurred between chunks.

If you are writing a program for which throughput is an important performance metric, you will want to change the send and receive buffer sizes using the SO_RCVBUF and SO_SNDBUF socket options. Although there is always a system-imposed maximum size for each buffer, it is typically significantly larger than the default on modern systems. Remember that these considerations apply only if your program needs to send an amount of data significantly larger than the buffer size, all at once. Note also that wrapping a TCP socket in a **FILE**-stream adds another stage of buffering and additional overhead, and thus may negatively affect throughput.

7.4   TCP Socket Life Cycle

When a new TCP **socket** is created, it cannot be used immediately for sending and receiving data. First it needs to be connected to a remote endpoint. Let us therefore consider in more detail how the underlying structure gets to and from the connected, or "Established", state. As we'll see later, these details affect the definition of reliability and the ability to bind a socket to a particular port that was in use earlier.

7.4.1   Connecting

The relationship between the connect() call and the protocol events associated with connection establishment at the client are illustrated in Figure 7.6. In this and the remaining figures of this section, the large arrows depict external events that cause the underlying socket structures to change state. Events that occur in the application program—that is, method calls and returns— are shown in the upper part of the figure; events such as message arrivals are shown in the lower part of the figure. Time proceeds left to right in these figures. The client's Internet address is depicted as A.B.C.D, while the server's is W.X.Y.Z; the server's port number is Q. (We have depicted IPv4 addresses, but everything here applies to both IPv4 and IPv6.)

---

[1]The same thing generally applies to receiving, although calling recv() with a larger buffer does not guarantee that more data will be returned—in general, only the data present at the time of a call will be returned.

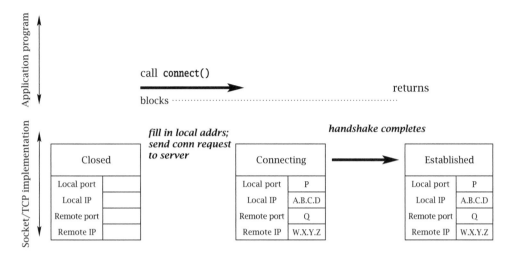

Figure 7.6: Client-side connection establishment. (Events proceed left to right in these figures.)

When the client calls connect() with the server's Internet address, W.X.Y.Z, and port, Q, the underlying implementation creates a socket instance; it is initially in the Closed state. If the client did not specify the local address/port with bind(), a local port number (P), not already in use by another TCP socket, is chosen by the implementation. The local Internet address is also assigned; if not explicitly specified, the address of the network interface through which packets will be sent to the server is used. The implementation copies the local and remote addresses and ports into the underlying socket structure, and initiates the TCP connection establishment handshake.

The TCP opening handshake is known as a *three-way handshake* because it typically involves three messages: a connection request from client to server, an acknowledgment from server to client, and another acknowledgment from client back to server. The client TCP considers the connection to be established as soon as it receives the acknowledgment from the server. In the normal case, this happens quickly. However, the Internet is a best-effort network, and either the client's initial message or the server's response can get lost. For this reason, the TCP implementation retransmits handshake messages multiple times, at increasing intervals. If the client TCP does not receive a response from the server after some time, it *times out* and gives up. In this case connect() returns −1 and sets *errno* to ETIMEDOUT. The implementation tries very hard to complete the connection before giving up, and thus it can take on the order of minutes for a connect() call to fail. After the initial handshake message is sent and before the reply from the server is received (i.e., the middle part of Figure 7.6), the output from netstat on the client host would look something like:

```
Active Internet connections
Proto Recv-Q Send-Q Local Address    Foreign Address    State
tcp      0      0 A.B.C.D:P          W.X.Y.Z:Q          SYN_SENT
```

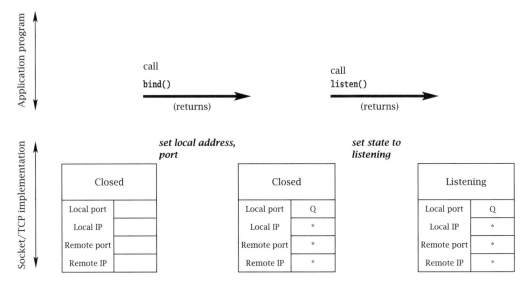

Figure 7.7: Server-side socket setup.

where SYN_SENT is the technical name of the client's state between the first and second messages of the handshake.

If the server is not accepting connections—say, if there is no program associated with the given port at the destination—the server-side TCP will respond (immediately) with a rejection message instead of an acknowledgment, and connect() returns −1 with *errno* set to ECONNREFUSED. Otherwise, after the client receives a positive reply from the server, the netstat output would look like:

```
Active Internet connections
Proto Recv-Q Send-Q Local Address    Foreign Address    State
tcp        0      0 A.B.C.D:P        W.X.Y.Z:Q          ESTABLISHED
```

The sequence of events at the server side is rather different; we describe it in Figures 7.7, 7.8, and 7.9. The server needs to bind to the particular TCP port known to the client. Typically, the server specifies only the port number (here, Q) in the bind() call and gives the special wildcard address INADDR_ANY for the local IP address. In case the server host has more than one IP address, this technique allows the socket to receive connections addressed to any of its IP addresses. When the server calls listen(), the state of the socket is changed to "Listening", indicating that it is ready to accept new connections. These events are depicted in Figure 7.7. The output from netstat on the server after this sequence would include a line like:

```
Active Internet connections
Proto Recv-Q Send-Q Local Address    Foreign Address    State
tcp        0      0 0.0.0.0:Q        0.0.0.0:0          LISTENING
```

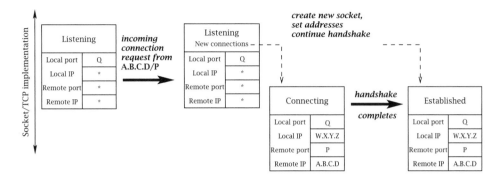

Figure 7.8: Incoming connection request processing.

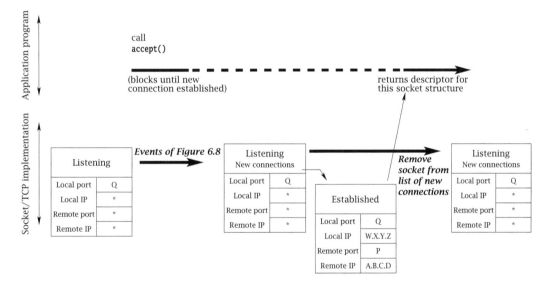

Figure 7.9: 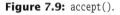.

Note that any client connection request that arrives at the server before the call to listen() will be rejected, even if it arrives after the call to bind().

The next thing the server does is call accept(), which blocks until a connection with a client is established. Therefore in Figure 7.8 we focus on the events that occur in the TCP implementation when a client connection request arrives. Note that everything depicted in this figure happens "under the covers" in the TCP implementation.

When the request for a connection arrives from the client, a new socket structure is created for the connection. The new socket's addresses are filled in based on the arriving packet.

The packet's destination Internet address and port (W.X.Y.Z and Q, respectively) become the socket's local address and port; the packet's source address and port (A.B.C.D and P) become the socket's remote Internet address and port. Note that the local port number of the new socket is always the same as that of the listening socket. The new socket's state is set to Connecting (actually called SYN_RCVD in the implementation), and it is added to a list of not-quite-connected sockets associated with the original server socket. Note well that the original server socket does not change state. At this point the output of netstat should show *both* the original, listening socket and the newly created one:

```
Active Internet connections
Proto Recv-Q Send-Q Local Address      Foreign Address      State
tcp      0      0 0.0.0.0:Q            0.0.0.0:0            LISTENING
tcp      0      0 W.X.Y.Z:Q           A.B.C.D:P            SYN_RCVD
```

In addition to creating a new underlying socket structure, the server-side TCP implementation sends an acknowledging TCP handshake message back to the client. However, the server TCP does not consider the handshake complete until the third message of the three-way handshake is received from the client. When that message eventually arrives, the new structure's state is set to "Established", and it is then (and only then) moved to a list of socket structures associated with the original socket, which represent established connections ready to be accepted. (If the third handshake message fails to arrive, eventually the "Connecting" structure is deleted.) Output from netstat would then include:

```
Active Internet connections
Proto Recv-Q Send-Q Local Address      Foreign Address      State
tcp      0      0 0.0.0.0:Q            0.0.0.0:0            LISTENING
tcp      0      0 W.X.Y.Z:Q           A.B.C.D:P            ESTABLISHED
```

Now we can consider (in Figure 7.9) what happens when the server program calls accept(). The call unblocks as soon as there is something in the listening socket's list of new connections. (Note that this list may already be nonempty when accept() is called.) At that time, the new socket structure is removed from the list, and a socket descriptor is allocated and returned as the result of accept().

It is important to note that each structure in the server socket's associated list represents a fully established TCP connection with a client at the other end. Indeed, the client can send data as soon as it receives the second message of the opening handshake—which may be long before the server accepts the client connection!

7.4.2   Closing a TCP Connection

TCP has a *graceful close* mechanism that allows applications to terminate a connection without having to worry about loss of data that might still be in transit. The mechanism is also designed to allow data transfers in each direction to be terminated independently. It works like this: the application indicates that it is finished sending data on a connected socket by calling close() or shutdown(). At that point, the underlying TCP implementation first transmits

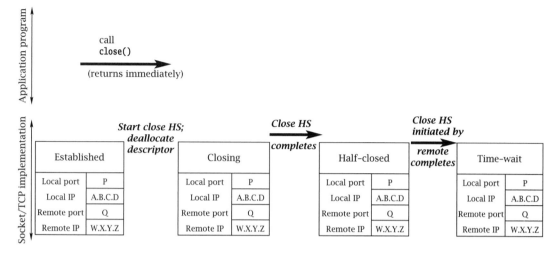

Figure 7.10: Closing a TCP connection first.

any data remaining in *SendQ* (subject to available space in *RecvQ* at the other end), and then sends a closing TCP handshake message to the other end. This closing handshake message can be thought of as an end-of-stream marker: it tells the receiving TCP that no more bytes will be placed in *RecvQ*. (Note that the closing handshake message itself is *not* passed to the receiving application, but that its position in the byte stream is indicated by recv() returning 0.) The closing TCP waits for an acknowledgment of its closing handshake message, which indicates that all data sent on the connection made it safely to *RecvQ*. Once that acknowledgment is received, the connection is "Half closed". The connection is not *completely* closed until a symmetric handshake happens in the other direction—that is, until *both* ends have indicated that they have no more data to send.

The closing event sequence in TCP can happen in two ways: either one application calls close() (or shutdown()) and completes its closing handshake before the other does, or both close simultaneously, so that their closing handshake messages cross in the network. Figure 7.10 shows the sequence of events in the implementation when the application invokes close() *before* the other end closes. The closing handshake (HS) message is sent, the state of the socket structure is set to "Closing", and the call returns. After this point, further attempts to perform any operation on the socket result in error returns. When the acknowledgment for the close handshake is received, the state changes to "Half closed", where it remains until the other end's close handshake message is received. At this point, the output of netstat on the client would show the status of the connection as:

```
Active Internet connections
Proto Recv-Q Send-Q Local Address      Foreign Address       State
tcp        0      0 A.B.C.D:P          W.X.Y.Z:Q             FIN_WAIT_2
```

(FIN_WAIT_2 is the technical name for the "half-closed" state at the host that initiates close first. The state denoted by "closing" in the figure is technically called FIN_WAIT_1, but it is transient and is difficult to catch with netstat.) Note that if the remote endpoint goes away while the connection is in this state, the local underlying structure will stay around indefinitely. Otherwise, when the other end's close handshake message arrives, an acknowledgment is sent and the state is changed to "Time-Wait". Although the descriptor in the application program may have long since been reclaimed (and even reused), the associated underlying socket structure continues to exist in the implementation for a minute or more; the reasons for this are discussed at the end of this section.

The output of netstat at the right end of Figure 7.10 includes:

```
Active Internet connections
Proto Recv-Q Send-Q Local Address      Foreign Address      State
tcp       0      0 A.B.C.D:P           W.X.Y.Z:Q            TIME_WAIT
```

Figure 7.11 shows the simpler sequence of events at the endpoint that does not close first. When the closing handshake message arrives, an acknowledgment is sent immediately, and the connection state becomes "Close-Wait." The output of netstat on this host shows:

```
Active Internet connections
Proto Recv-Q Send-Q Local Address      Foreign Address      State
tcp       0      0 W.X.Y.Z:Q           A.B.C.D:P            CLOSE_WAIT
```

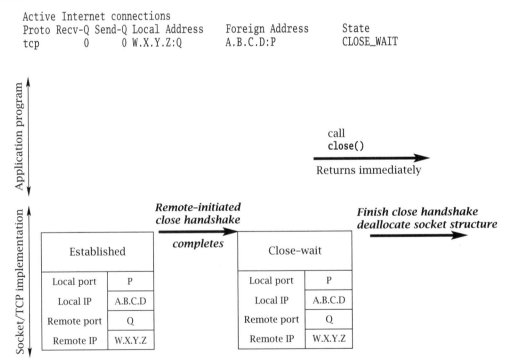

Figure 7.11: Closing after the other end closes.

At this point, it's all over: the implementation is just waiting for the application to call close(). When it does, the socket descriptor is deallocated and the final close handshake is initiated. When it completes, the underlying socket structure is deallocated.

Although most applications use close(), shutdown() actually provides more flexibility. A call to close() terminates *both* directions of transfer and causes the file descriptor associated with the socket to be deallocated. Any undelivered data remaining in *RecvQ* is discarded, and the flow control mechanism prevents any further transfer of data from the other end's *SendQ*. All trace of the socket disappears from the calling program. Underneath, however, the associated socket structure continues to exist until the other end initiates its closing handshake. In contrast, shutdown() allows the sending and receiving streams to be terminated independently. It takes an additional argument, one of SHUT_RD, SHUT_WR, or SHUT_RDWR, indicating which stream(s) are to be shut down. A program calling shutdown() with second argument SHUT_WR can continue to receive data on the socket; only sending is prohibited. The fact that the other end of the connection has closed is indicated by recv() returning 0 (once *RecvQ* is empty, of course) to indicate that there will be no more data available on the connection.

In view of the fact that both close() and shutdown() return without waiting for the closing handshake to complete, you may wonder how the sender can be assured that sent data has actually made it to the receiving program (i.e., to *Delivered*). In fact, it is possible for an application to call close() or shutdown() and have it complete successfully (i.e., not return −1) *while there is still data in SendQ*. If either end of the connection then crashes before the data makes it to *RecvQ*, data may be lost without the sending application knowing about it!

The best solution is to design the application protocol so that whichever side closes first, does so *only after* receiving application-level assurance that its data was received. For example, when our TCPEchoClient.c program receives the same number of bytes as it sent, there should be nothing more in transit in either direction, so it is safe for it to close the connection. Note that there is no *guarantee* that the bytes received were those sent; the client is assuming that the server implements the echo protocol. In a real application the client should certainly *not* trust the server to "do the right thing."

The other solution is to modify the semantics of close() by setting the SO_LINGER socket option before calling it. The SO_LINGER option specifies an amount of time for the TCP implementation to wait for the closing handshake to complete. The setting of SO_LINGER and the specification of the wait time are given to setsockopt() using the **linger** structure:

```
struct linger {
    int  l_onoff;   // Nonzero to linger
    int  l_linger;  // Time (secs.) to linger
};
```

To use the linger behavior, set *l_onoff* to a nonzero value and specify the time to linger in *l_linger*. When SO_LINGER is set, close() blocks *until the closing handshake is completed* or until the specified amount of time passes. If the handshake does not complete in time, an error indication (ETIMEDOUT) is returned. Thus, if SO_LINGER is set and close() returns no error, the application is assured that everything it sent reached *RecvQ*.

The final subtlety of closing a TCP connection revolves around the need for the Time-Wait state. The TCP specification requires that when a connection terminates, at least one of the sockets persists in the Time-Wait state for a period of time after both closing handshakes complete. This requirement is motivated by the possibility of messages being delayed in the network. If both ends' underlying structures go away as soon as both closing handshakes complete, and a *new* connection is immediately established between the same pair of socket addresses, a message from the previous connection, which happened to be delayed in the network, could arrive just after the new connection is established. Because it would contain the same source and destination addresses, the old message could be mistaken for a message belonging to the new connection, and its data might (incorrectly) be delivered to the application.

Unlikely though this scenario may be, TCP employs multiple mechanisms to prevent it, including the Time-Wait state. The Time-Wait state ensures that every TCP connection ends with a quiet time, during which no data is sent. The quiet time is supposed to be equal to twice the maximum amount of time a packet can remain in the network. Thus, by the time a connection goes away completely (i.e., the socket structure leaves the Time-Wait state and is deallocated) and clears the way for a new connection between the same pair of addresses, no messages from the old instance can still be in the network. In practice, the length of the quiet time is implementation dependent, because there is no real mechanism that limits how long a packet can be delayed by the network. Values in use range from 4 minutes down to 30 seconds or even shorter.

The most important consequence of Time-Wait is that as long as the underlying socket structure exists, no other socket is permitted to bind to the same local port. (More on this below.)

7.5 Demultiplexing Demystified

The fact that different sockets on the same machine can have the same local address and port number is implicit in the preceding discussions. For example, on a machine with only one IP address, every new socket accept()ed via a listening socket will have the same local address and port number as the listening socket. Clearly, the process of deciding to which socket an incoming packet should be delivered—that is, the *demultiplexing* process—involves looking at more than just the packet's destination address and port. Otherwise there could be ambiguity about which socket an incoming packet is intended for. The process of matching an incoming packet to a socket is actually the same for both TCP and UDP, and can be summarized by the following points:

- The local port in the socket structure *must* match the destination port number in the incoming packet.

- Any address fields in the socket structure that contain the wildcard value (*) are considered to match *any* value in the corresponding field in the packet.

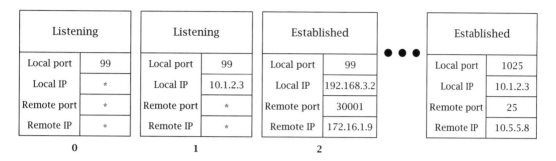

Figure 7.12: Demultiplexing with multiple matching sockets.

- If more than one socket structure matches an incoming packet for all four address fields, the one that matches using the fewest wildcards gets the packet.

For example, consider a host with two IP addresses, 10.1.2.3 and 192.168.3.2, and with a subset of its active TCP socket structures, as shown in Figure 7.12. The structure labeled 0 is associated with a listening socket and has port 99 with a wildcard local address. Socket structure 1 is also for a listening socket on the same port, but with the local IP address 10.1.2.3 specified (so it will only accept connection requests to that address). Structure 2 is for a connection that was accepted via structure 0's listening socket, and thus has the same local port number (99), but also has its local and remote Internet addresses filled in. Other sockets belong to other active connections. Now consider a packet with source IP address 172.16.1.10, source port 56789, destination IP address 10.1.2.3, and destination port 99. It will be delivered to the socket associated with structure 1, because that one matches with the fewest wildcards.

When a program attempts to bind() to a particular local port number, the existing sockets are checked to make sure that no socket is already using that local port. The call to bind() will fail and set EADDRINUSE if *any* socket matches the local port and local IP address (if any) specified in the argument to bind(). This can cause problems in the following scenario:

1. A server's listening socket is bound to some particular port *P*.
2. The server accepts a connection from a client, which enters the Established state.
3. The server terminates for some reason—say, because the programmer has created a new version and wants to test it. When the server program exits, the underlying system automatically (and virtually) calls close() on all of its existing sockets. The socket that was in the Established state immediately transitions to the Time-Wait state.
4. The programmer starts up a new instance of the server, which attempts to bind() to port *P*.

Unfortunately the new server's call to bind() will fail with EADDRINUSE because of the old socket in Time-Wait state.

As of this writing, there are two ways around this. One is to wait until the underlying structure leaves the Time-Wait state. The other is for the server to set the SO_REUSEADDR socket option *before* calling bind(). That lets bind() succeed in spite of the existence of any sockets representing earlier connections to the server's port. There is no danger of ambiguity, because the existing connections (whether still in the Established or Time-Wait state) have remote addresses filled in, while the socket being bound does not. In general, the SO_REUSEADDR option also enables a socket to bind to a local port to which another socket is already bound, provided that the IP address to which it is being bound (typically the wildcard INADDR_ANY address) is different from that of the existing socket. The default bind() behavior is to disallow such requests.

Exercises

1. The TCP protocol is designed so that simultaneous connection attempts will succeed. That is, if an application using port P and Internet address W.X.Y.Z attempts to connect to address A.B.C.D, port Q, at the same time as an application using the same address and port tries to connect to W.X.Y.Z, port P, they will end up connected to each other. Can this be made to happen when the programs use the sockets API?

2. The first example of "buffer deadlock" in this chapter involves the programs on both ends of a connection trying to send large messages. However, this is not necessary for deadlock. How could the TCPEchoClient from earlier chapters be made to deadlock when it connects to the TCPEchoServer from that chapter?

chapter **8**

Socket Programming in C++*

This book is for people who want to understand sockets. It's for people who want to know not only how to get a couple of programs to communicate over a network but also how and why the Sockets API works like it does. Or course, lots of developers use sockets all the time without really understanding these details. It's common to use sockets via a library that offers a simplified interface to socket creation, name resolution, and message transmission. This is particularly common in object-oriented languages like C++ and Java, where it's easy to wrap socket functionality in a collection of related classes.

The PracticalSocket library was developed to help expose students to the basics of socket programming without requiring a complete understanding of some of the material covered elsewhere in this book. This library is typical of object-oriented wrappers around socket functionality; it tries to offer a simple interface to the most commonly used functionality. The PracticalSocket library provides portability between Windows and UNIX platforms, and it can serve an instructional purpose since its source code is readily available.

A reader who is more comfortable in C or who prefers to start by understanding what's going on underneath should save this chapter for last. It can serve as a summary and application of many of the concepts introduced earlier. For a reader who is an experienced C++ programmer or who prefers to learn about sockets more selectively, this chapter can be read earlier and can serve as an overview of concepts covered in much more detail in earlier chapters. The examples presented here include many pointers to appropriate sections earlier in the text, so this chapter can serve as an entry point for many other sections of the book.

---

*Contributed by David Sturgill

In this chapter, we introduce the PracticalSocket library and demonstrate its use in a simple application. Through a series of more sophisticated applications, we expose additional features of the library and demonstrate how PracticalSockets or a similar library might be used in practice. Both the PracticalSocket library and the example programs used in this chapter to demonstrate it are available from the Web site for this text.

8.1 PracticalSocket Library Overview

Figure 8.1 illustrates the classes in PracticalSockets and their inheritance relationships. All the classes ending in "Socket" serve as wrappers around TCP or UDP sockets and provide a simple interface for creating a socket and using it for communication. The **SocketException** class provides support for error handling, and **SocketAddress** serves as a wrapper around an address and port number.

We can get started using this library without understanding everything about its classes and methods all at once. We'll start by covering just enough to write a simple application. From there, we can introduce new features gradually.

The **TCPSocket** class is the basic mechanism for communication over TCP. It is implemented as a wrapper around a TCP socket and serves as an endpoint in a bidirectional communication channel. If two applications want to communicate, they can each obtain an instance of **TCPSocket**. Once these two sockets are connected, sequences of bytes sent from one can be received at the other.

Functionality for **TCPSocket** is distributed across the class itself and its two base classes, **CommunicatingSocket** and **Socket**. The **Socket** class is at the top of the inheritance hierarchy, and contains only functionality common to all socket wrappers. Among other things, it has the job of keeping up with the underlying socket descriptor, and it automatically closes its descriptor when it is destroyed.

The **CommunicatingSocket** class is an abstraction for a socket that, once connected, can exchange data with a peer socket. It provides send() and recv() methods that are wrappers around the send() and recv() calls for the underlying socket descriptor. A successful call to the send() method of a **CommunicatingSocket** will send the first *bufferLen* bytes

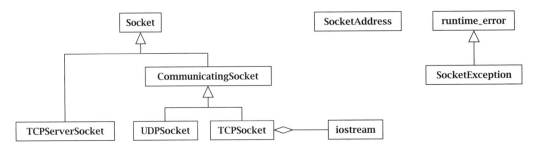

Figure 8.1: PracticalSockets class diagram.

pointed to by *buffer* to the peer **CommunicatingSocket**. A call to the recv() method of a **CommunicatingSocket** will attempt to read up to *bufferLen* bytes of data from the peer and store the result in the memory pointed to by *buffer*. The recv() method will block until data is available on the socket, and it will return the number of bytes received on the socket and written into *buffer*. After a socket is closed, recv() will return zero to indicate that no more data can be received.

---

void CommunicatingSocket::send(**const void** *buffer, **int** *bufferLen*) throw(**SocketException**)
int CommunicatingSocket::recv(**void** *buffer, **int** *bufferLen*) throw(**SocketException**)
int CommunicatingSocket::recvFully(**void** *buffer, **int** *bufferLen*) throw(**SocketException**)

The stream of bytes transmitted between sockets may be fragmented into packets and reconstituted by buffering on its way from the sender to the receiver. **A group of bytes sent in a single call to** send() **may not all be received in a single, corresponding call to** recv(). The recvFully() method is intended to help with this. It works just like recv(), except that it blocks until either exactly *bufferLen* bytes are received or the socket is closed. The return value from recvFully() reports the number of bytes received. Ordinarily, this will be the same as *bufferLen*. However, if the socket is closed before all the requested bytes are transmitted, a value less than *bufferLen* may be returned.

The PracticalSocket library uses C++ exceptions to report when something goes wrong. This is evident in the prototypes above. An instance of **SocketException** is thrown whenever an error occurs in the library. This exception object inherits from **runtime_error**, so it can be caught as an instance of **SocketException** by error-handling code specific to the communications portion of an application. A **SocketException** may be caught as a more general exception type by more general error-handling code. The what() method of a **SocketException** returns a string with a short description of the particular error that occurred.

The way to obtain an instance of **TCPSocket** depends on the role of the application. To establish a pair of connected **TCPSocket** peers, one application must function as a server and the other as a client. The server listens for new connections by creating an instance of **TCPServerSocket**. The other creates a **TCPSocket** directly. The **TCPServerSocket** class is derived from **Socket**, but not **CommunicatingSocket**. It is used to establish new TCP socket connections with client applications, but it is not itself used to send and receive bytes. The server must construct a **TCPServerSocket** with an application-defined port number. Afterward, a call to accept() will block until a client application attempts to connect by creating a **TCPSocket** with the same port number. When this happens, accept() will return a pointer to a new instance of **TCPSocket** that is connected to the **TCPSocket** peer on the client.

TCPServerSocket(**in_port_t** localPort) throw(**SocketException**)
TCPSocket ***TCPServerSocket**::accept() throw(**SocketException**)

The client application creates its end of the socket connection by simply constructing an instance of **TCPSocket** and providing the name or address of the server's host and the same port number. Once a pair of connected **TCPSocket** objects have been created, client and server can communicate using the send() and recv() methods until one of the endpoints closes its connection via the destructor or the close() method.

TCPSocket(**const char** *_foreignAddress_, **in_port_t** _foreignPort_) throw(_SocketException_)
void Socket::close()

8.2 Plus One Service

The few classes and methods introduced so far are enough to let us implement a simple client and server similar to the ones in previous chapters. Here, accessing sockets through the PracticalSocket classes yields somewhat shorter source code that hides many of the details of the underlying API. The "plus one" service is a client-server application that performs the increment operation. The client sends an unsigned integer to the server, and the server sends back a value that is one greater.

8.2.1 Plus One Server

PlusOneServer.cpp is the server portion of the application. It accepts client connections, reads a 32-bit unsigned integer from each client, increments it, and then sends it back.

PlusOneServer.cpp

```
1   #include <iostream>
2   #include "PracticalSocket.h"
3
4   using namespace std;
5
6   int main(int argc, char *argv[]) {
7     try {
8       // Make a socket to listen for SurveyClient connections.
9       TCPServerSocket servSock(9431);
10
11      for (;;) {                              // Repeatedly accept connections
12        TCPSocket *sock = servSock.accept(); // Get next client connection
13
14        uint32_t val;                        // Read 32-bit int from client
15        if (sock->recvFully(&val, sizeof(val)) == sizeof(val)) {
```

```
16          val = ntohl(val);              // Convert to local byte order
17          val++;                         // Increment the value
18          val = htonl(val);              // Convert to network byte order
19          sock->send(&val, sizeof(val)); // Send value back to client
20        }
21
22        delete sock;                     // Close and delete TCPSocket
23      }
24    } catch (SocketException &e) {
25      cerr << e.what() << endl;          // Report errors to the console
26    }
27
28    return 0;
29  }
```

PlusOneServer.cpp

1. **Application setup:** lines 1–6
   Access to the sockets API is hidden behind the PracticalSocket classes. The application only needs to include the header for the library and any calls we use directly.

2. **Error handling:** lines 7, 24–26
   Error handling is via exceptions. If an error occurs, it is caught at the end of the main function, and the program prints an error message before terminating.

3. **Create a server socket:** line 9
   The server creates a **TCPServerSocket** that listens for connections on port 9431. When constructed like this, the **TCPServerSocket** automatically makes the calls to socket(), bind() and listen() described in Sections 2.5, 2.6, and 2.7. If anything goes wrong in one of these steps, an exception is thrown.

   To keep the example simple, the server's port number is hard-coded in the constructor call. Of course, it would be more maintainable to use a named constant in a header file as the port number.

4. **Repeatedly accept client connections:** lines 11–12
   The server repeatedly calls the accept() method to wait for a new client connection. When a client connects, this method returns a pointer to a new **TCPSocket** for communicating with the client. This method is a wrapper around the accept() call described in Section 2.7. If something goes wrong in accept(), the catch block reports the error and the program terminates.

5. **Read an integer from the client and convert byte order:** lines 14–16
   Client and server have been written to exchange fixed-sized messages in the form of unsigned 32-bit integers. The server uses a stack-allocated integer, *val*, to hold the received message. Since the server is expecting a 4-byte message, it uses the recvFully()

method of **TCPSocket** to read the message directly into the storage for *val*. If the client connection is closed before the entire message arrives, recvFully() returns fewer than the expected number of bytes and the server ignores the message.

Although client and server agree on the size of a message, if they are running on different hosts, they may represent integers using different byte orders. To take care of this possibility, we agree to only transmit values that are in big-endian byte order. The server uses ntohl() to convert the received integer to local byte order if necessary.

Concerns over reading entire messages and adjusting byte order are really just the issues of framing and encoding. Chapter 5 focuses specifically on these topics and offers a variety of techniques for handling framing and encoding.

6. **Increment the client integer and send it back:** lines 17–19
   The server adds one to the client-provided value and then converts it back to network byte order. The server sends the value back to the client by sending a copy of the 4 bytes of memory used to represent *val*.

7. **Close client connection:** line 22
   When the server destroys its instance of **TCPSocket**, the socket connection is closed. If the server had neglected to destroy this object, it would have not only leaked memory but also leaked an underlying socket descriptor with each client connection. A server with this type of bug could very quickly reach an operating-system-enforced limit on per-process resources.

8.2.2 Plus One Client

PlusOneClient.cpp is the client counterpart of the plus one server. It connects to the server, sends it a copy of an integer value given on the command line, and prints out the value the server sends back.

PlusOneClient.cpp

```
1   #include <iostream>
2   #include <cstdlib>
3   #include "PracticalSocket.h"
4
5   using namespace std;
6
7   int main(int argc, char *argv[]) {
8     if (argc != 3) {                        // Check number of parameters
9       cerr << "Usage: PlusOneClient <server host> <starting value>" << endl;
10      return 1;
11    }
12
13    try {
```

```
14    TCPSocket sock(argv[1], 9431);    // Connect to the server.
15
16    uint32_t val = atoi(argv[2]);     // Parse user-suppled value
17    val = htonl(val);                 // Convert to network byte order
18    sock.send(&val, sizeof(val));     // Send to server.
19
20    // Read the server's response, convert to local byte order and print it
21    if (sock.recvFully(&val, sizeof(val)) == sizeof(val)) {
22      val = ntohl(val);
23      cout << "Server Response: " << val << endl;
24    }
25    // Socket is closed when it goes out of scope
26  } catch(SocketException &e) {
27    cerr << e.what() << endl;
28  }
29
30  return 0;
31 }
```

PlusOneClient.cpp

1. **Application setup and parameter checking:** lines 1–11
   The client uses the PracticalSocket classes along with support from a few other header files. On the command line, the client expects an address or hostname for the server and an integer value to send to the server. A usage message is printed if the wrong number of arguments is given.

2. **Error handling:** lines 13, 26–28
   As in the server, a socket-related exception is caught by code at the end of the program, and an error message is printed.

3. **Connect to the server:** line 14
   The client creates an instance of **TCPSocket**, passing in the user-supplied hostname and the hard-coded port number for the server. This constructor hides a lot of detail in the underlying sockets API. First, the given hostname is resolved to one or more addresses. As described in Chapter 3, getaddrinfo() returns all matching addresses for a given host and port. Some may be IPv4 addresses, and some may be IPv6. The **TCPSocket** constructor creates a socket for the first address and attempts to connect to it. If this fails, each successive address is tried until a connection can be established. If no addresses will connect, an exception is thrown.

4. **Parse, convert, and send value to server:** lines 16–18
   The client parses the user-provided value from the command line, converts it to network byte order, and sends it to the server by sending the 4 bytes starting at the value's starting address.

5. **Receive incremented value, convert, and print:** lines 21–24
   Using recvFully(), the client blocks until it either receives a 4-byte integer from the server or the socket connection is closed. If all 4 bytes arrive, the received value is converted to host byte order and printed.

6. **Close the socket:** line 25
   Since the client's **TCPSocket** is allocated on the stack, it is automatically closed and destroyed when the socket goes out of scope.

8.2.3   Running Server and Client

The executable PlusOneServer requires no command-line arguments. Once compiled, it should be started from the command prompt and permitted to run for as long as you want to try it out. While the server is running, you should run a copy of PlusOneClient from a different command prompt, possibly on a different host. Supply the name of the server's host and an integer value on the command line, and it should, with a little help from the server, produce a value one larger than the command-line argument. For example, if the server is running on a host named "venus," you should be able to run the client as follows:

PlusOneClient connecting to a server on host venus

```
% PlusOneClient venus 345318
Server Response: 345319
```

Exercises

1. Instead of simply incrementing the value from a single client, modify the server so that it will send back the sum of two values supplied by different clients. After a first client connects, the server will wait for a second client. The server will read integer values from both clients and send back the sum of these two values to both.

2. The client and server communicate using binary-encoded, fixed-sized messages. Modify these programs so that they use variable-length, text-encoded messages as described in Section 5.2.2. The sender will write its integer value to a character array as a sequence of ASCII-encoded digits. The receiver will read a copy of this array and parse out the integer.

8.3   Survey Service

Building on the concepts demonstrated in the plus one service and using techniques presented in Chapters 5 and 6, we can create a distributed application that does something a little more useful. The survey client and server implement a simple, distributed survey application. At start-up, the server reads a list of survey questions and responses from a text file. When a client connects, the server sends it copies of the questions and response options. The client prints each question and sends the user's response back to the server, where it is recorded.

The file, survey1.txt, is an example survey file the server might use. The first line gives the number of questions. This is followed by a description for each question. A question is described by a one-line prompt, followed by a line giving the number of responses and a line of text for each response. For example, the first question on the survey below is, "What is your favorite flavor of ice cream?" The three possible responses are "Vanilla," "Chocolate," or "Strawberry." As users take the survey, the server will keep up with how many selected each of these responses.

survey1.txt

```
 1  2
 2  What is your favorite flavor of ice cream?
 3  3
 4  Vanilla
 5  Chocolate
 6  Strawberry
 7  Socket programming is:
 8  4
 9  Surprisingly easy
10  Empowering
11  Not for the faint of heart
12  Fun for the whole family
```

survey1.txt

8.3.1 Survey Support Functions

The client and server depend on common functionality implemented in SurveyCommon.h and SurveyCommon.cpp. The header file provides a named constant for the server's port number, a **Question** type for representing survey questions and prototypes for provided functions.

SurveyCommon.h

```
1  #ifndef __SURVEYCOMMON_H__
2  #define __SURVEYCOMMON_H__
3
4  #include "PracticalSocket.h"
5  #include <string>
6  #include <vector>
7
8  /** Port number used by the Survey Server */
```

```
 9  const in_port_t SURVEY_PORT = 12543;
10
11  /** Write an encoding of val to the socket, sock. */
12  void sendInt(CommunicatingSocket *sock, uint32_t val) throw(SocketException);
13
14  /** Write an encoding of str to the socket, sock. */
15  void sendString(CommunicatingSocket *sock, const std::string &str)
16    throw(SocketException);
17
18  /** Read from sock an integer encoded by sendInt() and return it */
19  uint32_t recvInt(CommunicatingSocket *sock) throw(std::runtime_error);
20
21  /** Read from sock a string encoded by sendString() and return it */
22  std::string recvString(CommunicatingSocket *sock) throw(std::runtime_error);
23
24  /** Representation for a survey question */
25  struct Question {
26    std::string qText;                  // Text of the question.
27    std::vector<std::string> rList;     // List of response choices.
28  };
29
30  /** Read survey questions from the given stream and store them in qList. */
31  bool readSurvey(std::istream &stream, std::vector<Question> &qList);
32
33  #endif
```

SurveyCommon.h

SurveyCommon.cpp

```
 1  #include "SurveyCommon.h"
 2
 3  using namespace std;
 4
 5  void sendInt(CommunicatingSocket *sock, uint32_t val) throw(SocketException) {
 6    val = htonl(val);                    // Convert val to network byte order
 7    sock->send(&val, sizeof(val));       // Send the value through the socket
 8  }
 9
10  void sendString(CommunicatingSocket *sock, const string &str)
11    throw(SocketException) {
12    sendInt(sock, str.length());             // Send the length of string
13    sock->send(str.c_str(),  str.length()); // Send string contents
14  }
15
```

```cpp
16  uint32_t recvInt(CommunicatingSocket *sock) throw(runtime_error) {
17    uint32_t val;                          // Try to read a 32-bit int into val
18    if (sock->recvFully(&val, sizeof(val)) != sizeof(val))
19      throw runtime_error("Socket closed while reading int");
20
21    return ntohl(val);                     // Convert to host byte order, return
22  }
23
24  string recvString(CommunicatingSocket *sock) throw(runtime_error) {
25    uint32_t len = recvInt(sock);        // Read string length
26    char *buffer = new char [len + 1];   // Temp buffer to hold string
27    if (sock->recvFully(buffer, len) != len) {  // Try to read whole string
28      delete [] buffer;
29      throw runtime_error("Socket closed while reading string");
30    }
31
32    buffer[len] = '\0';                   // Null terminate the received string
33    string result(buffer);                // Convert to an std::string
34    delete [] buffer;                     // Free temporary buffer
35    return result;
36  }
37
38  bool readSurvey(istream &stream, std::vector<Question> &qList) {
39    int count = 0;
40    stream >> count;                      // See how many questions there are
41    stream.ignore();                      // Skip past newline
42    qList = vector< Question >(count);
43
44    // Parse each question.
45    for (unsigned int q = 0; q < qList.size(); q++ ) {
46      getline(stream, qList[q].qText);    // Get the text of the question
47
48      count = 0;
49      stream >> count;                    // Read number of responses
50      stream.ignore();                    // Skip past newline
51
52      // Initialize the response list and populate it.
53      qList[q].rList = vector< string >(count);
54      for (unsigned int r = 0; r < qList[q].rList.size(); r++)
55        getline(stream, qList[q].rList[r]);
56    }
57
58    return stream;                        // Return true if stream is still good
59  }
```

SurveyCommon.cpp

1. **Integer encode and decode:** lines 5–8, 16–22
   In this application, client and server communicate by exchanging values of type integer and string. Integers are handled much like they are in the plus one service. To encode a 32-bit integer, it is first converted to network byte order and then sent out over a socket. To receive an integer, we attempt to read 4 bytes from the socket and, if successful, convert them to host byte order and return the result. If 4 bytes can't be read, an exception is thrown. Since this type of error is not produced in the PracticalSocket library itself, the exception is reported as a **runtime_error** rather than a **SocketException**.

2. **String encode and decode:** lines 10–14, 24–36
   Encoding and decoding of strings is more complicated because they can be of arbitrary length. Strings are encoded by first sending the string length and following this by the content of the string. The decoder tries to read both of these values and, if successful, converts the received string contents to a **string** object and returns it.

3. **Parse survey:** lines 38–59
   The survey is stored in a text file. The readSurvey() function reads the survey from the given input stream and fills in the given *qList* parameter with the sequence of questions.

8.3.2   Survey Server

The survey server is responsible for maintaining the list of survey questions, keeping up with user response totals, and interacting with the client.

The plus one server was able to handle only one client connection at a time. If multiple clients wanted to use the service, they would have to take turns. This makes sense for a simple application, where we can expect very short exchanges with each client. However, it may not work for the survey service. Here, users may deliberate for as long as they want over each question. If two users want to take the survey at the same time, it isn't reasonable to make one wait until the other is finished.

To interact with more than one client at the same time, the survey server creates a separate thread to handle interaction with each client. As in Section 6.4.2, the new thread manages the session with the client. Each time the server receives a response, it tallies it in its response count. Mutual exclusion helps the server to make sure two threads don't modify the response totals at the same time.

SurveyServer.cpp

```
1   #include <iostream>
2   #include <fstream>
3   #include <pthread.h>
4   #include "PracticalSocket.h"
5   #include "SurveyCommon.h"
6
```

```
 7  using namespace std;
 8
 9  static vector<Question> qList;          // List of survey questions
10  static pthread_mutex_t lock;            // Mutex to Protect critical sections
11  static vector<vector<int> > rCount;     // Response tallies for each question
12
13  /** Thread main function to administer a survey over the given socket */
14  static void *conductSurvey(void *arg);
15
16  int main(int argc, char *argv[]) {
17    if (argc != 2) {
18      cerr << "Usage: SurveyServer <Survey File>" << endl;
19      return 1;
20    }
21
22    ifstream input(argv[1]);              // Read survey from given file
23    if (!input || !readSurvey(input, qList) ) {
24      cerr << "Can't read survey from file: " << argv[1] << endl;
25      return 1;
26    }
27
28    // Initialize response tally for each question/response.
29    for (unsigned int i = 0; i < qList.size(); i++)
30      rCount.push_back(vector<int>(qList[i].rList.size(), 0));
31    pthread_mutex_init(&lock, NULL);      // Initialize mutex
32
33    try {
34      // Make a socket to listen for SurveyClient connections.
35      TCPServerSocket servSock(SURVEY_PORT);
36
37      for (;;) {    // Repeatedly accept connections and administer the survey.
38        TCPSocket *sock = servSock.accept();
39
40        pthread_t newThread;              // Give survey in a separate thread
41        if (pthread_create(&newThread, NULL, conductSurvey, sock) != 0) {
42          cerr << "Can't create new thread" << endl;
43          delete sock;
44        }
45      }
46    } catch (SocketException &e) {
47      cerr << e.what() << endl;          // Report errors to the console.
48    }
49
50    return 0;
51  }
```

```
52
53   static void *conductSurvey(void *arg) {
54     TCPSocket *sock = (TCPSocket *)arg;     // Argument is really a socket
55     try {
56       sendInt(sock, qList.size());          // Tell client no of questions
57
58       for (unsigned int q = 0; q < qList.size(); q++) {
59         // For each question, send the question text and list of responses
60         sendString(sock, qList[q].qText);
61         sendInt(sock, qList[q].rList.size());
62         for (unsigned int r = 0; r < qList[q].rList.size(); r++)
63           sendString(sock, qList[q].rList[r]);
64
65         // Get the client's response and count it if it's in range
66         unsigned int response = recvInt(sock);
67         if (response >= 0 && response < rCount[q].size()) {
68           pthread_mutex_lock(&lock);         // Lock the mutex
69           rCount[q][response]++;             // Increment count for chosen item
70           pthread_mutex_unlock(&lock);       // Release the lock
71         }
72       }
73     } catch (runtime_error e) {
74       cerr << e.what() << endl;             // Report errors to the console.
75     }
76
77     delete sock;  // Free the socket object (and close the connection)
78     return NULL;
79   }
```

SurveyServer.cpp

---

1. **Access to library functions:** lines 1–5
   The server uses standard C++ I/O facilities and POSIX threads for interacting with multiple concurrent clients.

2. **Survey representation:** lines 9–11
   The survey is represented as a **vector** of **Question** instances. The variable, *rCount*, keeps up with user response counts, with each element of *rCount* corresponding to a survey question. Since each question has several possible responses, each element of *rCount* is a **vector** of totals, one for each response. Each time a user selects a response, the count for that question and response is incremented.

   If multiple clients connect to the server at the same time, it's possible that two or more of them will try to increment a counter at the same time. Depending on how this increment is performed by the hardware, this could leave the count in an unknown state. For example, an increment performed in one thread might overwrite the result of an increment that was just completed in another thread. The chances of this happening are remote, but this possibility should not be left to chance. The *lock* variable is a mutex that is used to manage concurrent access to *rCount*. By using this synchronization object, it will be easy to make sure only one thread at a time tries to modify *rCount*.

The server uses file-scoped variables to keep up with the survey and responses. This makes it easy to access these data structures from any of our threads. Using the static modifier prevents these variables from polluting the global namespace, since they are only visible to a single implementation file. However, this organization would be an impediment to code reuse if, say, we wanted to run multiple surveys from the same application.

3. **Initialize server state:** lines 17–31
The server parses the survey text from a user-supplied file. If anything goes wrong during this process, an error message is printed and the server exits. After the **Question** list has been successfully read, we know how many questions and responses there are, so we initialize the parallel response count representation. The mutex, *lock*, must also be initialized before it can be used.

4. **Create server socket and repeatedly accept clients:** lines 35–45
The server creates a **TCPServerSocket** listening on an agreed-upon port number. It repeatedly waits for client connections and for each connection creates a new thread to handle interaction with the client. When creating the thread, the server gives a pointer to the conductSurvey function as the starting point for the new thread and a pointer to the new **TCPSocket** as the thread's argument. From this point on, the new thread is responsible for the socket object and for interacting with the client. Of course, if a new thread can't be created, the server prints an error message and cleans up by deleting the socket immediately.

5. **Survey client handler:** lines 53–79
   - **Thread start-up:** lines 53–54
   The conductSurvey function serves as the main function for each new thread. The thread will execute this function once it starts up, and it will terminate once it returns out of the function. The parameter and return types of this function are determined by the Pthreads API. The void pointers are intended to let us pass pointers to any type of data we need. Here, we know we passed in a pointer to a **TCPSocket** instance, so the first thing we do is cast it to a more specific type to make it easier to use.

   Depending on the number of clients connecting, there may be several copies of conductSurvey running at the same time, each on its own thread. While all of these threads may be running in the same function, each has its own local variables, and each is communicating over the instance of **TCPSocket** that was provided at thread start-up.

   - **Send each question to client:** lines 56–63
   The server uses functions provided by SurveyCommon.cpp to simplify interaction with the client. It sends the client the number of questions in the survey and

then sends each question and its response list, waiting for a response between questions.

- **Get client response and tally it:** lines 66–71
  The client indicates the user's chosen response by sending its index back to the server. Before tallying the response, the server makes sure it's in the range of legitimate responses. This check is very important. If the server incremented *rCount* using an arbitrary client-supplied index, it would be giving the client permission to make changes at unknown memory locations. A malicious client could use this to try to crash the server or, worse, take control of the server's host. Of course, we wrote the client and the server code. You will see that we perform a similar check on the client before we even send a response, so what's the point of also performing the check on the server? We're not concerned about the behavior of properly functioning clients. We're more concerned about what will happen if a malicious user creates a client that doesn't behave as nicely as the one we wrote.

  If a legitimate response is received, the client thread locks the mutex to make sure no other threads are trying to modify *rCount* at the same time. It then increments the appropriate count and unlocks the mutex right away to let other threads make changes to *rCount* as needed. This is typical of the operation of a multithreaded application. In general, we want to lock out other threads for as short a period as possible. Consider what would happen if threads locked the mutex once at the start of conductSurvey and then released it when they were done. This would eliminate the need to lock and unlock the mutex on every response, but it would completely suppress concurrency; only one thread at a time could interact with its client.

- **Error handling:** lines 55,73–75
  An exception occurring in the client thread will terminate the thread, but the server will continue to run and accept new connections. This makes sense as such an exception may simply result from a client terminating unexpectedly. If an exception is caught during client interaction, execution falls through to the thread exit code. Note that the exception is caught as the more general type, **runtime_exception**, since it may be thrown either by PracticalSockets or by our own recvInt() or recvString() functions.

- **Close socket and exit:** lines 77–78
  Since the thread in conductSurvey is responsible for its dynamically allocated **TCPClient** instance, it must free the instance before it exits. Like a C++ stream, deleting the object automatically closes the underlying socket.

8.3.3   Survey Client

The survey client is not as complicated as its server. Here, we don't have to worry about multithreading, concurrency, or maintaining response counts.

SurveyClient.cpp

```
 1   #include <iostream>
 2   #include <iomanip>
 3   #include "PracticalSocket.h"
 4   #include "SurveyCommon.h"
 5
 6   using namespace std;
 7
 8   int main(int argc, char *argv[]) {
 9     if (argc != 2) {                       // Make sure the user gives a host
10       cerr << "Usage: SurveyClient <Survey Server Host>" << endl;
11       return 1;
12     }
13
14     try {
15       // Connect to the server.
16       TCPSocket sock(argv[1], SURVEY_PORT);
17
18       // Find out how many questions there are.
19       int qCount = recvInt(&sock);
20       for (int q = 0; q < qCount; q++) {
21         // Show each the question to the user and print the list of responses.
22         cout << "Q" << q << ":  " << recvString(&sock) << endl;
23         int rCount = recvInt(&sock);
24         for (int r = 0; r < rCount; r++)
25           cout << setw(2) << r << " "  << recvString(&sock) << endl;
26
27         // Keep prompting the user until we get a legal response.
28         int response = rCount;
29         while (response < 0 || response >= rCount) {
30           cout << "> ";
31           cin >> response;
32         }
33
34         // Send the server the user's response
35         sendInt(&sock, response);
36       }
37     } catch(runtime_error &e) {
38       cerr << e.what() << endl;            // Report errors to the console.
39       return 1;
40     }
41
42     return 0;
43   }
```

1. **Access to library functions:** lines 1–4
2. **Connect to server:** lines 9–16
   The client expects the hostname of the server on the command line. If it's not given, an error message is printed and the client exits. The client attempts to create a **TCP-Socket** object using the hostname and the server's port number defined in SurveyCommon.h. If a connection can't be established, the exception-handling code will report an error and exit.
3. **Receive and print survey questions:** lines 19–25
   Using functions provided by SurveyCommon.cpp, the client reads the number of questions and then reads each question and its list of responses.
4. **Read user responses and send them to the server:** lines 28–35
   For each question, the user is prompted for a response. The client checks to make sure the response is in the proper range before sending it to the server.

8.3.4   Running Server and Client

The SurveyServer requires one command-line argument, the name of the file containing the survey questions. For a survey file like the one above, we can run the server like:

SurveyServer offering questions from survey1.txt
```
% SurveyServer survey1.txt
```

The SurveyClient requires one command-line argument, the server's hostname or address. If the server is running on a system named "earth," we could run the client as:

SurveyClient connecting to a server on host earth
```
% SurveyClient earth
Q0: What is your favorite flavor of ice cream?
0 Vanilla
1 Chocolate
2 Strawberry
>
```

From this point, the user can respond to questions by entering the index of the desired response. The client terminates once all questions have been answered.

8.4   Survey Service, Mark 2

Although it performs a modestly useful function as it is, the survey service is ripe for enhancement. In this section, we add an administrative interface to report on response counts, we have the server keep a list of IP addresses of clients completing the survey, and we explore an alternative technique for encoding and decoding messages between client and server. A few additional features of the PracticalSocket library are needed to make these enhancements to the survey service.

8.4.1 Socket Address Support

The PracticalSocket library provides a **SocketAddress** class that encapsulates an IP address and a port number. It's actually just a wrapper around the **sockaddr_storage** structure introduced in Section 2.4. Objects of this type are handy for keeping up with the endpoints of a socket connection, and the library uses them in many different places.

Through its constructors and static `lookupAddresses()` methods, **SocketAddress** provides a simple interface to name resolution. An instance of **SocketAddress** can be constructed with either an address or a hostname and a port number. Alternatively, the port can be described using a service name instead of a number. Both of these constructors are wrappers around the `getaddrinfo()` function described in Chapter 3. The underlying `getaddrinfo()` actually returns a list of matching addresses, and these constructors simply use the first address that's returned. The static `lookupAddresses()` methods take the same parameters as these constructors and return a list of all matching addresses in an STL **vector**. This could be useful for an application that needs to choose between IPv4 or IPv6 or when multiple network interfaces are available on a single host.

SocketAddress(**const char** *`*host`*, **in_port_t** *`port`*) throw(**SocketException**)
SocketAddress(**const char** *`*host`*, **const char** *`*service`*) throw(**SocketException**)
static **std::vector**⟨SocketAddress⟩ **SocketAddress**::lookupAddresses(**const char** *`*host`*,
                                               in_port_t *`port`*) throw(**SocketException**)
static **std::vector**⟨SocketAddress⟩ lookupAddresses(**const char** *`*host`*,
                                         const char *`*service`*) throw(**SocketException**)

Instances of **SocketAddress** can also be obtained by querying the addresses at the ends of a socket connection. The base class, **Socket**, provides a `getLocalAddress()` method that returns a **SocketAddress** for the local address to which a socket is bound. In the case of a **TCPServerSocket**, this will give the address on which the server is listening, and in the case of a **TCPSocket** this will give the address at the local end of the connection. The **CommunicatingSocket** class provides a `getForeignAddress()` method that returns a **SocketAddress** for the remote end of a connection. Once obtained, the host address and port number of a SocketAddress can be examined via the `getAddress()` and `getPort()` methods.

SocketAddress Socket::getLocalAddress() throw(**SocketException**)
SocketAddress CommunicatingSocket::getForeignAddress() throw(**SocketException**)
std::string SocketAddress::getAddress() const throw(**SocketException**)
in_port_t SocketAddress::getPort() const throw(**SocketException**)

For the user who wants to take more control over how a socket is set up, bind() and connect() methods are provided that take an instance of **SocketAddress** as a parameter. An application can create a **TCPSocket** or a **TCPServerSocket** using the default constructor. The socket can then be bound to a local address with the bind() method and, in the case of **TCPSocket**, connected to a remote server with the connect() method. This lets the programmer manage socket creation with a level of control more similar to what's described in Chapter 2.

---

void TCPSocket::bind(**const SocketAddress &***localAddress*) throw(**SocketException**)
void TCPSocket::connect(**const SocketAddress &***foreignAddress*) throw(**SocketException**)
void TCPServerSocket::bind(**const SocketAddress &***localAddress*) throw(**SocketException**)

8.4.2   Socket iostream Interface

The send() and recv() methods provided by **CommunicatingSocket** serve as a very thin veneer over the send() and recv() functions for the underlying socket. This kind of interface is natural for some types of messages, but it isn't the most familiar for handling text-encoded messages, as described in Section 5.2.2.

The getStream() method of **CommunicatingSocket** returns a reference to an **iostream** that's backed by the socket. For a C++ programmer, this can serve as a very convenient interface for reading and writing text-encoded information. It's a C++ analog to the fdopen() mechanism described in Section 5.1.5. Character sequences written to the **iostream** will be sent over the socket, and the sequence of characters received from the network can be read from the **iostream**. With this interface, the programmer can use the familiar techniques for working with **istream** and **ostream** to encode and decode messages.

---

std::iostream &CommunicatingSocket::getStream() throw(**SocketException**)

The **iostream** interface to a **CommunicatingSocket** provides fixed-sized buffers for storing part of the character sequence being sent and received. Text written to the **iostream** will be held in memory until the buffer is full or until it is flushed. This can offer some performance advantages since a message can be written to the **iostream** one field at a time and then pushed out to the network after it's complete. However, this level of buffering makes it problematic to mix I/O operations via the **iostream** with direct calls to the send() and recv() methods. Consider, for example, some message *A* written to the socket via its **iostream**. If the stream isn't subsequently flushed, part of message *A* may remain buffered in the **iostream**. If message *B* is then sent directly via the socket's send() method, *B* will be pushed out to the network before the buffered portions of *A*.

8.4.3 Enhanced Survey Server

The enhanced server uses **SocketAddress** objects to keep up with a list of addresses for clients completing the survey. For each client, the server records the host address by saving a copy of the **SocketAddress** representing the remote end of the socket.

The server also provides an administrative socket interface for reporting the current state of the survey. The server restricts access to the administrative interface by only permitting connections from clients running on the same host. To do this, the server cannot use the convenience constructor for **TCPServerSocket** used in previous examples. The server must create a **TCPServerSocket** in the unbound state and then explicitly bind it to a **SocketAddress** for the loopback interface.

The enhanced survey server makes extensive use of the **iostream** interface of **CommunicatingSocket**. This makes the sending and receiving of messages look a lot like reading and writing a file. It also permits some additional code reuse between the client and server. Instead of using a new format to send survey questions to the client, the server encodes them in the same format as the survey file it reads at start-up time. The client can use the same readSurvey() function provided by SurveyCommon.cpp to read the list of survey questions all at once.

SurveyServer2.cpp

```
 1  #include <iostream>
 2  #include <iomanip>
 3  #include <fstream>
 4  #include <pthread.h>
 5  #include "PracticalSocket.h"
 6  #include "SurveyCommon.h"
 7
 8  using namespace std;
 9
10  static vector<Question> qList;            // List of survey questions
11  static pthread_mutex_t lock;              // Mutex to Protect critical sections
12  static vector<vector<int> > rCount;       // Response tallies for each question
13  static vector<SocketAddress> addrList;    // Address list for client history
```

```
14
15  /** Thread main function to administer a survey over the given socket */
16  void *conductSurvey(void *arg);
17
18  /** Thread main function to monitor an administrative connection and
19      give reports over it. */
20  void *adminServer(void *arg);
21
22  int main(int argc, char *argv[]) {
23    if (argc != 2) {
24      cerr << "Usage: SurveyServer <Survey File>" << endl;
25      return 1;
26    }
27
28    ifstream input(argv[1]);              // Read survey from given file
29    if (!input || !readSurvey(input, qList) ) {
30      cerr << "Can't read survey from file: " << argv[1] << endl;
31      return 1;
32    }
33
34    // Initialize response tally for each question/response.
35    for (unsigned int i = 0; i < qList.size(); i++)
36      rCount.push_back(vector<int>(qList[i].rList.size(), 0));
37    pthread_mutex_init(&lock, NULL);       // Initialize mutex
38
39    try {
40      pthread_t newThread;
41
42      // Make a thread to provide the administrative interface.
43      if (pthread_create(&newThread, NULL, adminServer, NULL) != 0) {
44        cerr << "Can't create administrative thread" << endl;
45        return 1;
46      }
47
48      // Make a socket to listen for SurveyClient connections.
49      TCPServerSocket servSock(SURVEY_PORT);
50
51      for (;;) {     // Repeatedly accept connections and administer the survey.
52        TCPSocket *sock = servSock.accept();
53        if (pthread_create(&newThread, NULL, conductSurvey, sock) != 0) {
54          cerr << "Can't create new thread" << endl;
55          delete sock;
56        }
57      }
58    } catch (SocketException &e) {
```

```
59        cerr << e.what() << endl;          // Report errors to the console.
60     }
61
62     return 0;
63  }
64
65  void *conductSurvey(void *arg) {
66     TCPSocket *sock = (TCPSocket *)arg;    // Argument is really a socket.
67     try {
68        // Write out the survey in the same format as the input file.
69        iostream &stream = sock->getStream();
70        stream << qList.size() << "\n";
71
72        for (unsigned int q = 0; q < qList.size(); q++) {
73           stream << qList[q].qText << "\n";
74           stream << qList[q].rList.size() << "\n";
75           for (unsigned int r = 0; r < qList[q].rList.size(); r++)
76              stream << qList[q].rList[r] << "\n";
77        }
78        stream.flush();
79
80        // Read client responses to questions and record them
81        for (unsigned int q = 0; q < qList.size(); q++) {
82           unsigned int response;
83           stream >> response;
84           if (response >= 0 && response < rCount[q].size()) {
85              pthread_mutex_lock(&lock);       // Lock the mutex
86              rCount[q][response]++;           // Increment count for chosen item
87              pthread_mutex_unlock(&lock);     // Release the lock
88           }
89        }
90
91        // Log this client as completing the survey.
92        pthread_mutex_lock(&lock);
93        addrList.push_back(sock->getForeignAddress());
94        pthread_mutex_unlock(&lock);
95     } catch (runtime_error e) {
96        cerr << e.what() << endl;          // Report errors to the console.
97     }
98
99     delete sock;  // Free the socket object (and close the connection)
100    return NULL;
101 }
102
103 void *adminServer(void *arg) {
```

```
104  try {
105    // Make a ServerSocket to listen for admin connections
106    TCPServerSocket adminSock;
107    adminSock.bind(SocketAddress("127.0.0.1", SURVEY_PORT + 1));
108
109    for (;;) {   // Repeatedly accept administrative connections
110      TCPSocket *sock = adminSock.accept();
111      iostream &stream = sock->getStream();
112
113      try {
114        // Copy response counts and address lists
115        pthread_mutex_lock(&lock);
116        vector<vector<int> > myCount = rCount;
117        vector<SocketAddress> myList = addrList;
118        pthread_mutex_unlock(&lock);
119
120        for (unsigned int q = 0; q < qList.size(); q++) {
121          // Give a report for each question.
122          stream << "Q" << q << ":  " << qList[q].qText << "\n";
123          for (unsigned int r = 0; r < qList[q].rList.size(); r++)
124            stream << setw(5) << myCount[q][r] << " " << qList[q].rList[r]
125                   << "\n";
126        }
127
128        // Report the list of client addresses.
129        stream << "Client Addresses:" << endl;
130        for (unsigned int c = 0; c < myList.size(); c++ )
131          stream << "   " << myList[c].getAddress() << "\n";
132
133        stream.flush();
134      } catch (runtime_error e) {
135        cerr << e.what() << endl;
136      }
137
138      delete sock;   // Free the socket object (and close the connection)
139    }
140  } catch (SocketException e) {
141    cerr << e.what() << endl;          // Report errors to the console.
142  }
143  return NULL;                         // Reached only on error
144 }
```

SurveyServer2.cpp

1. **Access to library functions:** lines 1–6
2. **Survey representation:** lines 10–13
   This version of the server adds a **vector** of **SocketAddress** objects to keep up with the list of clients completing the survey. Since multiple client threads may attempt to access this list at the same time, use of the list is protected by the mutex, *lock.*
3. **Initialize server state:** lines 23–37
4. **Create a thread for the administrative interface:** lines 43–46
   The server must accept connections over its primary **TCPServerSocket** and its administrative **TCPServerSocket**. If the same thread tried to serve both of these sockets, calling accept() on one of them would leave it blocked and unable to accept connections from the other. To serve both, the server creates a new thread to handle connections over its administrative interface. The adminServer() function implements this interface.
5. **Create server socket and handle each client with a new thread:** lines 49–57
6. **Survey client handler:** lines 65–101
   - **Encode survey and send to client:** lines 69–78
     A client thread first writes a copy of the whole survey to the client, using the same format as the original input file. It uses getStream() to obtain a copy of the **iostream** for its **TCPSocket** and then writes out the survey as if it were writing to a file. Instead of using *endl* to end each line, we use the newline character. Using *endl* would flush the stream after each line. As much as possible, we would like to buffer all or large portions of the message and then send when the message is complete. The server writes the entire message and then calls the stream's flush() method to initiate the sending of any buffered data.
   - **Get client responses and tally them:** lines 81–89
     The client has the entire survey, so the server only needs to read its responses one after another.
   - **Log the client:** lines 92–94
     Once the client has completed the survey, the server records a copy of its address.
7. **Administrative client handler:** lines 103–144
   - **Create administrative socket:** lines 106–107
     The administrative interface uses a port number offset by one from the survey port. Since the server is intended to only accept administrative connections from the local host, we have to go through more explicit steps to construct the **TCPServerSocket** and bind it to a local address.
   - **Repeatedly accept administrative connections:** lines 109–110
     Administrative clients are served with a single thread. If two administrative clients try to connect, the second will have to wait for the first to be served.

- **Snapshot reported structures:** lines 115–118
  Before sending a report, the server makes a copy of the client address history and the response count lists. This frees the server from having to lock these structures repeatedly as it writes out the report, but, more importantly, it provides a consistent snapshot of the state. The reported list of client addresses won't grow while the server is printing it out. If the server had simply locked the mutex for the entire report generation instead of copying these lists, all client threads would have been blocked while the server tried to send the report to the administrative client. A malicious administrative client could fail to read from its socket and suspend the conducting of surveys indefinitely.

- **Write administrative report:** lines 120–133
  We make the server responsible for formatting the administrative report. It writes a tally for each question and response to the socket's **iostream**, followed by the host addresses for every client completing the survey.

8.4.4 Enhanced Survey Client

To communicate with the server using text-encoded messages, the client requires a few changes. First, instead of reading survey questions individually, it obtains the socket's **iostream** and uses readSurvey() to read the whole survey at once. The client offers the survey to the user one question at a time and sends corresponding responses by writing to the stream.

SurveyClient2.cpp

```
1   #include <iostream>
2   #include <iomanip>
3   #include "PracticalSocket.h"
4   #include "SurveyCommon.h"
5
6   using namespace std;
7
8   int main(int argc, char *argv[]) {
9     if (argc != 2) {                    // Make sure the user gives a host
10      cerr << "Usage: SurveyClient <Survey Server Host>" << endl;
11      return 1;
12    }
13
14    try {
15      // Connect to the server.
16      TCPSocket sock(argv[1], SURVEY_PORT);
17      iostream &stream = sock.getStream();
18      vector<Question> qList;            // Read the whole survey
19      readSurvey(stream, qList);
```

```
20
21     for (unsigned int q = 0; q < qList.size(); q++) {
22       // Show each the question to the user and print the list of responses.
23       cout << "Q" << q << ":  " << qList[q].qText << endl;
24       for (unsigned int r = 0; r < qList[q].rList.size(); r++)
25         cout << setw(2) << r << " "  << qList[q].rList[r] << endl;
26
27       // Keep prompting the user until we get a legal response.
28       unsigned int response = qList[q].rList.size();
29       while (response < 0 || response >= qList[q].rList.size()) {
30         cout << "> ";
31         cin >> response;
32       }
33
34       stream << response << endl;        // Send user response to server
35       stream.flush();
36     }
37   } catch(SocketException &e) {
38     cerr << e.what() << endl;            // Report errors to the console.
39     return 1;
40   }
41
42   return 0;
43 }
```

SurveyClient2.cpp

8.4.5 Administrative Client

A very simple client is sufficient to access the administrative interface. Since the server writes out response counts and address list in a human-readable format, the client can just copy each byte it receives from the server to the console. The administrative client first attempts to connect to a server running on the local host. Since the client is attempting to connect using the administrative port number, the server will automatically send it a report and then close the socket connection.

The client creates a fixed-sized buffer and then copies one buffer full after another to the console. Even though the server writes to the socket using its **iostream** interface, the socket simply conveys the sequence of bytes written, and the client is free to read the sequence using the recv() method. In this case, recv() is probably a more convenient interface than **iostream** for echoing the server's output to the console. The client doesn't have to worry about how the server's report is formatted, how many lines it contains, or how long each line is.

The server's administrative report is just a sequence of printable characters, with no null terminators anywhere in the report. To print out a buffer full of the report as if it was a string, the client must mark the end of the buffer with a null terminator. Since the recv() method returns the number of bytes successfully saved in *buffer*, it's easy to fill in a null terminator at the end. Of course, the client has to be certain to leave room for this extra character each time a buffer is read. That's why the client's call to recv() advertises the buffer as one byte shorter than its actual capacity.

AdminClient2.cpp

```
1   #include <iostream>
2   #include "PracticalSocket.h"
3   #include "SurveyCommon.h"
4
5   using namespace std;
6
7   int main(int argc, char *argv[]) {
8     try {
9       // Connect to the server's administrative interface.
10      TCPSocket sock("localhost", SURVEY_PORT + 1);
11
12      // Read the server's report a block at a time.
13      char buffer[ 1025 ];
14      int len;
15      while ((len = sock.recv(buffer, sizeof(buffer) - 1)) != 0) {
16        buffer[len] = '\0';              // Null terminate the sequence
17        cout << buffer;                  // And print it like as a string
18      }
19    } catch(SocketException &e) {
20      cerr << e.what() << endl;          // Report errors to the console.
21      exit(1);
22    }
23
24    return 0;
25  }
```

AdminClient2.cpp

8.4.6 Running Server and Clients

The enhanced survey server and its survey client are run with the same arguments as the original. The administrative client doesn't require any arguments since it automatically tries to connect to an instance of the survey server running on the local host at a known port number.

Exercises

1. In the server's code for the administrative interface, we made an effort to get a consistent snapshot of the response tally and the client address list before we started generating the report. However, since the server's `conductSurvey()` function records client responses as soon as they are received, the administrative report may still include results for partially completed surveys. Modify the server so that responses are tallied only after the client completes the survey. In this way, both the response tallies and the list of client addresses will reflect only clients that actually completed the survey.

2. As it is written, it's possible for a client to cause a server crash. If the client closes its socket connection while the server is sending it a message, the server will receive a SIGPIPE signal. Consult Section 6.2 and modify the server so that it will not terminate under these circumstances.

3. The survey server maintains an open socket and a thread on behalf of each client taking a survey. If a client never completes the survey, the server never reclaims these resources. Extend the server so that sockets are closed and client threads are permitted to terminate automatically five minutes after the client begins taking the survey. When a client thread starts up, you will also start up another thread that we'll call the sleeper. The sleeper will simply wait for five minutes and then check to see if the client thread is still running. If it is, the sleeper will close the client's socket, which will unblock the server thread and give it a chance to exit. Doing this the right way will require the server to maintain some additional per-client state and to perform some additional synchronization. For example, a sleeper thread should not make a call to `close()` if its client thread has already finished and deleted the socket.

References

[1] Comer, Douglas E. *Internetworking with TCP/IP,* volume 1, *Principles, Protocols, and Architecture* (fifth edition). Prentice Hall, 2005.

[2] Comer, Douglas E., and Stevens, David L. *Internetworking with TCP/IP,* volume 2, *Design, Implementation, and Internals* (third edition). Prentice Hall, 1999.

[3] Comer, Douglas E., and Stevens, David L. *Internetworking with TCP/IP,* volume 3, *Client-Server Programming and Applications* (BSD version, second edition). Prentice Hall, 1996.

[4] Hinden, R., and Deering, S. "IP Version 6 Addressing Architecture." Internet Request for Comments 4291, February 2006.

[5] Deering, S., and Hinden, R. "Internet Protocol, Version 6 (IPv6) Specification." Internet Request for Comments 2460, December 1998.

[6] Gilligan, R., Thomson, S., Bound, J., McCann, J., and Stevens, W. "Basic Socket Interface Extensions for IPv6." Internet Request for Comments 3493, February 2003.

[7] Srisuresh, P., and Egevang, S. "Traditional IP Network Address Translator (Traditional NAT)." Internet Request for Comments 3022, January 2001.

[8] Mockapetris, Paul. "Domain Names: Concepts and Facilities." Internet Request for Comments 1034, November 1987.

[9] Mockapetris, Paul. "Domain Names: Implementation and Specification." Internet Request for Comments 1035, November 1987.

[10] Peterson, Larry L., and Davie, Bruce S. *Computer Networks: A Systems Approach* (fourth edition). Morgan Kaufmann, 2007.

[11] M-K. Shin, et al. "Application Aspects of IPv6 Transition." Internet Request for Comments 4038, March 2005.

[12] Postel, John. "Internet Protocol." Internet Request for Comments 791, September 1981.

[13] Postel, John. "Transmission Control Protocol." Internet Request for Comments 793, September 1981.

[14] Postel, John. "User Datagram Protocol." Internet Request for Comments 768, August 1980.

[15] Stevens, W. Richard. *TCP/IP Illustrated,* volume 1, *The Protocols.* Addison-Wesley, 1994.

[16] Stevens, W. Richard. *UNIX Network Programming: Networking APIs: Sockets and XTI* (second edition). Prentice Hall, 1997.

[17] Wright, Gary R., and Stevens, W. Richard. *TCP/IP Illustrated,* volume 2, *The Implementation.* Addison-Wesley, 1995.

Index